The Muttart Fellowship Program—unique in Canada—was created in 1996. A project of The Muttart Foundation, a private foundation based in Edmonton, Alberta, the program is designed to:

- develop research and other materials that will benefit the charitable sector in Canada.

- provide senior managers within the social-services sector with an opportunity for a sabbatical year—a chance to recharge and renew themselves.

Up to five fellowships are awarded each year to people working in senior-management positions in social-service charities within the Foundation's funding area—Alberta, Saskatchewan, Northwest Territories and Yukon.

During the Fellowship year, the Fellow leaves his or her agency to work on the chosen project. The Foundation makes a grant equal to the salary and benefit costs for the Fellow's position, and provides a budget for expenses related to the project. At the end of the Fellowship year, the Fellow returns to his or her agency for at least a year.

For more information about the project, please contact:

Executive Director
The Muttart Foundation
1150 Scotia Place 1
10060 Jasper Avenue
Edmonton, Alberta T5J 3R8

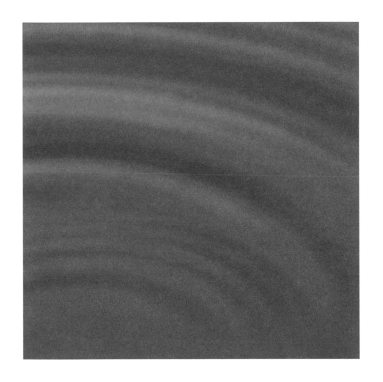

Political Asylums

Ronald A. LaJeunesse

March 2002

Published by:

The Muttart Foundation

National Library of Canada Cataloguing in Publication

LaJeunesse, Ronald A., 1944-
  Political asylums/Ronald A. LaJeunesse.

(Muttart fellowship series)
Includes bibliographical references.
ISBN 0-9730679-1-8

  1. Mental health services--Alberta--History. I. Muttart Foundation.
II. Title. III. Series: Muttart fellowships.

RA790.7.C3L33 2002   362.2'097123   C2002-901786-6

Dedication

This book is for the tens of thousands of Albertans who were well treated, supported, and cared for through Alberta's mental health services. It is also for the thousands who were not.

Acknowledgements

To my wife, Wendy, and our family, who supported me unconditionally and advised me personally, editorially, and politically. A special thanks to my son, Paul, who saved me technologically on what seemed a daily basis.

To the board and staff of the Canadian Mental Health Association, who supported my leave from work and who helped me with advice and research. Particular thanks to David Allen who shared his considerable research and editing talent.

To The Muttart Foundation, whose Fellowship made the research, writing, and publication of this book possible. Special recognition to Executive Director Bob Wyatt who has an extraordinary sensitivity to the issues and politics surrounding mental health reform and personal development.

To the 12 people who formed my editorial board and who reviewed material, some anonymously, from the perspective of consumers/users/survivors (patients and clients and those formerly so), families, psychiatrists, lawyers, psychologists, psychiatric nurses, educators, civil servants, politicians, publishers, and academics.

To Kathie Kennedy and Beckie Garber-Conrad, who so ably assisted in the editing of the original and revised manuscripts. To Dr. Haroon Nasir, who verified source documents, prepared the reference sources at the end of each chapter, and provided invaluable editorial and scientific advice.

After that, the list is too lengthy to detail. It includes: consumers/users who are and were patients and clients; family members, friends, and volunteers who supported consumers; current and former staff in mental hospitals, general hospitals, and community clinics; authors, researchers, and reference staff in libraries and archives; psychiatrists and lawyers; politicians, their secretaries, and assistants; civil servants, and journalists.

My sincere thanks to them all.

Table of Contents

Table of Contents

Appendices

Introduction

Introduction

Introduction

Political Asylums is first and foremost a history of the experiences of people with mental illness in Alberta. It is not an academic textbook, but rather is written as a novel, attempting to capture the experiences of people over the past century. It differs from a novel, however, in that there is no fiction. All of the events are recorded or reported history, detailed in studies, reports, books, files, and personal records, or as recalled by people who lived the events. Generally speaking, there was such a rich body of information available in archives, libraries, newspapers, and through personal interviews that the author had no shortage of raw material and needed only to organize the details into story format.

All of the people are real, set within real events. There are no composites or fictional accounts. In order to protect identities, the names and places of residence for some of the people have been changed. A listing of real names and pseudonyms can be found in the nominal record.

There were so many individuals and so much interesting material that the author could not possibly include all of the key historical figures that helped shape the mental health services of their time. Time and again, the author was tempted into one or another historical detour, and he hopes that his choices will neither offend nor disappoint the many people who have worked in, or have been treated by, Alberta's mental health system.

In the interests of disclosure, it may be important to note that while the author's own "character" is only rarely reported in the text, he personally witnessed and was sometimes intimately involved in the events recounted in these pages. His role however, was generally as a facilitator of others and whereas their action is reported, describing the details of his personal involvement was seen as redundant and irrelevant.

During the author's research, he interviewed many former staff members of Alberta's mental health services. One of them, a former psychiatric nurse from the Alberta Hospital at Ponoka in the 1950s, was particularly informative and colourful in the presentation of his experience. To the author's question about staff competence, he thought for a moment and then expressed a personal view. "The rule of thirds would apply," he said. "One-third were dedicated, compassionate, caring, and thoughtful. One-third put in the day with little care, and one-third were goons—cruel, harsh goons."

While this book paints several stories of people, programs, and practices that were in many ways cruel and harsh, it is important to remember the many compassionate individuals who worked most of their lives under very difficult conditions. It takes a special kind of caring and a very real sense of purpose to see through the illness and to encourage the strengths of people who sometimes seem to need so much.

As noted earlier, this is not a typical history book chronicling the events of an era. Rather, the focus is on people who lived the events of the day. It is a story of people who wielded extreme power and influence and of others who often lacked control—and hope. It is a story of inadequate resources for society's most marginalized. It is a story about the disconnected components of a "non-system" of mental health care. It acknowledges that there were good services—programs that worked. But for the most part, mental illness was the 20th century's equivalent of leprosy, a misunderstood disease so thoroughly stigmatized that it almost invariably engendered fear, rejection, isolation, and poverty. It still does.

This book is also about the very meaning of madness, the influence of politics, and the power of economics. Finally, it is about giving the reader an opportunity to experience a place in time and in so doing, to learn from the events and lessons of history.

There is one caution. It is important to understand the historical context in which treatment occurred and to guard against imposing today's values on past practices.

And a final note. It would have been unrealistic to present this history without using the classifications and labels of the past—no matter how repugnant, inappropriate or discriminatory they may appear today. "Lunatic," "feeble-minded," and similar diagnoses were an integral part of the values of the time and provide a true picture of the past.

A person's lifetime likelihood of suffering from one or another of the various mental illnesses now stands at 20 per cent—one in five— and some categories of illness are increasing as our population ages. While most people will recover with early and appropriate treatment, many will avoid going for help due to stigma and discrimination. And the five per cent of the population that is afflicted with severe and persistent illnesses like schizophrenia, dementias, and severe forms of bipolar disorder may never recover without a broad range of support services.

Any one of us might suffer a mental illness in our lifetime. No one is immune. In reality, whether directly or indirectly, poor mental health affects us all. This book therefore, may be of interest to us all: the users of mental health services; family members, friends, professionals, and just interested and concerned citizens.

"Those who cannot remember the past are condemned to repeat it."

– George Santyana

"Fear has a greater grasp on human action than historical evidence."

– Jeremy Siegel

"Man's treatment of the mentally ill has no steady march to enlightenment but a concrete expression of the prejudices and passions of changing cultures."

– New York Academy of Science

4

**Prologue
Jeopardy**

Prologue
Jeopardy

Prologue
Jeopardy

2001

The pain continued in the aftermath. Chad sat anxiously in the Bowden prison waiting to return home in the late autumn of 2001. Brent resigned from the police department after 10 years of service and moved to Arizona. Keith stayed with policing but wrestled with loneliness and sadness. "I feel like a part of me died that day in the field." Randy left his cherished canine service following the loss of his dog Caesar. Chad and his family suffered unspeakable anguish. Countless others dealt with intense post-traumatic stress. A single event had placed all of their lives in jeopardy.

Three years earlier, only 20 years of age and a high school graduate, Chad Yurko was a polite, quiet, almost withdrawn individual. No one thought him capable of creating such chaos. Chad was unemployed and aimless, living at home with his parents. He saw a psychiatrist for what his parents described as depression, but only his family seemed to realize the desperation in his soul. A prescription for Prozac and a monthly meeting with his doctor were evidently not enough.

On a warm Wednesday morning in June, Chad awoke in excruciating pain. The sadness would have to be stopped. After drinking heavily in an attempt to numb the pain, he went to his father's gun cabinet, took out a 12-guage shotgun and inserted several shells. He then went into the back yard, placed the gun in his mouth, and, paused. "Why can't I do it?" he sobbed as he fired the gun into the air.

Clad only in blue and white jogging pants, the depressed and now frustrated Chad walked down the driveway, through the back lane,

5

and into a school playground. As he walked, he waved the shotgun—pointing it, firing aimlessly, and periodically moving the barrel in and out of his mouth. There was pandemonium. Teachers and children ran for the safety of the three schools that occupied a common playground. Fearing the schools were the gunman's intended destination, teachers began securing doors and windows.

Among the first to respond to the 911 call were two officers patrolling in separate vehicles. The first cruiser sped down 105th Street to the Yurko residence. Officer Keith Smith yanked the trunk-mounted shotgun from its mooring and, hearing a noise behind him, turned to see a shotgun aimed at his back. He bolted for the cover of a hedge and trees. The second police car mounted the 103rd Street curb and skidded over the sidewalk. It then sped around the school and onto the playground, three metres from where Chad Yurko slowly raised his gun and aimed at the windshield. As he stared in disbelief, time seemed to stand still for constable Brent LaJeunesse. Yet later it all seemed to have happened so very fast. Adrenalin does that. He unsnapped his seat belt, yanked the car door open, rolled onto the grass and then ran for the cover of the school buildings. In the meantime, Chad raised the gun high, turned, and continued his meandering walk across the schoolyard.

Amid a sea of screaming children, the two constables regained their composure and began a cautious walk in pursuit of the gunman. Moving from the shelter of buildings and light standards, they were joined by Constable Randy Goss and a police Rottweiler named Caesar. Each policeman in turn demanded that Chad throw down his weapon.

Yurko's seemingly aimless walk took him further into the playground and then back towards Lorelei Elementary School. Hunching down, the three officers moved cautiously toward the gunman from behind—two constables and the dog from one direction, the third approaching Yurko at an angle. As they came within 50 metres, Goss released the dog. Hearing them now, the young man turned and fired. The police dog collapsed in an explosion of pellets and bloodied flesh. As Yurko's shotgun was lifted toward the officers, constables Smith and LaJeunesse fired simultaneously. The police shotgun pellets, fired from 40 metres, struck Yurko with immense force and his body crumpled—shattered and bloodied.

More police cars, including a tactical unit, arrived as the two constables walked numbly from the scene; the third was still bent in

Police subdue suspect, grieve their dog, and console fellow officers. (Photograph with permission of *The Edmonton Journal*.)

grief over his dog. In the school, teachers and students continued to cry, scream, and pray. Reporters and cameramen blanketed the school ground and, as the story hit the airwaves, distraught and panicked parents came racing in search of their children.

Hundreds of lives were altered that day. For weeks and months to come, students and parents would have nightmares and panic attacks. The teachers would report anxiety and tension. The three police officers would never approach their jobs in quite the same way again. Uncertainty, anxiety, and sadness would haunt them for months and even years.

Chad Yurko and his family would suffer for the rest of their lives.

In the aftermath of the tragedy, mental health officials and media representatives speculated as to whether or not Mr. Yurko was attempting "suicide by cop" and if a comprehensive mental health system might have made a difference. Attempting suicide by provoking police action appeared to be a late 20th-century phenomenon, caused by people suffering from one or a combination of mental illness, suicidal tendencies, and substance abuse. The idea was to end your life in a dramatic form—and to have someone else do it for you.

"Suicide by cop" was rare, but suicide was not. Chad Yurko's attempt was by no means an isolated case. Only weeks before,

University of Alberta astrophysicist Dr. Barry Harold killed himself in the dark protective privacy of a basement. Dr. Harold suffered from depression and had tried unsuccessfully to admit himself to hospital. In fact more than 350 Albertans commit suicide every year, often because help is unavailable or comes too late. Or because stigma and prejudice keeps them from asking for help.

More Albertans die from suicide every year than from auto accidents. Thousands of other people attempt to kill themselves after failing to cope with hopelessness and despair. Even young children are affected. In the decade between 1989 and 1998, an astonishing 389 children and youth between the ages of 10 and 19 killed themselves—the children of "normal," everyday Alberta families.

Three hundred and eighty-nine young people. That's enough to empty 15 classrooms and leave behind more than 7,000 bereaved classmates and school staff, along with an estimated 2,700 grieving family members and close friends. And suicides are but one statistic. If Yurko had actually entered Lorelei School in Edmonton, would he have replicated the massacre in Littleton, Colorado, or the tragedy in Taber, Alberta? "Perhaps," said the Canadian Mental Health Association's (CMHA) acting director Tony Hudson, "but it is more likely that he was much more of a risk to himself than to others." Study after study has demonstrated that, taken as a group, people with a mental illness represent less of a threat to public safety than does the general population. They are, though, extremely dangerous to themselves. Just prior to his release from prison, Chad Yurko described the allegation that he would have hurt children as "absolutely ridiculous. My only plan was to die."

8   Many troubled people do find help. Every year in Alberta, more than 28,000 people are treated in community mental health clinics and over 2,100 are admitted to psychiatric hospitals. Thousands of others are assisted in general hospitals; thousands more see psychologists and charitable organizations. Psychiatrists and family physicians see hundreds of thousands more in their office practices. In fact, each year between 1995 and 2000, mental illnesses including anxiety and depression were the most common doctor services accounting for 39 per cent of all patient contacts with Alberta physicians.

Yet there never seems to be enough help. According to a survey done by the Alberta Medical Association, an urgent admission to a psychiatric unit of a general hospital can take almost six weeks. Family physicians report that, after six months, 30 per cent of their referrals to psychiatrists have never been seen. Waiting lists for community organizations that provide rehabilitation, life skills, jobs, housing, and other community supports run as long as 40 months. People simply can't get help early enough, and mental illnesses, like physical illnesses, respond best when treated early.

Although Chad Yurko was on an anti-depressant and was seeing a psychiatrist monthly, his father alleges it was not enough. Chad was "not a victim—he was responsible for his own actions," said Allan Yurko, "but in retrospect, much could have been done to help us." Was it all preventable? There had been a previous attempt at suicide, and Chad's parents feared he was at risk. There was no counseling available to either Chad or the family. The parents knew of no support group and they were unsure about how they should best respond to their son. Everyone seemed to be relying on the anti-depressant drug Prozac to make a difference. It didn't.

Then Chad became part of the 23 per cent of inmates in Alberta prisons with a diagnosis of depression. Some mental health advocates describe prisons as today's mental hospitals. Ironically it appears that prison is where Chad has received help. Different medication, counseling, and treatment for alcohol abuse have left Chad's family optimistic about the future. What if the help had been provided earlier? What difference in consequence? What difference in cost?

Clearly, more resources are needed, but even more importantly, the available money needs to be spent differently. There is no system of care. High-cost services such as hospital beds are used time and again for the same people, who are then discharged into their communities without the benefit of adequate housing, income, training, and support. The illness returns and they begin their "revolving-door" journey all over again. Others remain in hospital longer than necessary because the community support services that do exist have no space for them. Still others cannot get in to hospitals for early treatment because the beds are filled. Such a "non-system" is costly and ineffective.

Attempts at reforming mental health programs in Alberta have been made since 1911 when the Hospital for the Insane at Ponoka was built to provide "moral treatment." But for many, "moral treatment" didn't work. The root of what would later be referred to as "deinstitutionalization" was firmly grounded in early attempts to reform the institutions themselves. Each reform flourished briefly, then was forgotten until a kind of institutional rot set in, whereupon another reform effort took place.

Early intervention and community services close to home were proposed as early as 1921, when the Canadian National Committee for Mental Hygiene (predecessor to the Canadian Mental Health Association) surveyed Alberta's system at the request of the government of Herbert Greenfield's United Farmers. Early intervention and community-based services were recommended again in 1971, when Premier Peter Lougheed dedicated his office to mental health reform. The same recommendations were made in 1992, when Health Minister Nancy Betkowski released her vision for New Directions and yet again in 1995, when Health Minister Shirley McClellan oversaw the plan—and in dozens of reports and studies in between.

In every case, the interest in developing new approaches ended in a few innovations, along with the building, rebuilding, and maintenance of yet more asylums and mental institutions. According to Hudson of the CMHA, McClellan's Building a Better Future became Health Minister Halvar Jonson's, "in the future, better buildings." And once again, available money was siphoned off for bricks and mortar with little left for early intervention or for community services to support the patients after discharge.

That's not to say that Alberta institutions weren't downsized. Like the rest of North America, de-institutionalization started in the 1960s, when new knowledge and treatments paved the way for what American President John F. Kennedy described as "a bold new approach." The idea behind de-institutionalization was that mental hospitals would open their doors and allow the mentally ill to take their rightful place in the community. Modern drugs and a more tolerant society would be expected to give people who had historically lived in a highly controlled environment new-found freedoms, including the essential feelings of inclusion, affection, and control over their own lives.

It hasn't worked out that way. Former patients are rarely included in community activities. Many of them have very few friends, their families can't cope with recurring illnesses, and "control" is little more than a word. The highly touted medications proved to be less than perfect and long-term use of the early drugs caused side effects and irreversible complications for many people.

As deinstitutionalization came to be known as a failure through media stories and devastating personal experiences, the practice developed a bad name. Until it was shown to be less than a success, the movement had attracted little public attention. Mental illness is, after all, one of the things the public would rather not think about. And when mentally ill people are placed in isolated institutions, it is much easier not to think about them.

Nevertheless, there have been some remarkable people in Alberta's ongoing battle over the care and treatment of those with mental illnesses, brave individuals whose efforts should be recorded and applauded. There were asylum superintendents who pushed for "moral treatment" and released patients from hideous restraint devices like "electric cabinets" and "cage beds." There were premiers and health ministers who, in spite of limited resources, fought for and allocated new dollars for improved services. There were news reporters who committed portions of their careers to promoting reform and professionals who worked with dedication beyond any reasonable expectation. There were also volunteers and family members who devoted much of their lives to assist people in difficulty. Possibly of most importance, there were "consumers" or "users," people who had lived through an illness and then provided one another with the help and support they so desperately needed.

Alberta's history also had failed leaders: hospital superintendents who used punishment as the treatment of choice; premiers and health ministers who tolerated populations of more than 1,700 patients in an institution designed for fewer than half that number; news editors who defended cruelty; and hospital staff who abused and killed.

This is a story about these people. Human beings whose work and whose treatment was affected to some degree by science and knowledge. But to a greater extent, their lives were placed in jeopardy by economics, politics, and sheer raw power.

References

Anonymous. Teacher—interview with author, 1998.

Alberta Health. *Mental Health Services in Alberta–Sharing a Vision of Better Health.* Alberta: Government of Alberta, November 1988.

Alberta Health. *Future Directions for Mental Health Services in Alberta.* Alberta: Government of Alberta, February 1992.

Alberta Health. *Working in Partnership: Building A Better Future for Mental Health–Final Report.* Alberta: Mental Health Strategic Planning Advisory Committee, Government of Alberta, August 1993.

Alberta Health Care Insurance Plan. *Statistical Supplement.* 1999-2000. July, 2001.

Alberta Medical Association. "Waiting Times are Increasing: Quality of Care is Declining," *Alberta Digest.* July/August, 23(4), 1998

Alberta Mental Health Board. *Fact Sheet — The Alberta Mental Health System.* May, 2001.

Bland, Roger C. *et.al.* Psychiatric Disorders in the Population and in Prisoners. *International Journal of Law and Psychiatry,* Vol. 21, No.3. 1998.

Clarke Institute of Psychiatry, Health Systems Research Unit. *Best Practices in Mental Health Reform: Discussion Paper.* Prepared for the Advisory Network on Mental Health 1997. Ottawa, Ontario: Health Canada, 1977.

Hudson, Tony. Edmonton, AB. Interview with author, 1998.

LaJeunesse, Brent. Phoenix, AZ. Interview with author, July, 2001.

Smith, Keith. Victim Impact Statement. February, 2000.

Statistical records. Suicide Information and Education Centre, Calgary. 1998.

Yurko, Allan. Edmonton, AB. Interview with author, 2001.

Yurko, Chad, Edmonton, AB. Interview with author, 2001.

14

Chapter 1
Bedlam

Chapter 1
Bedlam

Bedlam

1832

Andrew Ferguson was a derelict. He wandered the streets of Hanwell, Middlesex in England. He was in his early 40s with a weathered face, large dirty hands, matted hair, and a long crusty beard. He wore layer upon layer of clothing to fight the cold and the damp English air; he slept in alleys and cared for an abandoned cat, his only friend. Andrew was active, running from place to place, often changing directions before he reached his destination. And when he was alone, he would yell.

Then Andrew began yelling around other people. Most of them would walk around him, glaring disapprovingly. Others wanted this unpredictable lunatic removed. The English constabulary responded by delivering him to the Pauper Lunatic Asylum just outside of Hanwell. The asylum was one of many run in the manner of the original "Bedlam" madhouse opened in 1547.

Andrew was placed in a small stone room. The derelict was accustomed to sleeping on a floor, but by the time he awoke on the third morning, his hunger was unbearable. He moaned and begged for food and a keeper took pity on him. When he finished his morning porridge, Andrew became agitated. He wanted out. He had done no harm and his cat needed his attention. He began screaming and banging the walls with his fists. It was time for the arm-chair.

The Asylum Superintendent, Sir W.C. Ellis, believed that when "the patient begins to be ungovernable, the kindest and least afflicting" method of treatment was to "procure such an overwhelming power to restrain him as to make him feel it useless to resist." Three or four "determined persons" could do the job of holding one person down, according to Ellis, but his "simpler" methods were more efficient. The first option was a jacket with long canvas sleeves and a leather band to prevent the hands from grasping anything. Two straps across the back and three across the front secured the arms in a "natural" position. The front straps could be buckled or locked when there were many patients to be attended by one keeper.

The attendants, on the other hand, preferred the arm-chair. It would stop Andrew's incessant walking. Each of the arms of the chair formed a padded box into which his arms were forcefully thrust, up to his elbows. The boxes were then closed. A hinged board connected the two boxes across Andrew's chest and a leather strap was placed around his waist, through two holes in the chair and then buckled from behind. His feet were also strapped and for "comfort" a foot board, elevated from the floor and perforated with holes, was placed over a "vessel constantly filled with hot water." The arm-chair, according to experts, would "oppose the impetus of blood toward the brain," reduce the "force and frequency of the pulse," and "favour the application of cold water and ice to the head and warm water to the feet." All of which were considered an "excellent remedy in this disease."

Insanity, according to Superintendent Ellis, could be traced to three causes—"Direct physical injuries of the brain, over-excitement from moral causes, [and] diseased action from sympathy with other parts of the body." The superintendent thought little could be done to prevent injury, but the moral causes were far more frequently to blame anyway, and "generally the result of our having an undue estimate of the things of this life." But asylum inmates were considered by the public to be animals and criminals. Many people believed the lunatics were agents of Satan, thereby justifying the cruelest of punishment. Inmates were restrained and denied food; they had their heads shaved and they were placed in dark cells. Ellis disagreed. If the cause of most insanity, at least according to his theory, was "over-excitement due to moral causes," then it seemed logical that treatment should be "moral."

The best treatment, Ellis said, was "constant, never-tiring, watchful kindness."

Andrew Ferguson was one of the majority of patients in the Middlesex madhouse who were in constant restraint for an average of 12 hours each day. Andrew failed to see this as "watchful kindness." At meal times, attendants would force food into the inmates' mouths with crude spoons. Andrew watched several people choke and die. When not in restraint, he was locked behind heavy doors.

The institution used treatment methods such as "bleeding," to remove the body's toxins, lengthy cold water baths, and physical restraint in all its forms. "Patients are ordered to be bled about the latter end of May, or the beginning of June, according to the weather, and after they have been bled, they take vomit once a week for a certain number of weeks; after that we purge them," said Ellis.

The restraint, the treatment, the stale air, foul odour, the too-many roommates, and the restless nights spent sleeping on a floor or wooden shelf were causing Andrew to crawl further and further into his own reality. The screaming continued—and so did the use of the arm-chair. Time passed, but Andrew's world remained unchanged for seven years.

In 1839, the madhouse employed a new superintendent, John Conolly. A kindly man who abhorred cruelty to others, he introduced the non-restraint methods used since 1832 by Superintendent Robert Gardiner Hill of the Lincoln Lunatic Asylum at Lincolnshire. Over a five-year period, Hill boasted of reducing restraint from 55 of a total 81 inmates to only two of the asylum's population of 130. Hill's reforms also included granting the inmates water to wash with, room ventilation, heat, and the "watchfulness of strong, active attendants."

Superintendent Hill urged the use of the word "asylum" to replace madhouse. "Asylum," he argued, meant "a place of refuge, of shelter from injury, of comfortable retreat, until the storm be overpast: a place where every want is attended to, every reasonable wish gratified." He also preferred the term "insanity" to the alternative "lunacy." Insanity meant senseless, while lunacy was taken from the word lunar, or moon, and implied that the condition was caused by the strange effects of a full moon. Other doctors preferred the word "alienism" meaning that the insane seemed strange and alienated from the world.

17

Conolly's view, much like that of Superintendent Hill, was that governance of the "insane," or "alien," could best be achieved by creating in them a "kindly disposition" towards their keepers. It seemed to work. A study of Hill's Lincoln Asylum noted with amazement: "The condition of the patients is much improved, the quiet of the house increased, and the number of accidents and suicides is materially reduced in number." Hill was pleased and Conolly would follow his lead. The asylums would be a place "better than these wretched souls have ever before enjoyed."

It certainly worked for Andrew. His screaming continued, but for shorter periods. And he no longer smashed the attendants with his big knuckles. The madhouse was quieter, warmer, more tolerable. Five more years passed, and Superintendent Conolly wrote: "Since the abolition of the strait waist coat, the muff, the leg locks and handcuffs and the restraint chair," there had been no accidents which restraint might have prevented. There was also "marked improvement in the character of those parts of the asylum" in which restraint had been reduced.

Andrew Ferguson died at the Middlesex Asylum in the winter of 1847, exactly 300 years after King Henry VIII converted the monastery of St. Mary of Bethlehem into Bedlam, England's first madhouse for the insane. Mr. Ferguson died in non-restraint, on a wooden shelf in a locked ward, without his cat. Mercifully, his screaming had stopped.

English superintendents John Conolly and Robert Hill, like Ellis, were among the first to put "moral treatment" into practice. They took their lead from two distant colleagues. Phillipe Pinel of the Bicetre Asylum in Paris, France, dramatized the plight of his lunatics by personally removing their chains in 1792. The word moral according to Pinel was "the application of the faculty of intelligence and of the emotions in the treatment of alienation." In England, four years after Pinel released his inmates, the theory of "kindness, rest, and religion" was proposed by William Tuke. A Quaker, Tuke followed his beliefs and built an institution he called the York Retreat, where "patients could be treated with all the kindness which their condition allowed." A few asylums in the New World would take note—but not for another 25 years.

North American asylums had been influenced by Dr. Thomas Bond of Philadelphia, who travelled to England to find a model for treatment of the insane and feeble-minded. He toured Henry VIII's Bethlehem asylum and received what he described as "considerable inspiration." The first American public asylum was opened in the basement of the Pennsylvania Hospital in1751. The first stand-alone asylum was built in Virginia a few years later. Both were based on the English plan.

Over the next 75 years, another 12 asylums were built throughout the United States. The Bedlam influence continued, but gradually, the newer superintendents were swayed to "moral treatment" by the theories of Conolly, Hill, and Tuke. In New York, the Bloomingdale Asylum boasted "humane conditions" and a high cure rate. By 1844, that asylum claimed to have treated 1,841 patients and discharged 1,762, of whom, 672 were cured. "Cured" was defined as "minimal function between the patient, his family, and society." When the Bloomingdale Asylum published its results, the improvements were widely copied throughout the original 13 United States asylums. The superintendents formed a formal group, the Association of Medical Superintendents of American Institutions for the Insane, later to be known as the American Psychiatric Association.

Not all asylums adopted moral treatment—at least not until they were pressured to do so. Dorothea Lynde Dix was a Boston school teacher with tuberculosis, which forced her into early retirement. She spent volunteer time teaching in an institution for women. The deplorable conditions in jails and asylums moved Dorothea to inform newspapers of abuse and to begin a crusade against these institutions in the same year that the psychiatrists were organizing their association. Ironically her attack on the superintendents would lead to an increase in their numbers. Dix embarrassed some state governments and convinced others of the "rightness" of her message. Succumbing to the pressure, state politicians approved the building of 32 new asylums to relieve the overcrowding and to expand the new philosophy of moral treatment. Each had a superintendent who would join the new association.

The State of New York, in a bold passage, declared that "science, aided by humanity, has dispelled ignorance, overcome prejudice, conquered superstition and investigated the causes, character and curability of mental disease." While the government of New York may have overstated conditions surrounding mental illness, if the momentum of the concept of moral treatment held, Dix would move thousands of insane people to the "kindness and care" of the new, improved asylums.

Moral treatment was also moving into Canada. Sixty years after the building of America's first asylum in Philadelphia, two men from Saint John, New Brunswick, George Matthews and Dr. George Peters, appealed to the city government to have a cholera hospital converted to an insane asylum. Dr. Peters had worked in the city's jail and in the almshouse, a house for the poor supported by charity. "The pauper lunatics," he complained to city councilors, "are found in the same room as felons and criminals... I found several unfortunate men, some of them perfectly naked and in a state of filth [which was] under the circumstances unavoidable, yet disgraceful to humanity." Influential and persuasive men with a passionate cause, Matthews and Peters were successful. The councilors agreed to a temporary facility while they awaited provincial action on the building of a permanent asylum. In November of 1835, Canada's first asylum opened in an old building on King's Square in Saint John, New Brunswick.

Eighty miles to the northwest, a small committee was campaigning in Fredericton to appear before the legislature with a petition "for the passing of a law for the better providing for and securing of lunatics within the province." The population of the province was still sparse and lunatics were few in number, but the public was concerned. Individual counties were left to deal with the lunatics and mental defectives as best they could, which usually meant shackles and chains, in jail. The legislature heard the petition, and a year later, a committee under the leadership of Rev. Frederick Coster was struck to prepare a plan for the permanent asylum. In addition, a commission was charged with overseeing the temporary institution that was being run by its founder, Dr. George Peters.

Rev. Coster's report computed the number of lunatics in the province to be 130—one lunatic for every 10,000 citizens. The cost of the proposed new building, land, and furnishings was calculated to be about £11,000.

In the meantime, Dr. George Peters' passion made him the natural choice to run the temporary asylum. The building was inadequate, but he made do. He divided the building into two sides, one for men and the other for women. He then subdivided the sections to separate the "more violent inmates." When he was finished, he concluded, without much comfort: "The place is altogether insufficient, either for their comfortable residence, their safekeeping, or their proper treatment." He qualified his comment by adding that the facility was, however, "greatly superior to anything which these poor unfortunate persons have ever before enjoyed."

In the first eight months of operation, Peters admitted 22 patients. Of these, only 12 remained in the asylum. One died and nine were discharged as "cured." From his experience, after setting the "idiots" aside, Dr. Peters viewed the major cause of insanity in women as "sudden fright." For men it was "the abuse of spirituous liquors—a fruitful cause of insanity, which will very likely in this country keep a lunatic asylum well-filled with patients."

A decade after Rev. Coster's report recommending a new asylum, Peters was still waiting. Part of the delay was a government proposal that one institution serve all of the Maritimes, but after heavy debate, the government of Prince Edward Island withdrew its support and the plan fell apart. Then the major dispute in the New Brunswick Legislature was over the proposed location. There was a strong lobby for a site near the capital of Fredericton, but the Saint John site was finally selected. The reason, according to news reports, was that "a friend of the government had land to sell." Ground was broken in September of 1846 and 18 months later—before the asylum's construction had even been completed—90 patients were transferred from the temporary site into Canada's first modern asylum, albeit one with no central heat, light, or water.

But moral treatment as a concept was not to last. In 1891, 43 years after the opening of the New Brunswick asylum, 50 beds were rapidly filled at the new Insane Asylum in Brandon, Manitoba. Built a year earlier as the Manitoba Reformatory for Boys, it originally opened with only one inmate, nine-year-old Billy Mulligan, who was to serve five years for stealing letters from a mailbox. The Brandon asylum was typical of others across North America: large, impersonal dayrooms, crowded dormitories and side rooms, few washrooms, little organized activity—and troubled souls pacing the floors, locked in their own emotional cells.

Known as "The Mental," the 1906 Brandon asylum consisted of four stately buildings set among trees and gardens on a slope overlooking the Assiniboine River and downtown Brandon. From a distance, the asylum's exterior had a certain majestic tranquillity. Inside, there was kindness, solitude, warmth, and food. There were also inmate beatings and patients who were locked in cupboards, placed in straitjackets for days on end, shackled with chains, strapped on beds with metal grills placed over them, and when the wards were too crowded, forced to sleep on wooden shelves.

Two years after the building opened, the Government of the Dominion of Canada arranged with the Manitoba government to construct an addition to the Brandon Institution for the purpose of housing lunatics from the Northwest Territories. Since 1879, "dangerous lunatics" from the west were removed to the penitentiary at

The Brandon Asylum in 1906 served the Canadian West. (Reproduced courtesy of the Brandon Mental Health Centre Historical Museum Inc.)

Stony Mountain, Manitoba. The jail was overcrowded and Canada's health minister wanted to "more humanely" incarcerate the lunatics. He urged the asylum be expanded with Manitoba money. The national government would then pay Manitoba for each day it provided care for an inmate from anywhere in what was then called the Northwest Territories. The lunatics now in jail would be housed at less cost in the "Mental."

It was March during the savage winter of 1906-07, and a young Mountie rode through deep snow on his regular patrol between Cypress Hills and Wood Mountain. The journey was long, and Constable Braddock of the North West Mounted Police survived by using patrol posts stocked with supplies and wood. As he neared the community of Bigstick, he saw in the distance a pair of horsemen riding toward him, waving their arms. The men were brothers who, with a third man, were attempting to keep 2,000 cattle alive in the rolling hills. There were about 200 cowboys just like them trying to tend cattle over more than 10,000 square miles of territory. The job was tough and lonely, and the brothers were fighting a losing battle. Almost half the herd had starved or frozen to death.

The third cowboy, Hank Saunders, had been behaving strangely for weeks. Saunders, the brothers reported, had begun to "talk about nonsense." He would pace the shack talking to himself or sit in a chair quietly rocking back and forth. "Some days he would see things we couldn't," said a brother. "Things no one could—like spring time. Then this morning he saddled his pony and rode away without any provisions or proper clothing." Constable Braddock asked the brothers to show him the pony's tracks, then followed the hoof prints through the snow for four hours, expecting to find a stiff body. But Hank Saunders had already been found by a "wolfer," who had taken the cowboy to a hut near his trapline. The wolfer built a fire and dragged Saunders into his shelter, but he couldn't get him to talk. Saunders stared into the air. The wolfer was "damn glad" to see the Mountie at his door. He couldn't send the cowpuncher back into the cold, but he sure wanted him to go somewhere else.

The three men bunked together for the night, and the next morning Braddock, with his mute companion, rode to Wood Mountain. There, he found a magistrate who ordered the man to be transported to the Brandon Asylum, more than 700 miles to the east. It was 1907 and the new government of the two-year-old Province of Alberta had just passed an Insane Persons Act that provided for committal "in any asylum in the Province of Manitoba or elsewhere." There were no asylums in Alberta. The new province had adopted the Dominion government's arrangement with Manitoba and Alberta would pay for Saunders' care.

Almost a week later, the train chugged into Brandon Station carrying a tired Mountie and his charge. Saunders had given the officer no grief. Hank remained in handcuffs the entire trip, expressionless and staring at something only he could see. This was Braddock's first trip to the asylum and he knew nothing of the conditions to which Saunders was delivered. Seven hundred patients were in the care of one doctor who in his own words, spent all of his time "supervising the asylum farm" and "filling in death certificates." He had little time to treat patients and there were no trained nurses. Saunders and the other patients, some in straitjackets or shackles, dejected, staring vacantly into space, would sit in complete idleness on long, hard wooden benches—waiting for death to give them release.

23

Constable Braddock walked from the asylum with a shudder, feeling no regrets about the long trek home. At least he was going home. For Saunders, the chance of ever returning to Alberta seemed a very unlikely proposition—even if he wanted to.

References

Anonymous. Calgary, AB. Family of former inmate—interview with author, 1998.

Anonymous. Red Deer. Family of former inmate—interview with author, 1998.

Caplan, R.B. *Psychiatry and the Community in Nineteenth-Century America*. New York: Basic Books, 1969.

Conolly, John. *Treatment of the Insane without Mechanical Restraints*. London: Ayer Company Publishers, (Original work published 1856), 1973.

Ellis, Sir William Charles. *A Treatise on the Nature, Symptoms, Causes, and Treatments of Insanity*. London: Ayer Company Publishers, 1938.

Fallding, Helen. "Closing the 'mental.'" *Winnipeg Free Press*. November 15, 1998.

Goss, David. *150 Years of Caring: The Continuing History of Canada's Oldest Mental Health Facility*. Saint John, NB: Unipress, 1998.

Griffin, Jack. Toronto, ON. Interview with author, 1988.

Hill, R.G. *Non-restraint System of Treatment in Lunacy*. London: Longman, Brown, Green and Longman, 1857.

Johnstone, Christine, "The asylum's alienist," *The Medical Post*, June 13, 2000.

Martin, William. Winnipeg, MB. Interview with author, 1998.

Report of the U.S. Surgeon General. *The Fundamentals of Mental Health and Mental Illness*, 2000.

Ross, Ken. St. John, NB. Interview with author, 1998.

Rothman, David J. *The Discovery of the Asylum: Social Order and Disorder in the New Republic*. Boston: Little, Brown and Company, 1971.

Stanton, Alfred H. and Schwartz, Morris S. *The Mental Hospital: A Study of Institutional Participation in Psychiatric Illness and Treatment*. New York: Basic Books, 1954.

Tuke, Daniel Hack. *Chapters in the History of the Insane in the British Isles*. London: Trench and Co., 1982.

26

Chapter 2
Moral Treatment;
Then Bedlam Again

Chapter 2
Moral Treatment;
Then Bedlam Again

Moral Treatment; then Bedlam Again

1911

It was a magnificent building in a magnificent location. Situated high on rolling hills in prime agricultural land, the new hospital had a fine farm and a panoramic view of the countryside. Copied from a New York design after politicians and civil servants had examined the best American asylums, the three-storey brick structure was meant to bring Alberta into the forefront of treatment for the insane and feeble-minded—at a lower cost than treatments in the past. The province was paying the Dominion Government a dollar per patient for each day of care in the Brandon Asylum. The Provincial Hospital for the Insane at Ponoka, a town on the Canadian Pacific Railway line about halfway between Edmonton and Calgary, would provide care at a cost of about fifty cents a day. Agriculture Minister Duncan McLean Marshall, whose ministry included health services, was very proud.

The Ponoka Asylum built its first building in 1911. (Reproduced from public documents published by the Alberta Hospital Ponoka)

Premier A.C. Rutherford and his cabinet had approved funds for the hospital in the hope that it would serve Albertans well—and economically. This was to be a modern institution with care modelled on progressive "moral" techniques practiced in the best asylums of Europe and the United States. Officials had assured the Premier and the agriculture minister that Ponoka would be nothing like the infamous London Hospital of Mary of Bethlehem—which was better known by the name Bedlam.

Bedlam was infamous. A cold, damp, dark place where the insane were shackled, locked in cells, beaten and starved. Inmates were on public view for payment of a penny to the superintendent. Curious crowds of people would make a Sunday trip to Bedlam so they could watch outlandish behavior and perhaps thank God for their own better circumstances. The madhouse was so notorious that the word "bedlam" itself had come to mean "uproar" or "turmoil." But the English Bedlam was considered an advance over previous European treatments such as cramming people into "ships of fools" and casting them on the open seas, or auctioning them off to any bidder who would "care for them" at no cost to the public.

Alberta would have none of that. The Minister of Agriculture, Duncan Marshall, was described as a caring man who believed in the need for asylum—a place of solitude, escape, and comfort where one dealt with his or her problems. Marshall also espoused the philosophy of "moral treatment," begun more than a century earlier in England and France. Although the philosophy was less prevalent in the 20th century, it was being practised in the most impressive of the American asylums that the Alberta government had visited.

28   Moral treatment meant that the Bedlam madhouses of the world were to be replaced by new, caring asylums. The idea was to build a small place serving a maximum of 250 patients who would be provided with solace and protection in a relaxed rural setting. The asylum would be big enough to provide anonymity but small enough to allow people to know one another. Personnel would be friendly and approachable, and the superintendent would govern in a "fatherly sort of way." The staff would, said Minister Marshall, "create a family-like, tolerant, and loving environment." He believed patients and their families would take great comfort in these idyllic surroundings and great hope from a medical superintendent who could "control disruptive thoughts and impulses" and then teach patients to act

"normally." The selection of a superintendent, therefore, was all-important.

Provincial Secretary A.J. McLean visited and interviewed applicants from throughout Canada and the United States before recommending the appointment of a medical health officer from Calgary. Originally from Edinburgh, Scotland, Dr. Thomas Dawson was well-liked by most everyone he met. Although he had no training in psychiatry, he had a kind nature and firmly believed that patients would benefit from "exposure to social situations." He was just the man for the job! The 108 men and 56 women arriving shortly from the Brandon Asylum, most of who were never expected to return to Alberta, were considered fortunate.

A hot July day in 1911 found 164 people walking, hobbling, or being carted on horse-drawn wagons over the one and three-quarter miles from the Ponoka railway station to the hospital. Although he had never expected to see Alberta again, Hank Saunders, the rancher delivered to Brandon by the Mountie, was among them. The rag-tag group would join 16 other patients who had been admitted earlier in the month. As they travelled up the narrow dirt road to the hospital, they were seemingly unimpressed by the majesty of the brick building which was to become home.

Basing his design on the asylum in Utica, New York, architect A.M. Jeffers had strived to create a warm, safe, and functional building that would last for decades. While the hospital was in the centre of good farming land, the building site was marshy and Jeffers had to start with 25-foot pilings. Built in the form of a cross, the building had a central administration area and separate wings for the male and female patients.

Each wing included work rooms, sleeping dormitories, and sitting rooms. Parallel to each corridor was a sunroom for exercise in bad weather. Built of brick, Calgary sandstone, terra-cotta block and plaster, the asylum was a fortress. Fireproof materials were used wherever possible, and the rock was smashed on site, using steam-driven crushers. Steam-radiant heat served the dormitories and warm air was blown into the small side rooms. The day room was bright and cheery, with a bay window and a fireplace. An electric powerhouse was connected to the main building by a tunnel. A sewage plant, a water tower, and a fully equipped farm rounded out the 800-acre site. This was most certainly not Bedlam.

The Ponoka Asylum shown around 1911. (Reproduced from public documents publshed by the Alberta Hospital Ponoka)

But Marshall and McLean's vision of an idyllic centre ran into problems almost immediately. Unlike the successful American asylums, which operated privately, Dr. Dawson's public hospital could not restrict admissions. The Brandon patients, most of who were "in a weak and collapsed condition," were eventually joined by 52 Alberta admissions. The population of the province was growing, and admissions were growing with it. The new premier, Arthur Lewis Sifton, who had been elected just before the hospital officially opened, believed that Marshall's vision of a small facility providing humane treatment needed to be abandoned. Expanding an existing building was far more economical, he thought, than building another institution at some other location. The new hospital was still landscaping when the government approved the addition of a second building, on the same site, for male patients. It was to be another four-storey building, called "Male 4 and 5," and would contain work and recreation rooms on the lower level, two floors for patients, and a top floor for farmhands and other outside workers. In addition, two six-room brick cottages would be built for the medical superintendent and his financial manager.

By 1915, yet another building, "Female 4, 5, and 6," was opened to accommodate a surge in the number of female patients. The site was rapidly taking the form of the large rural asylums so prominent in many American states. A year later, the hospital's population passed 500 and plans were drawn up for yet another building, planned for completion within two to three years. Dawson was managing a very different institution from the one he had visualized in 1911, and he didn't like it.

Simultaneously, the Home for Mental Defective Children, operating in south Edmonton, had become overcrowded after less than a year in operation. It too, needed relief and the government was being pushed to act. An address to members of the Alberta Legislature by Clare Hincks of the Canadian National Committee for Mental Hygiene, seemed to influence the legislators. Hincks preferred smaller sites in a variety of locations, and the government was, as a result, now leaning towards a new site situated near the capital, separate from Ponoka. An institution in Edmonton would relieve pressure in Ponoka, but the plans were very preliminary, and Superintendent Dawson was unwilling to tolerate the hospital's explosive growth any longer. He resigned and returned to Edinburgh.

Five years later, in 1920, Premier Charles Stewart proudly announced "a farm and site for a permanent institution." The 1,000-acre site, just north of Edmonton at Oliver, was "admirably suited in every way," proclaimed the government. "The land is high ... the acreage is arable (and) in the summer there is bus service on the trail." The Department of Education saw the new institution as a permanent home for the estimated 600 severely retarded people in the province. "Alberta's feeble-minded will no longer be a menace to society," the government declared.

By 1921, the Department of Public Works had completed design drawings for a facility which would accommodate 1,000 to 1,500 patients. Hincks' proposal, encouraging smaller institutions had obviously been abandoned. Excavation was begun and tenders were let. The Education Department would run the institution as The Home and Training School for Mental Defectives.

Oliver/
TALE

31

Then the government changed again. The United Farmers of Alberta, under Herbert Greenfield, replaced Liberal Premier Charles Stewart—and the new Health Minister, George Hoadley, had his own ideas. Construction on the new school proceeded while his department did a reassessment. The government also asked Dr. Hincks to return to the province to undertake a "thorough canvass of the effect of mental sub-normality upon the welfare of the community." The new home/training school was completed in the spring of 1923, about the same time as Hoadley's department completed its review. The National Committee's work had been finished two years earlier and Hincks' recommendations, he was promised, would be considered in the department's plans.

The government's assessment concluded that the Oliver facility should be an institute for the insane and not a training school for the retarded. It further concluded that the number of severely retarded people was greater than originally thought, and that the underused Hospital for Returned Soldiers in Red Deer would make a better location for the idiots and imbeciles. Dr. W.J. McAlister, who was training in Massachusetts to run the Oliver school, would be reassigned to the renamed School Hospital in Red Deer. Dr. D.L. Dyck, of the soon-to-be-defunct Red Deer Soldier's Hospital, would take over at what was now to be called the Provincial Institute near the town of Oliver.

The plan would allow the overcrowded home in south Edmonton to be closed after sending the children to Red Deer. The mentally ill adults from the Red Deer hospital were to be sent to Ponoka, and the sickest of the Ponoka inmates would be sent to Oliver. All in all, an efficient plan. It would, boasted the Public Health Department, "obviate the necessity of building" for at least three years.

The recommendation by Hincks for a small "psychopathic hospital" was lost in the efficiency of the bureaucracy. "With a larger institution," warned Hincks, "there would be a tendency to harbour patients for long periods, and such a course is not recommended." Hincks was saddened. People would continue to be shuffled about the province with no regard for family and community relationships. Economic and political considerations always seemed to drive the agenda.

On the evening of July 1, 1923, a crowd of eminent government and medical leaders and their wives awaited the arrival of special guests,

Premier Herbert Greenfield and Attorney General John Brownlee. The group gathered in the administration section of one of the pair of three-storey buildings that would soon house the inmates. A power house, water tower, bakery, laundry, greenhouse, store, and the superintendent's mansion surrounded the two buildings on 100 acres of fine land nine miles north of Edmonton. An additional 900 acres of farm land would provide the necessary food and work for the inmates.

As the Premier's luxurious McLaughlin automobile navigated the narrow road, Health Minister Hoadley and other MLAs gathered to greet him. They were in formal attire: gowns, black suits, and uniforms. It was an auspicious occasion. The Premier greeted the guests warmly and described the opening as a milestone in the province's history. The crowd applauded as he cut the opening ribbon. Then refreshments were served, and the guests danced late into the evening, celebrating both Dominion Day and the official opening. This would be the last dance in the institution for a very long time.

Later in the month, some of the "better patients" from Ponoka were sent to Oliver to help prepare the grounds. By the end of summer, 47 patients who needed continuing care were transferred from the Hospital for Returned Soldiers. Hundreds of others would soon follow from the newly named Provincial Mental Hospital in Ponoka. The old name, Hospital for the Insane, was obsolete, and the Edmonton "Institute"—pointedly not a hospital—was expected to meet Alberta's needs for dealing with the sickest of the sick for many years to come.

However, only five years later, Health Minister Hoadley and Education Minister Perren Baker were expressing concern about the constantly growing population of the provincial institutions. They knew the cautions that Clare Hincks and the Canadian National Committee for Mental Hygiene had expressed about large institutions and they invited Hincks back to Alberta. He was joined by Dr. C.B. Farrar, a man considered to be one of Canada's leading psychiatrists. Hincks and Farrar had recently traveled extensively, and they apparently knew about worldwide trends and innovations. They conducted another survey and in 1928, Baker and Hoadley were given a confidential report.

To the question of building new asylums, they wrote: "In the old days the asylum was placed in outlying districts away from the centres of population, not necessarily in the interests of the afflicted to be cared for there, but rather for the assumed advantage of the community at large." Their advice followed: "The policy which now finds acceptance is just the opposite. Hospitals for mental patients are brought in as close contact as possible with centres where clinical and other urban advantages may be made available." Their conclusion was that "the closer the relationship between hospital and populace, the better for all concerned."

In the meantime, construction of facilities at Ponoka and Oliver stopped dead—but not because of the Hincks-Farrar Report. There was no money. The "dirty '30s," a decade of drought, dust, poverty, and hopelessness, eliminated any possible consideration of new projects. While construction stopped, the increase in patients didn't. Dr. C.A. Baragar, considered one of the most progressive psychiatrists in Alberta, had been appointed the new Provincial Commissioner of Mental Health in 1930. He agreed in principle with Hincks and Farrar, but the government was broke. The insane would have to be placed wherever space could be found.

Isolated sites away from the population might not be best for treatment, but the public didn't seem to care. Minister Hoadley rarely heard complaints from family members. He also viewed himself as a realist. Many of the patients in Ponoka would never recover, and it made sense to transfer them to places like the Oliver Institute where fewer treatment staff were needed and costs were lower. Institutes or auxiliary hospitals, rather than active treatment hospitals, made good economic sense.

In 1933, Hoadley converted a school of agriculture into a provincial auxiliary hospital on the outskirts of the small southern Alberta community of Claresholm. It had 100 beds and would care for the most chronic of patients for whom Ponoka Superintendent George Davidson had little hope. Davidson transferred 100 women, to be cared for by a single medical director. Eight years later, there would be no medical staff, only the occasional visit by local physicians who were "on call."

Hoadley then closed the University of Alberta's innovative "Psychopathic Ward," opened only three years earlier as the province's first and only psychiatric ward in a general hospital. The closure was "owing to the economic situation," he said. Patients were transferred to the other institutions or discharged. In spite of all the transfers out, within four years the Ponoka hospital patient population reached an all-time high of 1,707, in a facility designed for less than half that number. Conditions were disastrous, and money kept getting tighter.

By then, Ponoka had a new superintendent, Randall McLean, who refused to accept the status quo. He was outspoken and aggressive and would not be ignored. McLean bombarded Dr. Baragar and Minister Hoadley with requests. As a result, 238 men were transferred to the institute at Oliver. Overcrowding in an institute or auxiliary hospital was apparently not as bad as in a treatment hospital. The problems were being shuffled around rather than being solved.

The government then reviewed the Claresholm experiment where very little medical attention was provided. It seemed to have worked well. Costs were low and few problems were reported. So a second agricultural school was converted to an auxiliary hospital in Raymond, a tiny village in Alberta's deep south. In 1939, another 113 patients were transferred from Ponoka to the converted school under the medical care of "on-call" physicians.

As the decade and the Great Depression ended, Canada went to war. Hospital staff enlisted in great numbers, and good replacement nurses could not be found. Four doctors, including Superintendent Randall McLean, would have to deal with over 1,600 patients in Ponoka. At Oliver, near Edmonton, Dr. William McAlister was the only physician. The institute now held over 1,000 people. The staff hours were increased to 12 a day, and morale plummeted. More staff left to join the forces or take better paying jobs in the war industry.

A further problem was the increasing state of disrepair in the hospitals. Mattresses lying side by side on floors were soaked by rain from leaking roofs. And there were simply no resources to fix the ailing buildings. The 1935 "rainbow sky" promises of Premier William Aberhart had not materialized for the mentally ill in Alberta.

By the end of the war, Aberhart's successor, Premier Ernest Manning, felt a renewed optimism about the economy and agreed to act on the overcrowding in mental institutions. His solution, like that of most leaders in the preceding 37 years, was to provide yet another custodial institution. Converted from a normal school for teachers and more recently used as a World War II basic training camp for the army, the Rosehaven Centre in the central Alberta town of Camrose was opened in 1947. Medical services would, as in other institutes and auxiliary hospitals, be provided by on-call doctors. The centre accommodated 200 old and infirm patients from the Ponoka hospital. By the early 1950s, two dormitories had been added, and there were more than 450 patients in residence.

Still the Ponoka Hospital population continued to grow, with more than 680 patients admitted in 1953 alone. There were more than 125 patients in a single dayroom, every corner was crowded and the lack of privacy resulted in frequent fights. Some of the patients had their teeth removed to prevent them from biting staff. At night, mattresses were taken from a large pile in the corner and spread out over the dayroom floor. There was enough room in the dormitories for about half of the patients—and even that was more than three times the number recommended in the original hospital designs. The overcrowding was out of control, and in 1955 the government committed to adding buildings for another 786 beds. They would also move more "feeble-minded" patients to Deerhome, a new institution in Red Deer.

Once again patients would be shuttled between institutions with little regard for their families or for the location of their homes. In most cases, the first admission to hospital had taken people far from home, and each new move made visiting even more difficult. Most families and friends eventually gave up. With contact lost, patients faced years—and sometimes their entire lives—in impersonal institutions. Institutionalization and the stigma connected to mental illness virtually guaranteed they would never return to a normal life. Many were too afraid to leave. For those who tried, public reaction often drove them back.

Meanwhile, plans consistent with the 1928 Hincks-Farrar recommendations for early and intense treatment in small hospitals near patients' homes were beginning to serve as the foundation for modern programs in other parts of North America. In 1953, the World Health Organization called for an end to large centralized hospitals and proposed manageable "units" for the care of small groups of patients.

But across the prairies, the recommendations were lost among political considerations. In 1955, in Manitoba, the Brandon Asylum was again enlarged. According to the Premier, the public wanted it that way. The same year, in Saskatchewan, Premier Tommy Douglas was publicly disagreeing with his civil servants, who were proposing smaller psychiatric units around the province. In a letter to a constituent, Douglas wrote," You can be sure if there is any extension of mental hospital facilities, I will be on the job to see that Weyburn is not overlooked as the logical place for additional buildings, rather than scattering them all over the province as was suggested." A 950-bed mental hospital was Weyburn's largest employer, and Premier Tommy Douglas represented that constituency.

Mental hospitals were important. The public wanted them and politicians needed them. And for many of the inmates and patients, it was really their only option. Some people got better, but many didn't. Some just learned to do what was expected of them.

References

Alberta Health. *A History Of The Health System In Alberta.* Research and Planning Branch, February, 1991.

Anonymous. Family of former patient—interview with author, 1998.

Anonymous. Former psychiatric nurse—interview with author, 1998.

Abt, Mary Frances McHugh. *Adaptive Change and Leadership in a Psychiatric Hospital.* Edmonton, Alberta: Ph.D. Thesis, University of Alberta, 1992.

Abt, Mary Frances McHugh. Ponoka, AB. Interview with author, 1998.

Baragar, C.A. *Annual Report,* Provincial Mental Hospital, Department of Public Health, Alberta. Alberta: Provincial Archives, 1931.

Beers, Clifford Whittingham. *A Mind that Found Itself.* New York: Doubleday & Company, 1908.

Caplan, R.B. *Psychiatry and the Community in Nineteenth-Century America.* New York: Basic Books, 1969.

Cooke, E.H. *Annual Report.* Provincial Mental Hospital, Department of Public Health. Alberta: Provincial Archives, 1928-29.

Cooke, E.H. *Annual Report.* Provincial Mental Hospital, Department of Public Health. Alberta: Provincial Archives, 1930-31.

Dawson, T. *Annual Report: The Hospital for the Insane.* Government of Alberta. Alberta: Provincial Archives, 1912.

Dickinson, Harley D. *The Two Psychiatries: The Transformation of Psychiatric Work in Saskatchewan, 1905-1984.* Regina: Canadian Plains Research Center, University of Regina, 1989.

Goffman, Erving. Asylums: Essays on the Social Situation of Mental Patients and Other Inmates. Garden City, NY: Doubleday, 1961.

Johnson, J.O., *et. al.* A History of Dedication and Caring 1911-1986. Ponoka: Alberta Hospital Ponoka, 1986.

Johnson, J.O. Ponoka, AB. Interview with author, 1998.

Krewski, B.E. *Alberta Mental Health Services in Alberta: A brief History.* 1986.

Rothman, David J. *The Discovery of the Asylum: Social Order and Disorder in the New Republic.* Boston: Little, Brown and Company, 1971.

Rules and Regulations of the Provincial Mental Hospital. Alberta Hospital Museum, 1918.

Simmons, Harvey G. *Unbalanced: Mental Health Policy in Ontario, 1930-1989.* Toronto: Wall & Thompson, 1990.

Slater, R. *Ponoka Panorama.* Ponoka: Ponoka and District Historical Society, 1973.

Stanton, Alfred H. and Schwartz, Morris S. *The Mental Hospital: A Study of Institutional Participation in Psychiatric Illness and Treatment.* New York: Basic Books, 1954.

40

Chapter 3
Water, Weaving, Gardens, and Guesswork

Water, Weaving, Gardens, and Guesswork

1916

"As with a dumb animal, obedience must first be learned." Superintendent Cooke was explaining his philosophy of treatment. "The very ground rung of the treatment when a patient arrives at Ponoka begins with obedience," he declared, "or there can be no hope of recovery... Like a child, he must be taught the fundamentals of life all over again." In conclusion, he stated convincingly, "Obedience will give them everything they desire."

It was 1916 and Dr. E.H. Cooke was serving his fourth year at the Provincial Hospital for the Insane at Ponoka. His firm, authoritarian style had been solidly established. Born in England, Dr. Edelston Harvey Cooke graduated as a physician from that country's Durham University and then immersed himself in a four-month training program on mental diseases. He was recruited to the Ponoka medical staff shortly after the asylum opened and was more than pleased to assume the superintendency when the first "super," Dr. D.T. Dawson, resigned after five years of service. Cooke could not wait to get started.

He introduced a smooth, efficient hospital run in a businesslike manner. His style was crisp and authoritative. He had precise regulations for the staff. He also classified patients with a new system developed by the Americans and then maintained statistical tables and detailed annual reports. The government was pleased.

All treatment decisions were made according to Cooke's philosophy, and his five methods of treatment were clearly detailed for the staff. The first treatment was discipline. Patients would do as and when they were told. Punishment was to be given freely. The second treatment was bed rest which was connected with punishment. "Keep him in bed until he promises to correct the disobedience," declared Cooke. "He is then let out on his honour. If he breaks it he is placed in bed for a longer period." The superintendent then added confidently, "They rarely have to be put to bed more than twice." The third treatment was bathing in Epsom salts to eliminate toxins. Treatment number four was a strict daily routine. Patients would have to develop regular habits. Finally, staff had to help the patients understand themselves better by learning about their personal limitations and weaknesses. Any flaws should be pointed out daily.

The staff learned Cooke's lessons well. In addition to bed restraint, which was achieved by tying a metal cage over the bed, there were wrist and leg shackles. There were also camisoles, or straitjackets of heavy canvas, to tie the patient's arms across his chest. They were effective; they had, in fact, been used in English asylums for more than 400 years.

In 1924, the government granted Cooke an eight-month leave of absence to pursue post-graduate studies in psychiatry. He chose the "Bedlam" Hospital in London where most of his new training simply supported much of what he was already doing.

A typical treatment was the continuous bath in which Cooke had people immersed in warm water with Epsom salts. By 1918, the use of water had taken on added emphasis through the promotions of Dr. T.W. MacNeill, a Scot who was superintendent of the new Saskatchewan asylum in North Battleford. MacNeill believed in the value of the "two W's"—work and water. They were, he believed, the most effective way to treat insanity. He had constructed open metal showers with up to 17 spray heads apiece and patients would stand in the spray for long periods. MacNeill also recommended leaving patients in continuous baths for "two to 24 hours." And he reported, there were excellent results—the patients found the showers "relaxing." One of his strategies to encourage male patients into the water was to have the nurses attend the bathers in "abbreviated bathing suits."

North Battleford Asylum in Saskatchewan creates special showers for therapy. (Reproduced courtesy Saskatchewan Archives Board.)

Not to be outdone, Cooke would eventually have 22 continuous baths. But scantily clad nurses were out of the question for the conservative Cooke, who had his own innovations. In his continuous bath, the patient was placed on a hammock suspended in the tub with the temperature kept at a continuous 92 to 95 degrees Fahrenheit. Occasionally a sheet was drawn over the fully exposed tub to provide some privacy.

43

The only drug available was a foul-tasting liquid called Paraldehyde. It usually calmed patients or put them to sleep for a short time—if they could be convinced to take it. Sedative packs were also used to settle manic, hysterical, and aggressive patients, and they were more easily applied. Either a cold or hot wet sheet was placed on a bed. The patient would then lie on the sheet and an attendant would wrap him tightly with arms by his sides. If it was a hot pack, the patient was then wrapped in two heavy blankets. In either pack, he was

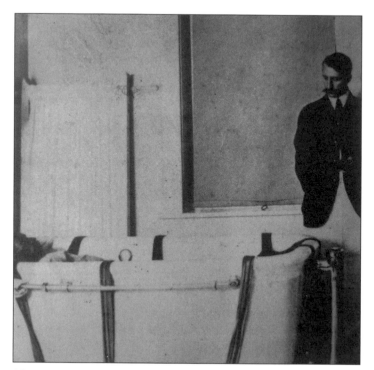

"Continuous baths" immerse patients in tepid water for up to 24 hours. (Photo courtesy CMHA — original source unknown.)

strapped tightly to the bed and would perspire profusely or shiver uncontrollably and it was hoped, fall asleep—a state which was, according to Cooke, "favoured by the brain in this situation."

Restraints were used only as long as necessary, but in some cases that was forever. Charlie McKenzie was an example. He would continually eat his own feces. "He would be in the bathroom all the time," the staff complained. Ten-year-old Hank Freedman was another. He would bite anyone who came near him.

For agitated patients who were not violent, Cooke introduced the "electric cabinet," or "heat box," as the staff preferred to call it. Patients were stripped and locked in a rectangular wooden box with a hole in the top to allow the head to protrude. The box contained electric bulbs which, if they did not touch the skin, provided a "warm relaxing sensation" followed by "perspiration and obedience." According to nursing staff, Cooke apparently never personally tried the device.

Other innovations included canvas cuffs and straps or sheets to tie people into their beds or chairs. For older people, shortening the back legs of the chairs would improve the effectiveness of the sheets. The staff preferred the sheets to the cuffs because they weren't officially considered restraint, and therefore didn't need the doctor's approval.

One of Cooke's most difficult challenges was treating "General Pareses," a mental illness caused by syphilis. Cooke was seeing more and more people who had contracted the sexually transmitted disease during the "Great War." He was also beginning to see an increasing number of inmates in the advanced stages of the disease. Most of these advanced cases had strange beliefs and suffered terrible visions.

The superintendent's trip to "Bedlam" in England had introduced him to at least one new treatment. Cooke learned from a published German experiment that raising the body temperature seemed to keep syphilis in check. The Germans had been awarded the Nobel prize for their findings. A high fever was required, so Cooke obtained live malaria parasites and injected patient Eldon Snipps, who was still in the early stages of the disease. Cooke hoped to arrest his condition and, if it worked as promised, to apply the treatment to others.

In three days, Eldon began to shiver. He was experiencing extreme chills and the staff, afraid he might be contagious, wrapped him carefully, and locked him in a side room. In a few hours, he began to sweat profusely. His chills would come back at intervals. As he lay on a mattress on the floor of the tiny room, Eldon stared at the ceiling and prayed for death. The staff watched closely through a tiny porthole in the door. Twelve hours later, Dr. Cooke injected Snipps with the drug Quinine to kill the malaria parasite. The treatment was over. The technique worked and Eldon experienced a general improvement in his mental and physical condition. In the next year, Cooke would treat 58 cases with a 60 per cent success rate—with almost half of that number going into complete remission.

As money became scarcer in the late 1920s, the malaria parasite became more difficult to acquire. Desperate times required desperate measures, so some inmates were selected to be carriers of malaria. They were innoculated with the parasites and as new syphilis patients were diagnosed, Cooke had simply to transfer blood from the carrier. A ready source was always available. To ensure proper diagnosis, all new patients would require a spinal tap, the painful introduction of a needle into the spinal column to remove fluid. More than 400 patients were being admitted every year and Cooke was finding syphilis in 60 to 70 of these cases.

Like his Scottish counterpart in North Battleford, Cooke also believed in the value of work. It was part of what he perceived as his patients' need for routine. The hospital should reflect the community's standards, declared Cooke, who mandated that each day should consist of "eight to 12 hours work, eight hours of sleep, and the remainder in personal activity." Working patients were also essential to keeping the asylum open. There were only 80 people on staff and they could not possibly handle all of the work. Ever since it opened, the hospital had required able patients to work on the farm, on the ward, in the kitchen, and on the grounds.

Harvey Slater was typical of the labourers. A tall muscular man with no teeth, he looked forward to working on the farm or grounds whenever possible. Slater would shovel dirt with a scoop rather than a spade; he got more done that way. Farm staff loved to see him arrive each morning, and they told him so. What they did not do was teach Harvey new skills, promote him, or encourage him to leave the institution. The main objective of work therapy was to match people to the tasks that needed to be done. For example, Randy Winkley was an electrician's helper. Seven feet tall and gangly, Randy was a natural to change ceiling light bulbs.

While nursing staff received a maximum of $60 per month, Slater, Winkley, and the other male patients were paid in tobacco—two packages per person, per week. The women did "domestic work" and so did not require pay. Tobacco wasn't an issue either because "women don't smoke." said the superintendent. He may have meant "shouldn't."

Ironically, Cooke's most lasting innovations were introduced before he traveled to the Bedlam hospital. By 1922, his inmates numbered over 800, and his first priority had been to house them. He complained he had been too long preoccupied with constructing new buildings, and he now needed to spend time looking at new treatments. During that year, he would introduce dental care, psychiatric social work to investigate cases in the field, and, as a priority, occupational therapy.

Cooke assigned two large rooms on the third floor of the main build ing and hired Occupational Therapist Miss C. Dingman and three teachers to assist her. Patients were brought in at regular intervals throughout the day to do weaving, basketry, toy making, tailoring, and carpentry items such as birdhouses and lawn chairs. In later years, when a therapist from Europe became intrigued with totem poles, they became the new therapy. The work appealed to only a small number of patients and many resisted. Others seemed to enjoy it, lending credibility to the departmental slogan, "Through hands and mind to health."

The last few years of his superintendency were difficult ones for Cooke. He seemed to be losing his firm grip on the hospital's affairs. The patient population had grown to almost 1,200, more than double the number he had been responsible for when he started in 1916. And the government, facing an economic depression, had no new funds for construction. Staff turnover was high and most of Cooke's charges were untrained. Families were beginning to complain about abuse, and the beating death of patient Dr. Arthur Hobbs had caught the attention of Premier Brownlee. The government was no longer happy and invited the National Committee for Mental Hygiene to undertake a review. They issued an unflattering report and many of the solutions they proposed were beyond the superintendent's control. Dr. E.H. Cooke resigned to enter private practice in 1931.

Cooke was replaced by Dr. Charles Baragar, who would also serve as Commissioner of Mental Institutes and Director of Mental Health for the province. Baragar was a progressive man and his emphasis on new treatments changed the face of services across the province. But the greatest changes for people living in the Ponoka institution were brought about by a 28-year-old. In 1936, Dr. Randall R. MacLean was appointed Acting Superintendent. The staff feared his youthful, liberal ideas, which they considered to be naïve. MacLean had travelled to Boston, London, and Zurich for special training and returned with fresh treatment ideas. He would introduce Ponoka's patients to shock therapy and other new treatments he had learned during his travels. He would also advocate for better hospital conditions.

The patient population grew to almost 1,500 during MacLean's administration. From the time he accepted the job, MacLean had courageously and persistently challenged the government to correct the conditions of overcrowding. With strongly written statements like "great concern is felt for the safety of a large number of defenseless patients," "services are taxed to the utmost," and "the situation has become not only serious but very grave." MacLean tried hard to push his superiors in Edmonton.

His second intention was to eliminate restraint. The 1928 survey of Cooke's institution by the National Committee for Mental Hygiene concluded that restraint and seclusion would "aggravate symptoms and jeopardize recovery"; MacLean agreed. He also agreed with the report's recommendation that seclusion could be replaced by reduced overcrowding and by providing occupational therapy, continuous baths, and skilled nursing care.

The government would have to solve the overcrowding issue, but the rest of the problems, MacLean could manage. The staff would require his approval for all restraint and seclusion and he intended to give it rarely. Nursing rules were developed in which the staff was urged to keep calm and collected and "maintain a friendly bearing" when faced with a violent patient. The rules also cautioned that "those who have not sufficient good nature and self-command to meet even serious provocations without losing their tempers are unfit to be nurses."

"We will be killed," complained the staff as they secretly continued the restraint practices. But MacLean was persistent. He toured wards unexpectedly and, when he found patients in restraints, growled at the staff to "get them out of there." He had restraint devices removed from the wards; when senior staff resisted, he replaced them with young, trained, registered nurses. His expectations were explicit. It is "absolutely forbidden to strike a patient, to trip or throw down, to twist the arms or wrist, or hold by the hair," he wrote. It was also forbidden "to place the weight of the body or knees on the chest or abdomen or to choke or place anything over the mouth that interferes with breathing."

MacLean also introduced clinical teaching for the staff, who had worked for years without any formal training. Continuous baths and occupational therapy were expanded. By far, his most popular initiative was reducing the working day to eight hours. MacLean's popularity soared and the use of restraint dropped dramatically. Staff still used seclusion in side rooms for the most disruptive of patients, but less restraint had not seemed to pose a great problem. Certainly, no one was killed or seriously injured, and the staff were surprised.

In 1948, MacLean was promoted to the position of Mental Health Director for the province, following the untimely death of Director C.A. Baragar. MacLean was replaced at the hospital by Dr. Thomas C. Michie. Soon after Michie took over, the use of seclusion and restraint began to creep back into the wards. It was easier and safer for the staff, he felt, and the new superintendent was more interested in introducing new medical procedures in order to cure and control patients. In the meantime, patients could be held down forcibly.

Michie had graduated from the University of Alberta and obtained a fellowship in medicine that earned him the opportunity to study at the famed Mayo Foundation in Rochester, Minnesota. A tall, striking man, he commanded respect and he intended, like Baragar and MacLean, to leave a legacy as a progressive psychiatrist.

At the Oliver Institute, Dr. Alexander D. McPherson, a rugged man who was a former Ponoka physician, was appointed superintendent the same year that Michie was instated at Ponoka. Like Michie, McPherson wanted to increase the use of shock treatment and introduce treatment techniques that had been in use in Europe and parts of North America for more than a decade. Born in Vermont at the beginning of the millennium, McPherson was keen to bring the Oliver Institute into the 20th century. Like Michie, he had been educated at the University of Alberta, but his post-graduate training was from the Colorado Psychopathic Hospital.

49

McPherson and Michie would work well together, although it would take McPherson eight years to convince the government to open an admissions unit and provide active treatment at Oliver. The two superintendents also hoped that the new medical procedures might help bring psychiatry into the mainstream of medicine. Psychiatrists were not highly regarded by the public—or by the medical profession itself.

One such procedure was shock treatment. No treatment was as popular with McPherson and Michie as convulsive therapy. In this technique, an epileptic seizure was induced to "improve mental functioning." The procedure was first attempted in 1934 by

Hungarian psychiatrist Ladislas von Meduna, who injected camphor-in-oil into a patient who had reportedly been in a stupor for four years. According to Meduna, the patient recovered.

Meduna later substituted the drug Metrazol, a technique that had been tried at Ponoka in 1938 by Dr. MacLean, a year after he began using insulin shock therapy. MacLean used both procedures very little because of poor results and terrible side effects. The patients would suffer violent convulsions and frequently break bones, often in the vertebrae. They would choke, tear muscles, and lose their memories for months or even years. Even the mention of Metrazol caused anxiety in patients and it became known as "the roller coaster to hell." Following the purchase of an electro-shock machine in 1945, MacLean and his staff increased the use of shock slightly, but the side effects remained troublesome and MacLean was cautious.

But Dr. Michie liked the use of electro-shock, although he felt that insulin could be equally as effective. During his tenure at Ponoka, they were sometimes used together. Insulin coma therapy had been introduced in Austria about the same time as Metrazol, but quite by accident. Chronic mental patients had been given insulin to help them gain weight and relax. A few sensitive patients suffered unexpected seizures and doctors noticed an improvement in their mental conditions.

In Italy, doctors were interested in studying seizures, but they were convinced that electricity would be more effective than chemicals like camphor, insulin, or Metrazol—and with fewer side effects. In experiments, an electrode was attached to the mouth and anus of animals. Seizures were created, but half of the animals died. The problem was solved by moving the electrodes to the side of the head. When the electric current did not pass through the heart, the animals lived; the procedure was now ready for man. In 1938, the first recipient of electro-shock was an unnamed catatonic man found in a stupor in a Milan railway station. After nine treatments, he was diagnosed as having "improved markedly."

Michie and McPherson also subscribed to the "clean slate" theory—the patient's mind, following unconsciousness, was blank. Unhealthy thoughts would be wiped out, and the patient could then learn new coping skills. But there was little evaluation of the treatments and no standards as to how many to administer or how often

Early electro-shock (convulsive) machine with uncontrolled current caused severe patient injuries. (Photo taken with permission at Alberta Hospital, Edmonton.)

they should be given. Dr. Ewan Cameron, a former Brandon Asylum Superintendent who worked for American intelligence organizations in Quebec asylums, administered up to 60 treatments per case, with as many as 12 treatments in a single day. At the Alberta School Hospital in Red Deer, Dr. L.J. LeVann would administer "ticklers," small jolts which would be repeated until patients promised to behave in proper ways.

Ponoka's first electro-convulsive therapy machines were crude, their voltage irregular. A decade later, there was little improvement in the equipment—but there were drugs to relax the muscles and control the saliva, thereby reducing the high number of physical injuries. Out-of-control seizures continued to occur. This was terrifying for the poor patients who could not lose consciousness. Years later, poet Sylvia Plath described her own similarly nightmarish experiences with electro-shock treatments that had been administered in an American institution:

> "Something took hold of me and shook like the end of the world. It shrilled through an air crackling with blue light, and with each flash a great jolt drubbed me till I thought my bones would break and the sap fly out of me like a split plant."

51

Doctors Michie and McPherson would supervise more than 10,000 electro-shock treatments and more than half as many insulin coma seizures. Insulin coma shock was stopped entirely in 1962, largely because electric shock was easier to control and had fewer side effects.

In 1953, both physicians instituted group therapy at their respective institutions. Initially the medical staff led all of the groups, but within a year, the nurses were extensively involved. While most of the staff had very little formal training in group psychotherapy, the daily sessions provided an opportunity for nurses and patients to discuss problems and concerns. The staff reported seeing patients in a different light. The nurses seemed more interested in supporting new recreation activities such as dances, tea rooms, beauty parlours, and, in Ponoka, even a small British pub—"the most popular treatment in the hospital."

The activities, according to a male nurse, were "an island of reality in a world where there was none." The staff interest in patients' conditions began to expand beyond the institution walls, and in 1953, Michie started an after-care program in Calgary. Located at the Foothills Hospital, Ponoka staff, including psychiatrists, would try to help families and patients adapt to community life.

While these humane innovations were fine, both superintendents remained focused on the more technical treatments. McPherson still had no operating room at Oliver, but the two men were intrigued by lobotomy. The as-yet-unnamed technique had been developed more than a decade earlier at Yale University. Two chimpanzees, Becky and Lucy, had been trained to solve elaborate problems in order to obtain food but they became quite agitated when their efforts were frustrated. They banged their cages, pulled their hair and threw feces at the scientists. The researchers then removed the frontal lobes of their brains and the chimps seemed to become immune to frustration. While their skills diminished, they were no longer upset by failure.

Then a Portuguese neurologist by the name of Egas Moniz, a man with little apparent concern for the diminishing of skills, adapted the procedure for humans and called it a leucotomy. The term came from the Greek words "leucos," meaning white, and "tomos," meaning cutting. Moniz received a Nobel Prize for his work—one of only two ever awarded in the field of psychiatry. The procedure, according to Michie, who helped teach the operating room nurses, "was refined by Americans Dr. Walter Freeman and Dr. James Watts." Freeman described his patients as "trophies" and named the procedure "lobotomy" because "only the nerve fibres of the brain are cut."

The procedure began with shock treatment to render the patient unconscious and eliminate any sense of pain. The surgeons then used two special instruments: first, a hand drill to grind a pair of holes, one on each side of the forehead; second, a "leucotome," which had a shaft which was inserted through the drilled holes until it reached the desired brain fibres. The surgeon would then depress a plunger, forcing a sharp wire into the brain where it was rotated to cut the brain tissue.

Freeman's procedure was complex; it also required a neurosurgeon and was costly. Michie looked for an alternative. He soon became interested in a new American method of psychosurgery and adapted it for Ponoka. In what was called a transorbital lobotomy, the surgeon drew the upper eyelid away from the eyeball and tapped an ice-pick-like instrument with a hammer to get through the tissue. He would then sever fibres in the frontal lobe of the brain. The patient

Shown are early surgical instruments at the Alberta hospitals. (Photo taken with permission at Alberta Edmonton Hospital)

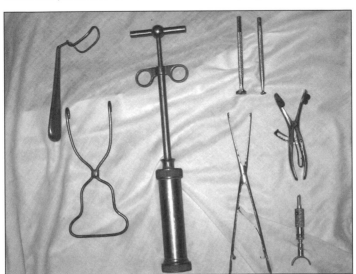

would awaken with black eyes, but recuperation time was far shorter. The procedure took less than five minutes and could be done by most physicians in a modest operating room. Best of all, the treatments seemed to work. Dr. Freeman's view of his patients' bizarre thinking, was that "the idea is still there, but it has no emotional drive." "I think," he said, "we have drawn the sting as it were out of the psychosis and neurosis."

Although several patients previously thought to be incurable were discharged by Michie, his hospital staff were less positive about the technique. The treatment seemed to be effective in controlling patients who were particularly agitated or had compulsions that required them to repeat rituals like pacing or washing their hands for most of the day. But active, thinking, busy patients became mute and withdrawn. The staff referred to them as "vegetables."

Timmy Beach was a particularly sad case. At 13 years of age, Timmy was admitted after frequent arrests by the Calgary police. He had a poor home, difficulty learning, and was easily manipulated by other kids. His goal in life was to get back to Calgary, buy a bottle of whisky, steal a car, and drive down Eighth Avenue screaming "fuck you" to the world. In spite of his belligerent attitude, Timmy liked the staff and they liked him. He pleaded with several of them to adopt him. But no treatment seemed to work for the kid. After two suicide attempts, doctors decided on a transorbital leucotomy. Timmy Beach suffered a brain hemorrhage and paralysis. Whisky and cars would now be out of the question.

The Ponoka Hospital had been doing surgical procedures since shortly after sterilization was approved in 1928, and, in spite of the occasional complication, these technical procedures would enhance the hospital's reputation as a treatment centre. Between 1950 and 1968, visiting surgeons performed psychosurgery on 89 patients— most of them under the supervision of Superintendent Michie. At the Edmonton hospital, McPherson would participate following the opening of an operating room and a tuberculosis unit in July of 1952. Psychosurgery, when added to Alberta's world leadership in sterilization, would bring the Alberta hospitals into the mainstream of modern medicine.

Neither McPherson nor Michie saw the procedures as guesswork. They were important additions to the gardens, the water therapy, and the basket weaving. They had a modern mental hospital that they believed bore no resemblance to the past.

References

Abercrombie, Sheila. *Alberta Hospital Edmonton 1923 to 1983—An Outline of History to Commemorate the 60th Anniversary*. Edmonton, Alberta: Alberta Hospital Edmonton, 1983.

Abt, Mary Frances McHugh. *Adaptive Change and Leadership in a Psychiatric Hospital*. Edmonton, Alberta: Ph.D. Thesis, University of Alberta, 1992.

Abt, Mary Frances McHugh. Ponoka, AB. Interview with author, 1998.

Anonymous. Family member of former patient—interview with author, 1998.

Anonymous. Former Alberta Hospital Manager—interview with author, 1998.

Anonymous. Former psychiatric nurse—interview with author, 1999.

Baragar, C.A. *Annual Report*, Provincial Mental Hospital, Department of Public Health, Alberta. Alberta: Provincial Archives, 1931.

Blair, W.R.N. *Mental Health in Alberta: A Report on the Alberta Mental Health Study 1968*. Edmonton, AB: Human Resource Research and Development Executive Council, Government of Alberta, 1969.

Brownlee, John. Premiers Papers, Provincial Archives. 1930.

Caplan, R.B. *Psychiatry and the Community in Nineteenth-Century America*. New York: Basic Books, 1969.

Cooke, E.H. *Annual Report*. Provincial Mental Hospital, Department of Public Health. Alberta: Provincial Archives, 1928-29.

Cooke, E.H. *Annual Report*. Provincial Mental Hospital, Department of Public Health. Alberta: Provincial Archives, 1930-31.

Dickinson, Harley D. *The Two Psychiatries: The Transformation of Psychiatric Work in Saskatchewan, 1905-1984.* Regina: Canadian Plains Research Center, University of Regina, 1989.

Goffman, Erving. *Asylums: Essays on the Social Situation of Mental Patients and Other Inmates.* Garden City, NY: Doubleday, 1961.

Hincks, Clarence M. *Mental Hygiene Survey of the Province of Alberta.* Canadian National Committee for Mental Hygiene, 1921.

Hincks, Clarence M. and Farrar, C.B. *Report of Commissioners Appointed to Investigate the Provincial Training School at Red Deer, Provincial Mental Institute at Oliver, Provincial Mental Hospital at Ponoka.* Edmonton, AB: Government of Alberta, Provincial Archives, 1929.

Johnson, J.O., *et. al. A History of Dedication and Caring 1911-1986.* Ponoka: Alberta Hospital

Ponoka, 1986.

Johnson, J.O. Ponoka, AB. Interview with author, 1998.

Jones, Maxwell. *The Therapeutic Community: A New Treatment Method in Psychiatry.* New York: Basic Books, 1953.

MacEachran, J.M. *Report of the Alberta Board of Visitors for Public Institutions*, 1927. Province of Alberta Sessional Paper #31. Alberta: Provincial Archives, 1929.

Michie, T.C. *Annual Report.* Provincial Mental Hospital, Department of Public Health. Alberta: Provincial Archives, 1953.

Michie, T.C. *Annual Report.* Provincial Mental Hospital, Department of Public Health. Alberta: Provincial Archives, 1954.

Michie, T.C. *Annual Report*. Provincial Mental Hospital, Department of Public Health. Alberta: Provincial Archives, 1955.

Michie, T.C. *Annual Report*. Provincial Mental Hospital, Department of Public Health. Alberta: Provincial Archives, 1956.

Michie, T.C. *Annual Report*. Provincial Mental Hospital, Department of Public Health. Alberta: Provincial Archives, 1957.

Rules and Regulations of the Provincial Mental Hospital. Alberta Hospital Museum, 1918.

Simmons, Harvey G. *Unbalanced: Mental Health Policy in Ontario, 1930-1989*. Toronto: Wall & Thompson, 1990.

Slater, R. *Ponoka Panorama*. Ponoka: Ponoka and District Historical Society, 1973.

Stanton, Alfred H. and Schwartz, Morris S. The Mental *Hospital: A Study of Institutional Participation in Psychiatric Illness and Treatment*. New York: Basic Books, 1954.

58

Chapter 4
The Mad Physician
from the East

Chapter 4
The Mad Physician
from the East

The Mad Physician from the East

1918

It was his most troubling tour. Dr. Clare Hincks of the Canadian National Committee for Mental Hygiene was visiting the Portage la Prairie Home for the Incurables. Manitoba was the first province to ask the newly formed organization for a survey of its mental hospitals, and the home was the second institution Hincks and his assistant Marjorie Keyes would tour.

At the end of a long, dark ward, he found a coffin-shaped closet containing a naked woman. The tiny space had no furniture, not even a mattress. As the door opened, the deathly pale woman grabbed a ragged cloth and pressed it to her eyes to protect herself from the blinding light.

"How long has this woman been in here?" Hincks asked.

"Two years," replied the superintendent.

"How often has she been permitted out?" "Only once. She was put in a cage for 10 minutes but became restless, so we returned her to the cupboard."

The place had become a recuperation house for every kind of ailment from eczema to dementia. "Apparently any family in Manitoba which has a troublesome member sends them here," complained Hincks. "We have an unhappy conglomeration of idiots, imbeciles, epileptics, insanes, seniles, and normal people suffering from incurable diseases. There, but for the grace of God, go I."

He vividly remembered the circumstances of his own first attack. In 1901, Clarence Meredith Hincks, only 16 years old, had started university in Toronto. "I was playing bridge at the home of one of my pals on St. George Street. I had been feeling in fine health and excellent spirits, and then, during the game, a sudden change came over me. Without physical pain, my world cracked up. I lost all interest in the game I was playing. I felt completely different from my former self. My interest in friends and life completely vanished."

He became listless and refused to communicate. He did not feel overly sad, he said, but as he listened to those around him he could not understand how anyone could find anything to laugh about. He didn't know what was wrong and went home to bed—for two weeks. The young student thought that perhaps this was a "device of nature" designed to give his mind a rest.

Born in St. Mary's, Ontario, an only child, Clarence Hincks was thin and frail for most of his youth. The family physician predicted Clare would not live past the age of 15. His father, William, was a highly respected Methodist minister and his mother, Mattie, was a school teacher. Indeed, William, who was 14 years younger than Mattie, had once been her student. Mattie had seen great promise in William and, following high school, she financed him through university on the condition that he would never ask her to marry him. William didn't keep his end of the bargain.

Clare's father spent very little time at home as he built up almost a dozen parishes, and the family moved from community to community. Clare was sorry to leave each parish but the many moves taught him to make new friends easily. He was happy and gregarious and always fun to be with. His most successful summer jobs were in sales or promotions where he could use his slick tongue. He developed a reputation as "Hincks the Huckster."

Clare's mother showered him with affection and indulged his every wish. "My Mother's delusion," he said, "was that Dad and I were both great. The view was shared by us. We faced the world with extreme confidence and took chances without the slightest fear of defeat." With his mother's help, Clare managed his studies with ease and was ready for university at 15, a year before he was eligible. At that age, he still felt physically and emotionally dependent on Mattie.

When Hincks did go to university, he was lonely and insecure—and the mysterious attack in his first year was terrifying. When he returned to his studies, he had less energy and found he needed to go to bed by eight each evening. As a result, there was little time for social activities and his classmates thought him shy. Although the limited time for studying affected his grades, his entire class was offered a special option after third year—they would be given degrees in arts and medicine after only six years. Dr. Clare Hincks graduated as a physician in June, 1907, at the age of 22.

Only a minority of medical school graduates went on to intern, but Hincks won a year of internship at the Toronto General Hospital, after which he temporarily took over the practice of a colleague in Campbellford, Ontario. He began by diagnosing the town's mayor with paratyphoid fever, an acute infectious disease much like typhoid, but which lasts only 10 days, rather than six to eight weeks. The townspeople hadn't heard of paratyphoid and when the mayor returned to work within two weeks, they marvelled at Clare's skill.

A second patient, a young man critically ill with empyema, the build-up of pus in a body cavity, required urgent surgery. Clare located one of his university classmates and on a kitchen table in a rustic farm home, the two doctors withdrew large quantities of pus from the young man's chest cavity. When the patient went into shock, they administered strychnine and pulmonary resuscitation. The boy survived and recovered quickly. The whole neighbourhood heard about the surgery and Clare's waiting room began getting fuller by the day. Hincks remained humble. He was a terrible surgeon, he lamented, but the plight of his patients steadied his nerves. A poor surgeon perhaps, but he had a special gift for handling people in difficulty.

His fine reputation was cemented when he was called to a home where he found a tearful family. He asked if he was too late and was told that the grandmother had just passed on. Feeling for the old woman's pulse, he found it regular and strong. He leaned over the patient and said, "This is not St. Peter, just a neighbour. You will soon sit up and talk to your family. You are in good health." In a few minutes, she opened her eyes. Her family was convinced they had seen a miracle.

Eventually, Campbellford's permanent doctor returned to his practice, and Hincks moved back to Toronto. There he taught animal biology at the university, completed insurance examinations, and even located his own practice at a busy intersection known for accident injuries. None of these activities generated much money, and his repeated periods of depression made it difficult to follow through with his patients.

Hincks' chronic financial problems led to his taking an additional job as a part-time medical inspector in west Toronto. To his dismay, he found that 40 per cent of his cases were related to what he and others were beginning to call "mental hygiene." Nothing he had been taught in medical school helped him. The work proved to be a turning point in his career.

Hoping to gain more background in this area of treatment, Hincks enrolled in a psychology course. There he claimed to have learned "nothing about human nature and its operations." When he heard about a major conference on mental hygiene in Buffalo, New York, that he could not afford to attend, he decided to resume his career as Hincks the Hustler. He wangled an interview with the editor of the Toronto Star and convinced the man to send him to the conference as a special reporter.

One of the conference presenters had worked with the much-published psychologists Binet and Simon in Paris, helping to develop their intelligence test. Clare was trained to apply the test, and he returned to Toronto riding a wave of enthusiasm. The Toronto school system was interested in IQ testing, and Hincks had a new job. But working in the school and court systems did not provide him with opportunities to learn more about psychiatry, and Hincks discovered he had become obsessed with the subject. Perhaps expanding his knowledge in this field would help him come to grips with his own bouts of depression, which were coming more frequently and lasting much longer.

Most psychiatrists of the era were being trained in Vienna, but Hincks was poor and newly married to his college sweetheart. Europe was out of the question for now. His wife's father worked as the assistant medical superintendent at Ontario's Rockwood Asylum, and their discussions fuelled Clare's interest. Clare's boss, Dr. Helen McMurchy, was acquainted with Toronto's best-known psychiatrist, Dr. C.K. Clarke. They would introduce Dr. Clarke to Clare's work in assessing intelligence, and to his interest in psychiatry.

Dr. Clarke agreed to meet with Hincks, but he had his own agenda. He had opened the country's first outdoor clinic in psychiatry in 1909 at a house in the centre of Toronto. His plan had been to provide an informal setting where former patients of the asylum could receive help and support. "It was only too evident," said Clarke, "that patients would be reluctant to seek help in a hospital for the insane." Known as "the Nut House," the clinic, according to Dr. Clarke, did excellent work, sometimes preventing suicide or giving its patients a new start in life. It had been closed, however, when the new Toronto General Hospital was built. Clarke wanted it reopened.

Along with a young nurse, Marjorie Keyes, Hincks accepted the challenge. Within months, the new clinic was accepting referrals from schools, courts, doctors, and families, as well as seeing patients at their own instigation. Hincks observed an "endless flow of troubled and disordered people" whose illnesses he believed could have been prevented. "We are spending our time bailing out the boat rather than plugging the leak," he complained. After two years at the clinic, he knew what needed to be done. "It struck me like a thunderbolt," he said, "I want to dedicate my life to preventing mental illnesses."

After careful thought and many discussions with Dr. Clarke, Hincks detailed his four priorities. Asylums had to be assessed and reorganized, mental hygiene training had to be introduced, research was needed and prevention programs like mental hygiene screening for immigrants had to be put in place. The task was dominion-wide, but Hincks believed he was up to the job. He had recently come through a bout of black depression, and he now felt a certain restless, yet coherent and focused mania. But how was he to start?

63

In the fall of 1917, Hincks, at the insistence of Dr. Clarke, travelled to New York City, the centre of psychiatric education in North America. During his visit, he was introduced to an energetic young man named Clifford Beers, about whom he had reported in his Toronto Star columns from the Buffalo Conference four years earlier. When Hincks explained the project he was embarking on, Beers assured Hincks that he had come to the right place. Beers gave Hincks a copy of his book, A Mind that Found Itself, and asked him to return the next day.

Like Hincks, Beers had suffered from insanity, and his book detailed his two-year experience in private and public mental hospitals. After graduating from Yale's School of Engineering, Beers had become severely depressed. He jumped from a third-story window in his home but only broke his legs. He was immediately admitted to an asylum and eventually recovered, in spite of treatment that he described as brutal and lacking in understanding. Beers' book about his experiences was a success, and the author used the proceeds of its sale to launch the first mental hygiene society in the world.

Hincks was asked to help expand the society into Canada. He returned to Toronto highly motivated and with a plan. There was strong competition between the University of Toronto and McGill University in Montreal, and Hincks decided to use this to his advantage. Through an acquaintance, Dr. Colin Russell, a Montreal neurologist and university lecturer, Hincks arranged a meeting at McGill with the entire medical faculty. Hincks thought Russell must be very influential, but, in reality, the physicians thought Hincks was trying to recruit talent and they attended to defend their faculty. The University of Toronto had recently lured away some of McGill's most prestigious people and they didn't want it to happen again.

Whatever their reason for coming, Hincks had a captive audience, and his salesmanship was at its best. He spoke of his experiences in Toronto and New York, the challenges ahead, and the potential for McGill to make history by leading the way. McGill, he noted, was a national university while Toronto was provincial. It simply made more sense for McGill to lead a nationwide movement. When Hincks had finished, McGill Principal Sir William Peterson announced that he was convinced the need for a national mental hygiene organization was overdue. He would support the plan. Other faculty members agreed, including Dr. Charles Martin, who was to serve as the committee's first chairman. Back at the University of Toronto, Hincks generated support by playing up the reception he had received in Montreal.

He was then off to Ottawa. He had been granted an audience with the Governor General, the Duke of Devonshire. When Hincks arrived at Rideau Hall, the Governor General admonished him not to use medical jargon. "I would not understand you," said the Duke. "You know I am a farmer."

The two hit it off. Hincks repeated his stories, adding more passion and relevance for the Duke. "We have Canadian soldiers," he argued, "of such low mentality that they do not know who the enemy is." Other men, he went on, languished in jails when they had committed no crimes. The issue was of such importance that the entire medical faculty at McGill actively supported the aims. The Governor General was impressed.

"All right, I will be pleased to give you my patronage when your board requests me to do so," said the Duke.

"But," Hincks confessed, "we have no board."

"You want my patronage for something that does not exist?" asked the confused Duke.

"That is exactly what I want," said Hincks, "and I will be back with a board composed of the top leaders in Canada."

Hincks returned to Montreal, where, with the help of Principal Peterson, he prepared a list of 20 distinguished Canadians, many of them the country's biggest business tycoons. He visited each person on the list personally. Appointments were easily made when he announced he was calling on behalf of the Governor General. In a matter of days, he had recruited 18 of the 20 men. Each of them also agreed to donate $3,000. Ten of the appointees and the two professors of medicine from McGill and Toronto accompanied Hincks back to Ottawa for another meeting with the Duke. The Canadian National Committee for Mental Hygiene was formed on April 26, 1918. It had taken an enthusiastic and energetic Hincks only a few weeks to move from a plan to a national committee with vice-regal patronage.

But now he had to raise money. He approached Timothy Eaton, a neighbour in Muskoka, where the Hincks family had a cottage. He then prepared a list of successful businessmen like William Birks, Fred Molson, Edward Beatty, and R.B. Angus. Travelling to New York, he obtained a grant from the Rockefeller Foundation. In a few more weeks, he had collected thousands of dollars. "He can talk anyone into anything," said the publisher of the Toronto Star.

Dr. Colin Russell, the man who had arranged Hincks' first meeting with the McGill University faculty, was now in charge of neuropsychiatry for the Canadian Army. He was inspecting Canadian facilities for the treatment of shell shock and was appalled at the conditions he found in Manitoba. He proposed two options: move the soldiers to other centres or have the National Committee for Mental Hygiene conduct an inspection. The national government chose the second option, reasoning that "if the asylums are unsuitable for soldiers, they must also be unsuitable for civilians."

Hincks and Nurse Marjorie Keyes, who had also moved from the Toronto Clinic to work with the National Committee, were to conduct the inspection with the assistance of Dr. Clarke. They would look at three major institutions: Selkirk, Brandon, and Portage La Prairie. The Portage Home for the Incurable, keeper of the ashen woman in the coffin-like closet, housed 335 inmates in a building designed for less than 200. One room, measuring just eight feet by 18 feet, contained 16 beds. At least the woman in the closet had privacy. Many of the inmates were restrained with chains or muffs that tied the hands together and wrapped them in canvas. Other inmates were secluded in small cells without light or ventilation. No physicians worked in the home. The superintendent's rationale for the treatment was detailed in a book written more than a hundred years before by Dr. John Haslam. It read:

… the patient should be kept alone in a dark and quiet room, so that he may not be affected by the stimuli of light and sound…. the hands should be properly secured and the patient should also be confined by one leg… Should the patient, as frequently occurs, be constantly endeavouring to liberate himself, the friction of the skin sustained without injury will restrain him.

66

Hincks and Clarke agreed in advance that their reports would never attack individuals and that the contents would remain confidential, so as not to embarrass the governments. The governments were essential allies, for they must agree to improvements and provide more money for the operation of the Committee, they reasoned.

But the conditions were too serious. Hincks crafted a carefully worded report that he hoped would be critical but supportive of the staff. With respect to Selkirk, he said it was "totally unfit to meet the modern demands of a hospital for the insane," but "admirably managed, achieving such excellent results with such meagre equipment and resources." In Brandon, he noted, "it is scarcely fair to censure the officials who have a task imposed on them which they are not trained to take." In Portage la Prairie, Hincks observed that the institution was "devoid of any equipment." His report concluded: "The result has been tragic in the extreme, and we may well pass by most of the details of what might be the unpleasant task of describing what we saw, knowing that the government will take immediate steps to put an end to the abuses existing."

With report in hand, Hincks travelled to Winnipeg and demanded a meeting with Premier T.C. Norris. The Premier was busy with an important meeting. "No business can be more important than mine," shouted Hincks. "I have seen things in your mental hospitals this week that would put your government out of power!" That night he sat with the Premier and his caucus until 3 a.m. The politicians were exhausted, but Hincks was only beginning. Finally, Education Minister Dr. R.S. Thornton relented. "Gentlemen, we should get down on our knees ... we have failed our trust."

Shortly thereafter, the Manitoba Government passed new laws that had been recommended by Hincks and proposed by Dr. Thornton. They also opened a psychopathic ward at the Winnipeg General Hospital and voted more than $2 million in improvements to the Hospitals for the Insane, which would be renamed Hospitals for Mental Diseases.

The Ontario survey was next, but the province's government was quite unreceptive to recommendations. A frustrated Hincks spoke to the Ontario Educational Association and they seemed to like what he had to say. His enthusiasm grew and so did his use of sensational words. "My experience could be likened to a religious conversion," he said later, adding that "perhaps it would be nearer the truth to say that I got into a paranoiac condition with delusions of grandeur."

A Toronto Star reporter was in the audience, and the April 7, 1920, edition of the Star quoted Hincks as saying that Ontario was "far behind in mental diagnostics" and that he "had enough facts to blow up the Parliament Buildings." The Premier seemed to take the comments literally and called Hincks a Bolshevik and an anarchist. One Member of the Provincial Parliament complained that Hincks was "probably an immigrant," and even the opposition leader said that "men of this character are in the habit of getting on the stump or soap box in order to make sensational statements entirely unwarranted in point of fact."

Hincks was concerned. The front-page story could damage any possible relationship with other provincial governments, and he appealed to the publisher of the Star to arrange a meeting between himself and the Premier. This time, Hincks repeated the gist of his passionate speech from Manitoba but softened the condemnatory details. It worked. Hincks agreed to issue a new release supporting the government, and the Premier apologized for the government's inaction on the survey. Hincks was now more convinced than ever that his policy of avoiding extreme public statements in favour of small day-to-day gains was appropriate. In the future, he would submit private and confidential reports, no matter what his findings. Equally important was controlling his mania.

In a survey of the first asylum in New Brunswick, Hincks found one group of insane people who were put to bed in boxes filled with hay. Wooden slats were then nailed on top. All boxes except two were secured at night; these two belonged to patients designated as trustees. Their job was to deal with any noisy inmate by urinating through the slats.

In a Halifax asylum, a man was kept in an unheated room year-round. The staff were somehow convinced he could not feel the cold. In the Edmonton Institute, imbecile children were rolled in long strips of cotton with their arms and legs bound. They were then piled on shelves. Each of the governments received a confidential report.

The Alberta survey, which included an examination of the Edmonton Institute, was conducted in 1921 by Dr. Hincks with the assistance of Professor D.G. Revell of the University of Alberta. The survey was commissioned by the recently elected United Farmers of Alberta after news stories regarding the treatment of feeble-minded children. The Minister of Education, Perren Baker, was particularly interested and supportive, and his help would of course be acknowledged in the report.

As in his previous reports, Hincks used the forum to educate people to his mental hygiene movement, which he defined as "studying individuals so that their weaknesses and strengths can be determined." He planned to then use this study as a preliminary measure to "formulate treatment and training that will be productive of the best social results." The Hincks and Revell report classified the province's patients into three groups: the "insane," who were those with "brain disease"; the "deficient," who lacked "brain development"; and the "psychopathic," who were "neither insane nor deficient, but so unbalanced that they contribute to social problems." Each group's problems were then related to questions of morals, crime, prostitution, and immigration. The section on children placed most emphasis on "mental defectives," but Hincks was also interested in children with superior intelligence, those with nervous instability, and those with conduct disorders.

The survey was a bombshell, revealing much, much more than the government had expected. The physician from the east was as mad as his reputation reported. In 68 pages, his report gave credit to many Albertans and their programs; he also made far-reaching and costly recommendations. For the Hospital for the Insane at Ponoka, Hincks recommended a new building for male patients, an "outside house' for trial leaves, an assembly hall for entertainment, a training program for nurses, special programs for tuberculosis patients, the introduction of social work and occupational therapy, and provision for voluntary admissions. Hincks was particularly adamant that not all admissions be done through the courts. Patients were "mad, not bad."

The 1921 report went on to recommend institutional farms and training schools for the idiots and imbeciles and special classes in public schools for the defectives. Likewise, children of superior intelligence should receive scholarships and state assistance so that they "could receive extra educational advantage." For those with nervous instability, Hincks proposed a system whereby the public schools would "make provision for the mental examination of all children." They would then be classified into different groups and placed in segregated classrooms "where the rate of progress was suited to their developmental needs." Hincks had no recommendations to deal with children with conduct disorders, other than to say they needed to be understood.

69

Other urgent needs included a new mental hospital, a psychopathic ward in a general hospital, the establishment of psychiatric clinics, the supervision of inmates in the community, the instruction of teachers and students in good mental hygiene, and the strengthening of immigration laws. And, of course, the storing of wrapped children on shelves would have to stop. The process should begin urgently, Hincks wrote, with the appointment of a Mental Hygiene Commission to lead the way.

Governments move slowly, but Hincks was patient. When, seven years later, he was invited to return to Alberta for a second survey, he saw it as an opportunity to acknowledge progress and to restate unmet goals. He had spoken in Alberta many times over the past seven years, frequently to promote prevention and the sterilization of the feeble-minded. This visit was to be an official one, commissioned by a government in the throes of a public scandal.

A prominent veterinary surgeon, Dr. Arthur Hobbs of Medicine Hat, had died under questionable circumstances while a patient at the Ponoka Hospital for the Insane. A former member of the Royal North West Mounted Police, Hobbs had strong ties to the Canadian Legion. After eight staff members were charged by the police, the Legion demanded a full government investigation into conditions at the asylum. In addition to the Legion, the government had also begun to receive letters from patients, although very little in the way of frank correspondence was smuggled through the censored mails.

One young woman wrote Premier Brownlee and described in detail her confinement and abuse at the hands of the staff. Brownlee made only a courtesy response, indicating that the matter was under review by the Health Minister. On a copy of the letter sent to Health Minister George Hoadley, Brownlee scribbled, "From my reading of the letter I think you will have to be careful that she does not become a 'woman with a mission' and cause your department considerable embarrassment in the future in her zeal to improve conditions at Ponoka." He expressed no concern for the woman.

Seven of the attendants sentenced in the Hobbs death received two months' hard labour; the eighth was convicted of manslaughter and imprisoned for five years. Responding to criticism in the Edmonton and Calgary newspapers, Brownlee and his cabinet toured the hospital. They left with an "impression that the capacity of the institution was taxed" but stated they had been "highly gratified at the general air of cleanliness and efficiency in evidence." A survey by Hincks and the national committee would, they hoped, defer the matter and put it to rest.

The new survey was conducted by Hincks, Marjorie Keyes, and Dr. C.B. Farrar, an Ontario colleague. Their task was to compare conditions and treatment against the best standards in similar situations. Hincks had developed a checklist of 19 asylum standards and this report would be easy. Although the survey was officially to include the Red Deer Training School, the Oliver Mental Institute, and the Ponoka Mental Hospital, Hincks knew the government was most concerned about the Ponoka controversy. Two-thirds of the report would focus on that hospital.

Tabled in the legislature in February of 1929, the report repeated many of the recommendations from the 1921 survey while acknowledging progress on others. Central to the recommendations was a reduction in the size of the Ponoka patient population, now numbering over a thousand. Hincks also asked for an increase in staff, less use of restraining devices such as the cage beds and straitjackets, and more use of hydrotherapy and occupational therapy. Hincks and Farrar also believed in the therapeutic value of water and work. On the issue of staff abuse of patients, the surveyors heard many sad and harrowing stories from patients and former staff. But the report did not confirm abuse. Hincks and Farrar preferred to play down the controversy and to recommend training and the introduction of techniques that might prevent future occurrences.

Finally, the report recommended a nursing school, new mental health clinics, sexual sterilization, and, again, a Mental Health Commission to lead the way. With the support of Premier Brownlee and Health Minister Hoadley, a commission headed by Dr. C.A. Baragar was appointed, and within two years, the government would act on most of the recommendations. By 1930, the future for the insane in Alberta began to look a bit better. Then came the Great Depression and conditions worsened.

By September of 1947, a third survey was commissioned by government Order-in-Council. Premier Ernest Manning and Health Minister W.W. Cross were concerned about the conditions in mental hospitals that had been created by 17 years of impoverished budgets and poor staffing. The Depression and World War II had taken their toll. Earlier that year, some relief had been provided to Ponoka by the transfer of 100 patients to Rosehaven in Camrose, but the politicians wanted an independent review of conditions. Hincks and his committee were again commissioned to make a general survey of the conditions in mental institutions and mental hygiene clinics in the province. Hincks was now 62 years old and considering retirement. He could not attack the job with the same zeal and energy he had shown before, and he had only two months to devote to the project. He had to prepare for an all-important presentation to the federal government early in the new year—a presentation which could affect government research grants for decades to come.

The Alberta study would have to be superficial, but it would be honest. Hincks was genuinely impressed with what he saw as the progressive efforts in the mental hygiene clinics. While conditions in the hospitals remained poor, the government was interested in improvements and some change had begun. Perhaps this was an opportunity to encourage them. Hincks wrote a positive report. The institutions, Hincks wrote, had "attained a credible standard of humanitarian care." Premier Manning and Minister Cross were pleased. The report was submitted to the Queen's Printer for publication, and thousands of copies were proudly circulated throughout the province. Obviously, few changes were required.

Despite advancing age and diminishing energy, Clare Hincks worked harder than most men. The month of August he spent resting at the family cottage at Muskoka, where he became reacquainted with his family. Otherwise, he was rarely home. Mental hygiene was his personal and professional obsession. His family had always come second. Hincks readily admitted that he placed his work before his wife and children, yet he remained married for 40 years. His wife and three children had fond memories of an occasional Sunday and sometimes even a few weeks over the summer months at the cottage. Otherwise, Clare was usually away or withdrawn. His family did not understand why he was silent and moody, or why he disappeared to a small room above his boathouse, even when on holiday at Muskoka.

During all these years, Hincks' assistant, Marjorie Keyes, supported him, deferred appointments, transcribed letters, and in many other ways protected him from responsibilities. The black periods, which he referred to as his annual spring neurosis, would pass—usually within a few weeks, but sometimes taking as long as six months. Marjorie even purchased a boarding house near the Hincks cottage. The two were extremely close and it came as no surprise to his family when Clare and Marjorie married several years after his first wife's death.

Hincks' recurrent highs and lows shaped his life. He often felt ambivalent about treating the illness for fear it would "flatten him out." In his mania, he was able to work with super-human energy and drive. "I did not want to come down to earth," he said, " for heaven was too sweet."

"My job in life is pioneering," he added, "to be a pioneer you must be vigorous. Poised, steady people are priceless but in my work a touch of neurosis seems to be essential." But Hincks' tune changed during his lengthy depressions. He subjected himself to electro-shock treatment and travelled to Europe for psychoanalysis. Hincks had become quite interested in the theories of Sigmund Freud, and wondered about promoting them back in North America. But famed German psychiatrist Emil Kraepelin changed his mind. "If Freud had worked with psychosis rather than neurosis," Kraepelin advised, "he would never have been able to develop his interesting theories."

Although primarily interested in psychosis that he viewed to be more serious than his own illness, Dr. Hincks thought his "neurosis" might respond to psychoanalysis. While repulsive to him, he considered the psychoanalytic view that his problems stemmed from "incest passion from the parent of the opposite sex." Psychoanalysis proved to be no more helpful than the shock treatment. He read books, took drugs, and consulted with colleagues. Nothing seemed to work except work itself. When Hincks retired and then married Marjorie Keyes in 1957, his episodes of depression vanished. The reason, he guessed, was that he no longer worked 16-hour days and then paid for them by going into depression. Hard work had perhaps not been as helpful as he thought.

Just prior to his death from cancer, Hincks lamented, "I'm not at all impressed by what we know or what we've done." His efforts in running the mental hygiene movement in Canada and for almost a decade in the United States, had led to hundreds of innovations, many of them first implemented in Alberta. Hincks had directly inspired new laws, more humane care, reduced use of restraint, research, new treatments, community clinics, nursing education, and mental hygiene courses in the faculties of medicine, nursing, dentistry, and education. He had also influenced a registration system for psychiatrists, the beginning of a national citizens' mental health organization with divisions in every province, and an international federation for mental health. The doctor's single lingering controversy, it seemed, was the promotion of sexual sterilization.

The National Committee for Mental Hygiene changed its name to the Canadian Mental Health Association in 1950 and the Alberta Division was initiated five years later by Hincks and George Gooderham, one of Hincks' college friends from Calgary.

Upon his death on December 17, 1964, the *Toronto Star* described Dr. Clare Hincks as a "Moses for the mentally ill." He would not have agreed. The man who more than any other person changed the landscape of mental hygiene in Alberta and across Canada, complained from his deathbed that the mentally ill were still treated as animals. He would not have agreed with Doctors Mitchie and McPherson from Alberta that modern mental hospitals bore no resemblance to the past. "Future generations will weep for us," he said. "They'll call this the dark ages."

Dr Clare Hincks, 1885-1964, founded the Canadian Mental Health Association. (Photo courtesy CMHA)

References

Beers, Clifford Whittingham. *A Mind that Found Itself.*
New York: Doubleday & Company, 1908.

Brownlee, John. Premiers Papers,
Provincial Archives. 1930.

Canadian Mental Health Association, Alberta Division.
"The Amazing Claire Hincks," Viewpoints—"Then and
Now" 5(2), 1994.

Canadian Mental Health Association. *Let Just Praise be
Given—A Book of Tribute to John Douglas Morecroft
Griffin.* The Canadian Mental Health Association, 1971.

"Founder, Head of Canadian Mental Health Association,
Dr. Hincks Dies at 79," *The Globe and Mail*, December
18, 1964.

Griffin, John Douglas. Toronto, ON. Interview with
author, 1998.

Hincks, Clarence M. *Mental Hygiene Survey of the
Province of Alberta.* Canadian National Committee for
Mental Hygiene, 1921.

Hincks, Clarence M. and Farrar, C.B. *Report of
Commissioners Appointed to Investigate the Provincial
Training School at Red Deer, Provincial Mental Institute
at Oliver, Provincial Mental Hospital at Ponoka.*
Edmonton, AB: Government of Alberta, Provincial
Archives, 1929.

Katz, Sidney. "Clare Hincks' Crusade for the Mentally
Ill." *Readers Digest,* 1986.

Rohn, George. Toronto, ON. Interview with author, 1998.

Roland, Charles G. *Clarence Meredith Hincks: Mental
Health Crusader.* Toronto and Oxford: Hannah Institute &
Dundurn Press, 1990.

Weil, Robert. "A Pioneer in Psychiatry," *The Medical
Post*, April 4, 2000.

Chapter 5
The Rules of Law

Chapter 5
The Rules of Law

The Rules
of Law

1922

"She done stuff I don't consider appropriate." Little Joe was a trapper from Lac La Biche who, upon returning from his trapline, found that his wife had committed a few indiscretions. Joe beat her. His wife, Theresa, called the local priest, who called the local Mountie. When the constable asked if Joe had beat his wife, he said simply, "Yes—she done stuff I don't consider appropriate." Little Joe had very little understanding of the broader community, and he couldn't read or write. He was a very private person who lived a simple life. Joe was a Cree and a Catholic who knew about obedience. He had beaten his wife and that was okay, but out of respect for the priest and the Mountie, Joe agreed to go to the Ponoka "insane hospital." He viewed it as his penance. No one could say why the shy trapper had been taken to Ponoka, but presumably the priest and Mountie viewed Joe as insane or mentally deficient.

Alberta had new laws in 1922: *The Insanity Act* and *The Mental Defectives Act.* They allowed for committal to an institution in two ways. A Justice of the Peace could judge a person to be "insane and dangerous to be at large" or determine that the person was "inflicted with mental deficiency and incapable of managing himself or his affairs." In reality, the "new" law regarding the insane was basically the same law that had been passed in 1907, except that the original law had failed to include any provision for discharge. There simply was no official way to leave institutions! It seemed that when people checked in they rarely checked out! The 1907 Act had decreed that the insane would "remain subject to the custody of the officers and other persons in charge—until discharged under the provisions of this Act." A quick amendment in 1910 corrected the problem, and the provision was then incorporated into the 1922 Act.

The laws regarding the treatment of the insane were different across the Dominion of Canada. *The British North America Act* of 1867 required each province to make its own laws regarding "hospitals, asylums, charities" and alms, or "eleemosynary institutions." Only matters of criminal conduct resulting from insanity would be dealt with by national laws.

The government's interest in confining certain groups of people against their will was based on two concepts. The first was to provide a relationship similar to a parent and a child, in order to protect the insane from harm. The second was to relate to mentally ill people as jailers would—thereby protecting the public from harm. The idea went back to fifth century B.C. when Roman law stated that "if a person is a fool, let his person and his goods be under the protection of his family or his paternal relatives."

Although provincial laws differed, most of them had similar arrangements regarding commitment. The Justice of the Peace usually received his information from the local police and community leaders. In Joe's case, it came from the constable and the priest. If they thought Little Joe was insane, Little Joe was insane.

The Mountie's report specified Joe's name, his residence, his "calling," his means of support, his friends and relatives, and "the fact of his being married or single." The law also required the Mountie to state "the danger to be apprehended from his being at large" and the "alleged insanity." Insanity was not defined and a physician's opinion could be used if one was available. Joe had no right to appeal the Justice's decision; only a family member or friend could do that— and they had to do it within four days. Joe's wife certainly wasn't going to do it, and while neighbours viewed Joe as quiet, kind, and generous, they weren't about to get involved. After all, the priest and Mountie had decided.

The trapper was placed in the local jail to await transfer to Ponoka. Committal to the asylum required a warrant signed by the Attorney General and Section 18 of the new law stated that treaty Indians could not be removed to an asylum unless the expenses were guaranteed by the Superintendent of Indian Affairs. If Joe had not been Cree, his family would have been responsible for the daily costs— unless, of course, they were "indigent." The decisions by the officials would take several days, and Joe would wait patiently in the local jail.

A week later the Cree man arrived at Ponoka, prepared to do his penance. What and when his penance would be was at the sole discretion of the superintendent. The doctor would decide when Joe had been "restored to reason" and was "competent to act." Only the Attorney General himself could overrule the superintendent and order the release of a patient. The staff at the Ponoka Hospital for the Insane saw Joe the way his neighbours did—as quiet, kind, and generous—and he was soon given grounds privileges. The hospital was close to the river and town dump, and Joe spent his time scavenging, fishing, and trapping. On one occasion, he was found in a ward closet with a young lady, picnicking on cooked muskrat. It was delicious, she said. Little Joe sold most of his bounty in Ponoka and in time, he had earned enough to buy a 22-calibre rifle and a bicycle, which he hid beneath the garbage at the dump.

After several months, Joe decided he had done enough penance. On a warm September morning, he hung his rifle on his back, mounted his bike and headed for Lac La Biche. Within two days, he was picked up by the Mounties and returned to Ponoka. When the doctor asked Little Joe if he knew why he had been returned to the hospital, Joe replied, "Sir, I was carrying a rifle in white man's land." Joe's new time on the locked ward was spent preparing an elaborate map that would take him "out of white man's country," around Chip Lake, and back to Lac La Biche.

After several months on the closed ward, Little Joe was again given grounds privileges. It was now spring and on a late Friday afternoon, he walked away from the hospital, travelling at night when it was cold and sleeping in the heat of the day. He lived on a diet of duck eggs. The Lac La Biche Mounties were waiting for Joe when he got home, and he got another 300-mile trip back to Ponoka, courtesy of the Crown. Little Joe was discharged a week later. The hospital was tired of his coming and going, and no one considered him dangerous. He would be released on the condition he stay away from his former wife in Lac La Biche. The hospital's first psychiatric social worker had just been appointed and he would check on Joe to make sure he complied. Joe would.

The new law respecting "insane persons" was clear; Joe was on a trial leave for six months and any violation of the superintendent's order would "direct all constables" to see that Joe was "apprehended and taken back to the asylum from which he was discharged." If

Little Joe had been considered mentally defective rather than insane, his discharge might have taken much longer.

The 1922 *Mental Defectives Act* allowed any mentally defective person to be placed in an institution "upon application to the Minister of Health." In most cases, the application was made by families who would agree to pay a monthly cost of $10. In cases where families refused to consent to an admission, the situation would be reviewed by a Justice of the Peace, and an order would be made back to the Minister. For those people placed in an institution as defectives, the Act, like the 1907 *Insanity Act,* had no provision for discharge.

But Joe had been discharged and he was soon back on the trapline— away from his beloved Lac La Biche, but also away from wives, priests, Mounties, and doctors—spending his days trapping and cooking delicious rats.

In 1924, only two years after the government passed the new *Insanity Act*, things were changing rapidly. The opening of the Edmonton Institute, increasing admissions, and the transfer of hundreds of patients to and from various institutions, called for a more efficient law. The public seemed to want to make it easier for mental defectives and for the mentally diseased to be institutionalized. Society needed to be protected.

But society also appeared more interested in treatment for the disease and in discharge if, of course, it was warranted. Public Health Minister George Hoadley, through the influence of Ponoka psychiatrist Dr. Randall McLean, was becoming more and more interested in Alberta's asylums, and he wanted to see improvements. Hoadley wondered if medical doctors, rather than the courts, could make the admission and discharge decisions.

As psychiatrist Dr. Clare Hincks had said, "These people are mad, not bad." Historically, psychiatrists had not been regarded as true members of the healing arts. Described as "alienists," their function was to protect society from the insane by determining which of its members should be segregated. But new attitudes and therapies designed to treat—or at least maintain—the insane were giving the psychiatrists and the insane a new image and the potential for a new role in society.

Dr. Randall McLean was influential, and he believed new names might help medicalize psychiatry. A new law, *The Mental Diseases Act,* was passed and the word insanity was dropped. At the same time, the Ponoka hospital changed its name from the Hospital for the Insane to "Provincial Mental Hospital."

Then in 1925, the government appointed the first "Board of Visitors." The group of citizens was charged with touring the institutions and reporting back to the Public Health Minister. The board's first report led to a separate study on hospital working conditions, which in turn led to the 1928 assessment of services by Dr. Clare Hincks. As a direct result, Dr. C.A. Baragar was appointed Commissioner for Mental Health, community clinics were opened, and a training program for psychiatric nurses was begun at Ponoka. The *Sexual Sterilization Act* was passed, and plans were developed for a new psychopathic ward at the University of Alberta Hospital.

The 1931 amendments to *The Mental Diseases Act* enshrined these wards in general hospitals as official government policy. Psychopathic wards had existed in several American states since the turn of the century, and their goal was to provide early intervention. They also improved psychiatry's reputation as a bona fide part of the medical establishment.

The introduction by psychiatrists of insulin, Metrazol, electro-shock, and psychosurgery also gave psychiatrists the feeling they were using scientific methods. They were eager to impress their brethren in general hospitals as well as politicians and the public. They wanted desperately to show that psychiatry and mental hospitals were as deserving of respect and money as the rest of the medical profession and the general hospitals.

As the psychiatrists basked in a new scientific aura created by news stories of successful treatment, the public, too, began to better accept the profession. The prestigious *British Medical Journal* informed readers that the "tangibility" of the new psychiatric treatments made them "easily acceptable to the layman." The actual physical treatment of mental diseases, it maintained, "should have the effect on many people of bringing mental diseases within the same category of health as physical ill-health."

Moreover, the laws would give the psychiatrists mastery over the entire system. A mental hospital superintendent had the power to admit and detain anyone for examination and treatment "as he may deem proper to be so admitted and detained." There was still no definition of mental disease. Even the Minister, who previously could order an admission, now had to receive a voluntary request or a request from a close family member, or he had to be satisfied by the evidence of two "legally qualified medical practitioners." The detention could last no longer than 30 days. In the event a Justice of the Peace was satisfied a person was mentally diseased and too dangerous to be at large, he could still order a person to jail. The prisoner would there await the order of the Attorney General to transfer him to hospital. The superintendent always had the power to discharge, except when a warrant had been issued by the Attorney General, who would have to agree with the release.

In the new University of Alberta psychopathic ward, a person could also be admitted voluntarily, by warrant from a Justice, or by Ministerial Order. But the new Commissioner for Mental Health, a psychiatrist, would have to approve all discharges. No one could stay longer than three months. Patients who didn't respond to treatment would be transferred by the Commissioner to the mental hospitals. There was no appeal, except by families, and then only if they received "the approval and consent of the Minister." The appeal still had to be lodged within four days of the warrant or order. There were now numerous ways to get into hospital and only one way out—the psychiatrists had to approve.

For mental defectives under the age of 18, psychiatrists had to approve much more than their release from the institutions. A 1942 amendment to the *Mental Defectives Act* stated that the superintendent could discharge any patient in any case where he "considers that such person is capable of earning a legitimate livelihood" and of "conforming to the law," and that the "power of procreation of that person no longer exists." The sterilization scalpel would now become a discharge instrument.

Psychiatrists were also maintaining their job as "alienists." They were providing more and more advice to the courts as to who should be locked up and where. The *Canadian Criminal Code* had provisions which essentially asked the court to determine "responsibility." In essence, the law asked a simple question: "Should this person be made liable for punishment?" Psychiatrists could help. While most of them probably operated with the highest of motives, hoping to use the best knowledge in deciding the future of a fellow human, the science of forensic medicine was woefully inexact.

In 1955, a young man named Edward Brown was arrested following a botched attempt at purse snatching. He was 19 years old and this, his first time at the intersection of law and psychiatry, would change his life forever. During his first court hearing, Edward was asked if he intended to get a lawyer and enter a plea. He didn't need a lawyer, he said. He knew what he had done and he wanted to "get this over with." Because of Edward's young age, the Judge ordered a customary pre-sentencing report. It was discovered that Edward had received previous treatment at a mental health clinic, and his psychiatrist was asked to provide the court with his findings.

The *Criminal Code* allowed for the consideration of "expert" testimony by the courts at several points: when the court was trying to determine whether a person was fit to stand trial; when helping to determine responsibility for a defense of insanity; and when providing advice to a judge following a conviction or guilty plea just prior to sentencing.

Edward's judge was simply confirming that Edward understood the proceedings prior to sentencing. In the course of a 10-minute hearing, the psychiatrist described Edward as "mentally retarded— moron level." The doctor was apparently attempting to convey that Edward had some reduced degree of responsibility, and when the judge asked him if Edward would be capable of instructing a defense, the psychiatrist said, "I hardly think he would be able to instruct counsel or to give a coherent and logical story which would be acceptable to the court." Edward was dumbfounded. He had thought this man was on his side. The exchange persuaded the judge that he had made a mistake several weeks earlier in accepting Edward's guilty plea. He ordered that the plea be struck, declared Edward unfit to stand trial, and placed him under a "Lieutenant Governor's Warrant." He would be detained indefinitely in the provincial hospital.

As with any finding of being unfit to stand trial or insane, the *Criminal Code* required the judge to order that the person be kept in custody "until the pleasure of the Lieutenant Governor is known." In practice, this normally meant a decision by the provincial cabinet, or at a minimum, the provincial Attorney General. "Until the pleasure is known" could mean anything from a few months to life. A review of the case was not required in law.

The public, however, thought Edward "got off." He spent 16 years in detention for an offense which would normally have resulted in less than 30 days in jail. And Edward's story was hardly an exception to the rule. In 1969, Alberta's Ombudsman, George McClellan, reported on 34 Albertans who had spent up to 27 years in the Ponoka and Oliver institutions with no appeal of their conditions allowed. In at least one case, a formal plea to the Lieutenant Governor had been redirected by civil servants.

By the early 1970s, more and more stories like Edward Brown's were being made public in the popular press. New civil liberty groups—and, in some parts of North America, new "anti-psychiatry" movements—were emerging. Mental health advocates also began to enlist their most important recruits: lawyers. In the United States, young lawyer Bruce Innis gave rise to the "mental health bar" through his work with the New York Civil Liberties Union and through the publication of his book Prisoners of Psychiatry. Psychiatrist Thomas Szasz, who made a career describing the "myth of mental illness," wrote the preface. In the book, Innis portrayed psychiatry as a means to control or dispose of people who annoy others. Innis wrote: "How would we tame our rebellious youth, or rid ourselves of doddering parents, or clear the streets of the offensive poor without it?" For Innis, mental hospitals were places "where sick people get sicker and sane people go mad."

Within a few years, Innis, with the support of sympathetic lawyers, had organized well-attended conferences throughout the United States. Successful lawsuits by human-rights attorneys fuelled the cause and the Mental Health Law Project was formed. Its goal was to eliminate involuntary hospitalization, which was considered to be "incompatible with a free society." Influential articles in the law reviews of major universities demanded a limit to the "therapeutic orgies." In less than a decade, the mentally ill in most states could refuse hospitalization, no matter what the consequences or their ability to understand those consequences.

In Canada, the anti-psychiatry movement had trouble gaining steam. There were former patients who were vocal, and the Church of Scientology worked hard to recruit people who had poor experiences with mental health services. But Canadian lawyers were reluctant to get involved. They were more cautious than their American counterparts and addressed the involuntary "admission issues by working to tighten commitment standards rather than to eliminate certification. Canadian lawyers like Barry Swadron, Gail Czukar, Harvey Savage, and Carla McKague made strong criticisms of mental health law, but none of them advocated the more radical American stance.

In Alberta, the government of Peter Lougheed was dominated by young lawyers, and they had many supporters who viewed themselves as civil libertarians. Premier Peter Lougheed's commitment to reform of the mental health system also meant a commitment to certain rights for those being treated against their will. Prior to 1964, the province's mental health laws had remained pretty much the same for 30 years. Two ministers, W.W. Cross and J.D. Ross, had led the Health Department for that entire period, and neither had seen much need to rewrite the mental health laws until the mid-1960s. A 1955 review did little but change the term "psychopathic ward" to "psychiatric ward" and recognize the cyclical nature of many mental illnesses by limiting hospitalization to three months in any 12-month period. If patients didn't respond to treatment in that time, they would have to be transferred to the Ponoka or Oliver institutions.

In the early 1960s, following the release of popular, highly critical books by anti-psychiatry authors Erving Goffman, Thomas Szasz, and R.D. Laing, the public began to grow increasingly suspicious of psychiatric authority. According to the controversial psychiatrists, the profession had for years excised portions of people's brains, experimented with chemicals, sent patients into dangerous comas, passed electricity through the brain, removed sex organs, and committed people to institutions—frequently without any form of consent and almost always with no appeal or independent review. Public interest was kept alive by popular books and movies like Ken Kesey's One Flew Over The Cuckoo's Nest and dramatic media reports of hospital atrocities. In the United States and Ontario, the major controversy was crude lobotomies, even though very few American or Ontario physicians were still performing them in the mid-1960s.

In Alberta, lobotomies would continue for more than four years beyond the 1964 Mental Health Act, a law reputed to address human-rights issues. The 1964 act, according to Health Minister Ross, provided clarity to the definition of mental disorder, that being "suffering from mental illness or retardation." In essence, it said a mental disorder was a mental illness. And to demonstrate the government's support of the growing North America phenomena of freedom and rights, the new law proposed an independent review panel to consider complaints. In direct contrast to the American trend, the Alberta criteria for involuntary admission was based on concerns about the person's "welfare" rather than his or her "dangerousness."

Alberta's civil libertarians and advocates expressed outrage at the confusing definition and the vagueness of the welfare concept. Most psychiatrists and family members simply hoped it would help ensure early admissions. They had argued successfully that admissions should be based on the medical concept of disease and not the legal concept of dangerousness.

These "loose" or "humane" committal rules, depending on one's values, were not entirely unique to Alberta. While most American states were moving to a "dangerousness" criteria, the law in Massachusetts called for the committal of a person "likely to conduct himself in a manner which contravenes laws and morals." Pennsylvania permitted commitment if anything "lessens the capacity of a person to use his customary self-control," and even the National Institute of Mental Health in the United States had recommended committal "for those in need of care or treatment."

When the Lougheed government came to power, it agreed with the civil libertarians. The welfare concept was too loose and the Act too open to potential abuse. And the Alberta media had been having a field day throughout the late 1960s and early 1970s with stories exposing deficiencies in the provincial institutions. The public was ready. In 1972, a new act redefined mental illness as "lacking reason or control of behaviour" and required the appointment of a Citizens' Advisory Council in order to provide the Minister with public input. The notion of personal welfare was abandoned in favour of criteria that included "suffering a mental disorder" and "presenting a danger to himself or others."

A proposal was made to have registered therapists help with admissions in rural areas where psychiatrists were few or nonexistent.

A provincial judge or a policeman could also order an apprehension. These orders were intended to provide "conveyance certificates" to get people to hospital. But the orders would only be valid for 72 hours. To be admitted, a person would first need the evaluation of two physicians and then they could only be held for one month before renewal certificates had to be issued.

The act also allowed for new patients' rights, which included knowledge about review panel procedures, privacy, and access to visitors and written communications. Mail could no longer be censored. Relatives and the "referring source" would also need to be advised when a patient was discharged.

Many psychiatrists saw all this as an unnecessary encumbrance on their authority, and the Canadian Medical Association expressed concern over the proposed "increased use of non-medical personnel." But the lawyers liked it. In announcing the Act, Health and Social Development Minister Neil Crawford said the legislation would "set the pace for North America." The civil libertarians were pleased. And so was lawyer Lougheed.

In 1980, shortly after Bob Bogle was appointed Minister of Social Services and Community Health, he inherited mental health services from Hospitals Minister David Russell. Legislative changes were required to transfer responsibility to Bogle's department—and mental health officials used the opportunity to request a few additional amendments. The most significant change involved toughening up the rules on the confidentiality of patient records. Furthermore, the proposal to have "therapists" help with admissions had proven to be unworkable; no one, it seemed, could agree on what exactly constituted a therapist, so the conveyance certificates were still being left to the discretion of physicians, usually the family doctor.

Bogle thought that a complete review of the legislation was overdue. The 1972 Act had been introduced a decade earlier, Bogle complained, and it was "timely to undertake a major reassessment." Some staff in his department suspected this was a slippery strategy to assure the public how vitally interested the Minister was in mental health reform—while potentially delaying any changes for years.

Bogle's predecessor, Helen Hunley of Rocky Mountain House, had served as Social Services Minister between 1975 and 1979, and she had demonstrated a strong interest in mental health issues. Hunley had been instrumental in pushing for improved forensic services at the Alberta Hospital Edmonton, and her reputation in the mental health community was good. In fact the forensic "Pavilion" was named in her honour. Hunley was now retired from politics, and Bogle appointed her to replace psychiatrist Dr. Mary McIntosh as chairman of the Advisory Board that had been struck under the 1972 legislation.

"Helen," as Hunley preferred to be known, got along well with council members and seemed to develop a particular liking for young Edmonton lawyer Richard Drewry of Emery Jamieson. Bogle and Drewry also seemed to get along, and Hunley soon extended Bogle's invitation to have the 35-year-old chair a task force to, as Bogle had put it, "undertake a major assessment of the legislation and practices used in Alberta." He wanted them compared with other laws with a "focus on the society of today."

Drewry's interest in mental health law had developed during his education at the University of Saskatchewan. The young lawyer had also sat on provincial hospital review panels and represented the Law Society of Alberta on the Minister's Advisory Council. There were few Alberta lawyers who shared his strong interest in mental health law. Two others were Margaret Shone of the University of Alberta, a leading member of the Schizophrenia Society, and Calgary lawyer Aleck Trawick, Drewry's former Saskatoon class-mate, and the Canadian Mental Health Association's incoming President. Both of their organizations had pressed for legislative change, and Drewry knew he could work easily with them.

The two-year study was undertaken with enthusiasm by a nine-member group, which included Helen Hunley and Margaret Shone. They held public hearings in six provincial centres, received more than 80 submissions, and did comparative research in many other jurisdictions. More than three months were spent just debating issues and agreeing on recommendations. Ultimately, 199 recommendations saw the light of day. Many additional recommendations regarding the need for mental health service improvements were not included. While Drewry wrote at the outset of his report that the Minister had a "legislative obligation to establish and maintain a satisfactory system of community-based mental health services," he refused to make specific suggestions, noting that his group did "not see it as within our mandate."

The final report, entitled "The Report of the Task Force to Review The Mental Health Act," but commonly known as the "Drewry Report," was tabled with Health Minister Neil Webber in December of 1983. Minister Bogle was no longer in charge. Director of Mental Health Services, Dr. Roger Bland, and government lawyer Anne Russell reviewed the report with concern. It was their job to evaluate the recommendations and write them into law, a task that could take years.

The 191-page document dealt with types of facilities, admission procedures, rules for apprehension and admission, the rights of patients, the procedures for independent reviews, control of and consent to treatment, confidentiality, the need for advocacy, and, of course, miscellaneous administrative matters. The Bland and Russell review was further complicated by the 1986 *Charter of Rights and Freedoms*, which guaranteed "freedom of thought, belief, opinion, and expression," the right to "security of the person," and the right not to be subjected to "cruel and unusual treatment." Bland and Russell were in a medical and legal minefield.

A year earlier, in 1985, New York City Mayor Edward Koch ordered the police, in sub-freezing weather, to pick up people lying on the streets and take them to shelter. New York's Civil Liberties Union formed a "freeze patrol." They walked the streets and handed out pamphlets advising the street people, many of whom were ill, of their "right to freeze." The news outraged many Canadians. The pendulum, at least in Canada, appeared to be beginning its swing away from personal liberties at all cost.

The 1986 "Uniform Law Commission," a federal initiative to provide a framework for the many varied provincial mental health acts, released its draft report. Although the initiative coincided with the Charter of Rights in timing, the report was considered medically oriented, moving to the right of both Drewry's report and the Charter. The Commission recommended the commitment of persons who caused "emotional harm" to others and a system for "involuntary outpatients." Bland and Russell's job kept getting tougher.

More than four years after Drewry tabled his report, Alberta still had no new laws, and stakeholders were becoming impatient. The CMHA, under the leadership of Aleck Trawick, asked the courts for "intervener status" on behalf of a patient who was having difficulty and then sued the government for lack of action. Several months later, a new act was tabled in the legislature. It was coincidental and unrelated to the law suit, the government claimed. And the 1988 *Mental Health Act* was a disappointment for Drewry. While civil servant Dr. Bland argued that most of Drewry's recommendations were accepted, Drewry took solace "in a few significant items that were." Mental disorder was redefined, substitute decision-making based on the best interests of the patient was introduced, and the concept of the "least intrusive treatment" was agreed upon.

Further, restrictions were placed on treatments like lobotomies, some 15 years after American lobbyists and Massachusetts Senator Edward Kennedy had convinced a United States congressional committee to place severe restrictions on unwanted surgery. In truth, lobotomies were no longer being done in Alberta anyway. Still, the external review of complaints and objections was made more independent and a Mental Health Patients' Advocate was appointed to investigate complaints. The study was not a total loss.

Drewry's study had been designed to make a dramatic difference, but even the few proposals that had been accepted did not work as well as he had hoped. The highly touted Mental Health Patients' Advocate, for example, was so encumbered with legal limits on what he could do that many patients didn't even bother to call. Those who did were frequently told their issues were "outside his authority." Each year, between one and two thousand calls would be logged, with only about 10 per cent of them resulting in new files. The Advocate, Dr. Mervyn Hislop, believed in his responsibilities and complained that his office's activity reflected "the maximum productivity permitted by current staffing levels."

Hislop petitioned the Health Minister to change his narrow mandate, citing specific problems he had encountered with assisting "voluntary patients"—people outside his authority who were forced to receive treatments like electro-shock against their will. His complaints fell on deaf ears, and some members of the mental health community privately described him as the "Maytag man." When the regulations had originally been developed, Mental Health Association representatives met with Health Minister Nancy Betkowski to express concern. She asked them for some time to "give it a chance." Even Dr. Hislop believed that time was up long ago.

Richard Drewry's involvement with the task force whetted his appetite for more. In his report, he wrote "significant improvements to the mental health system cannot be achieved by legislation alone." He would now concentrate on services and systems. His particular interest was people with the most chronic conditions such as schizophrenia and bipolar depression. He feared that the increasingly broad categories of mental illnesses would minimize the public's perception of the devastating nature of the more serious diseases.

Drewry joined the Canadian Mental Health Association and was elected and then re-elected divisional president between 1994 and 1998. During his tenure, he pushed aggressively for system improvements, emphasizing the needs of the more "severe and persistently ill." It was Drewry's leadership that helped encourage the Alberta government's short-lived 1994 commitment to mental health reform. While Drewry's presidency was to be characterized as a system reform era, legal issues were never far away. He chaired a national task group on mental health law and led the CMHA through one of the most contentious issues facing the organization in years—the relationship of rights and involuntary treatment in the community.

The Canadian Schizophrenia Society had proposed a system of "community committal" in which mentally ill people living in communities could be kept on a kind of "psychiatric parole" and forced to receive treatment, including medication. This type of law had been in place in many American states for years and had been proposed in Canada by the Uniform Law Commission. The proposal was seen by many as a violation of the Canadian Charter of Rights, and it was vehemently opposed by civil libertarians.

The government of Saskatchewan included a similar proposal in its legislation of 1993, arguing that the built-in protections provided compliance with the Canadian Charter demands. Although the act's community-committal provisions were very rarely used, the debate stimulated interest across Canada. Views on the matter of community committal were emotional, strongly influenced by people's personal experiences. Many former patients who had survived negative experiences with involuntary committal in hospital described the proposals as "barbaric," "fascist," and "paternalistic." Family members who had watched their loved ones refuse treatment, especially medication, were naturally distressed by the suffering that was the usual result and they favoured forced committal. Most psychiatrists sided with family members, although some, likethe University of Alberta's Dr. Roger Bland, expressed major reservations.

Drewry carefully led both the Alberta and national boards of the CMHA through a consensus-seeking process that tried to bring the views of patients and clients, family members, physicians, and lawyers to the table. Predictably, there were many disagreements.

"People with a serious illness are sometimes unable to understand what is in their own best interests," protested a member.

"This will be a further erosion of rights that diminishes the ability of consumers to be in control," retorted another.

"Forced treatment will jeopardize relationships with caregivers."

"Community committal is less restrictive than hospitalization."

"If an adequate system were in place, community committal would not be required."

"Unless you have experienced the loss of a loved one, don't even comment."

"Forced treatment is more harmful than helpful."

And on it went.

In the end, a 10-page national CMHA discussion paper detailed the pros and cons of community committal. The association, at both the provincial and national levels, endorsed a policy that supported "the continued development of comprehensive systems of community-based support as a positive alternative to community committal."

Some critics argued that the policy was a "cop-out" that said neither yes nor no to the controversial proposal. What the policy stipulated, Drewry insisted, was that community committal wouldn't be need-ed if the government would provide comprehensive community services with assertive outreach, medication monitoring, and early intervention. But, he warned, if the government continued its prac-tice of treating the mentally ill in large mental hospitals and then abandoning them to the streets, community committal was probably essential.

In 1999, the Alberta government's Mental Health Advisory Board instructed Mary Marshall, their Director of Legal and Policy Development, to prepare a discussion paper on "Compulsory Community Treatment Orders." During her consultations, the Canadian Mental Health Association and the Self Help Network continued to push for a comprehensive system of care as an alternative to legislation. The Schizophrenia Society of Alberta persisted in demanding new legislation allowing community treatment orders. The debate continues.

References

Anonymous. Former psychiatric nurse—interview with author, 1998.

Anonymous. Former civil servant—interview with author, 1998.

Anonymous. Civil servant—interview with author, 1998.

Bland, Roger. Edmonton, AB. Interview with author, 1998.

Drewry, Richard. *Report of the Task Force to Review the Mental Health Act*. Alberta: Social Services and Community Health, Government of Alberta, 1983.

Drewry, Richard. Edmonton, AB. Interview with author, 1998.

Hudson, Tony. Edmonton, AB. Interview with author, 1998.

Laing, R.D. London, England. Interview with author, 1972.

Savage, Harvey and McKague, Carla. *Mental Health Law in Canada*. Canada: Butterworths, 1987.

Swadron, Barry B. *Detention of the Mentally Disordered*. Markham: Butterworths, 1964.

Swadron, Barry B. *The Law and Mental Disorder*. Toronto: Canadian Mental Health Association, 1973.

Chapter 6
Prevention on the
Cutting Edge

Chapter 6
Prevention on the
Cutting Edge

Prevention
on the
Cutting Edge

1928

The debate was emotional. Chairman J. M. MacEachran was adamant. "Since the state must assume most of the load of responsibility in connection with defective children, it is surely justified in adopting reasonable measures to protect itself against their multiplication." The chairman was keenly supportive of sterilization legislation and in 1928, he made speeches to whomever and whenever he could.

The founding chairman of the Department of Philosophy and Psychology at the University of Alberta, MacEachran was one of the most senior and respected academics in Alberta. He was also an elitist. He spoke with admiration of the philosopher Plato and his proposal for a state ruled by a class of philosopher-kings. The most intelligent among all citizens were to be intensively trained in music, art, science, and philosophy for the first 35 years of their lives. These individuals would then govern society based on knowledge "free from private interests and corrupt party politics."

95

Not too coincidentally, John MacEachran had been appointed to the university at the age of 35, after studying music, art, science, and philosophy. His goal for society was "the achievement of human perfection and the realization of human happiness." The purity of the race was to be found, he thought, through regulating marriage and reproduction. A eugenics law would be a good start. The "multiplication" of "defective" children needed to be stopped.

Thirty-nine years later, in 1967, the definition of "defective" was being interpreted very broadly. Métis Annie Smith was apparently defective. At 28 years of age, she had five children for which she was incapable of providing. She had a hard-drinking husband, no father, and a nomadic mother. She had no work and no money. She was a Métis chased from the reserve but also felt she was "unwelcome in white man's land." Annie Smith had no roots and no future.

Annie was depressed. She withdrew into her personal misery; sleep her only comfort. Driven by her husband to the Alberta Hospital at Oliver, Annie was left at the admissions unit. This would be her second admission to the hospital in less than two years. Exhausted and withdrawn, Annie begged to sleep. Nothing else mattered. Not the doctor who interviewed her, not the nurses who escorted her to the ward, not even the three women who shared her tiny room.

The next morning, as the sun peeked through the grilled windows, Annie was awakened by the nurses' call to rise. "Please God, more sleep," Annie muttered. Pulled from her bed, she had to be helped to dress. She shuffled to the dining room but could not eat. She had a fleeting idea that she should be embarrassed about being there. "I'm better than these other people," she thought. "I don't care what they think, I don't care what they do." After breakfast, Annie and several other patients were "herded" into occupational therapy sessions. Annie remembered occupational therapy from her first time in hospital and she hated it. The ward staff proposed many activities, but the proper materials never seemed to be available. She sat idle at a table while a young therapist tried to interest her in macramé, which was at that time the "in thing" for middle-class Albertans. Annie just wanted to be left alone. The black cloud of despair grew thicker, yet Annie refused drugs. Her mother had said they were evil and would have long-lasting effects. The effects were no problem, but the young patient could handle no more evil. The doctor suggested shock treatment. Mother had said nothing about shock. Annie didn't care.

The next morning, Annie Smith missed breakfast. She was escorted to a treatment room and sat in the hallway with a dozen others, waiting her turn. No one seemed concerned. About 20 minutes later, Annie was placed on a high gurney-like bed. She remembers the nurse's reassurance, the doctor's soothing words, and the needle. Annie trusted. She would have no memory of the electrodes placed on her temples, of the sustained electrical shock, of the violent contractions, or of the deep peaceful sleep that followed.

The following day, Annie missed breakfast again. The doctor wanted a series of treatments—five or six would likely be most effective. In fact, many of his patients went home after the series. One of Annie's roommates was such a person. "A most unpleasant experience in that room," the roommate advised Annie, "but entirely worth it. The cloud will lift, I assure you."

The cloud would not lift. Annie felt even more depressed. The treatments affected her memory, and that frustrated her. The hospital staff were also frustrated. Weeks had passed and they seemed to be getting nowhere with this depressed and, now agitated, woman.

"Your problem, Annie," said the ward doctor, "is your children. You have had too many in too short a period and you can't cope. We must consider the future." He paused. "I would like you to agree to sterilization." Although trained as a nursing aide, Annie had never heard the word "eugenics." She did, however, know about sterilizing animals. The thought was ugly. "It is best for you," the doctor persuaded, "and for your children." The doctor explained that eugenics was the science of ensuring fine offspring. "You could pass your illness on to them," he warned. Annie Smith's mother agreed. Her daughter had been pregnant at 17 and seemed to obsess over every new man in her life. Yes, sterilization was a good idea.

This particular "good idea" had originated as a treatment in England. A proposal for a eugenics law was widely accepted by many of the country's elite in the early 1900s, largely because they were obsessed with the British class system. In short, they feared that society would be swamped by lower-class degenerates. In 1912, the first International Eugenics Conference was held in London, presided over by Leonard Darwin, a son of Charles Darwin, author of the theory of evolution. The conference was attended by about 700 delegates, including the organization's two vice-presidents—Winston Churchill and Alexander Graham Bell—and other world leaders. Although the conference delegates were keen, academics and researchers in England pointed out that "many cases of mental defect are not hereditary" and "most cases arise from evidently normal parents." The British Parliament refused to pass a law.

In the United States, the situation was different. Americans were alarmed by the northward movement of blacks and the arrival of Eastern European immigrants. They vastly preferred Anglo-Saxons. The purity of the race was at risk. Sterilization and control of immigration were linked. A combination of the two would keep the country pure and minimize the costs to care for the degenerates. First legalized in Indiana in 1907, forced sterilization existed in the laws of 16 states by 1920. Although Canada was an important part of the British Empire, Alberta was close to the United States and more heavily influenced by American trends.

By the time Annie Smith was sterilized in 1972, more than 60,000 Americans in a population of 203.3 million had been sterilized. In Alberta, the only Canadian province with a sterilization law in effect and with a population of 1.6 million, the number of sterilizations was almost 2400—about five times the ratio of the United States. Alberta also had an additional 1885 patients approved for sterilization who had, thus far, somehow evaded the scalpel. While many Albertans had fought against the tyranny of Nazi Germany, few would realize that the Alberta ratio of sterilization was only slightly less than half of those performed by the Nazi regime, where more than 300,000 people were sterilized from a population of 78.3 million.

Many physicians favoured sterilization, but the most influential Canadian was Dr. Helen MacMurchy, the country's leading public health authority. She worked for the Ontario government, and her annual reports influenced medical leaders and politicians about both the numbers and the dangers of the feeble-minded. In her book, Almost: A Study of the Feeble-Minded, MacMurchy wrote that while the feeble-minded represented only 3 to 5 per cent of the population, "they account for half or more of alcoholics, juvenile delinquents and unmarried mothers, not to mention between 29 and 79 per cent of all prostitutes."

98

Describing herself as a "general" in the righteous war against mental defectives, MacMurchy argued that 80 per cent of feeble-mindedness could be eliminated within a generation through segregation and sterilization. Her message was supported by the National Council of Women and the National Committee for Mental Hygiene. The committee, under the leadership of Dr. Clare Hincks, was particularly influential. In a 1922 survey of seven Canadian provinces, the committee reported that the number of feeble-minded was high and represented a threat to society. Feeble-mindedness, said Hincks, was a primary cause of poverty, crime, and prostitution. Sterilization was an important tool of prevention.

The country's foremost geneticist, Professor Madge Macklin of the University of Western Ontario, supported the theory—but she went much further. She called for the sterilization of not only all patients with schizophrenia, but of their parents, children, and all other relatives of "schizophrenics" because they carried a "latent factor" which could cause the disease at any time.

Alberta's leader in the sterilization movement, Professor MacEachran of the University of Alberta, had some important allies. While the government of the United Farmers was a diverse movement with no official ideology, its Agriculture and Health Minister, George Hoadley, was personally supportive of eugenics. As a farmer, he was familiar with the laws of heredity as applied to his herd of cattle. He concluded that in a country of small population, some steps needed to be taken to prevent "weakening of the race by sub-normal individuals."

The superintendents of Alberta's mental hospitals and institutes were also strong advocates, each believing that feeble-mindedness and schizophrenia were hereditary. Another influential ally was Emily Murphy, the first female magistrate in the British Empire. In a petition to the Alberta Legislature in 1914, she described mentally defective children as "a menace to society and an enormous cost to the state." She argued that "mental defectiveness is a transmittable hereditary condition." She wrote to Hoadley about two women who already had several children. "In my opinion it is a crime to let these two women go on bearing children," she warned.

99

Dr. Hincks of the National Committee on Mental Hygiene helped mobilize the United Farmers Women of Alberta, the Women's Christian Temperance Union, and the physicians in the Department of Agriculture and Health. The doctors helped disseminate material on the "moral and spiritual decay" of society by degenerates who included the mentally handicapped. In 1924, the United Farmers Women formed a committee of influential women to encourage legislation that would prohibit entry into Canada of immigrants who were "feeble-minded, epileptic, tubercular, dumb, blind, illiterate, criminal, and anarchistic."

The Ku Klux Klan had also come to Alberta and found unlikely allies in the farm women who also opposed the immigration of Catholics. Even Charlotte Whitton, Canada's flamboyant director of the Canadian Council on Child Welfare and the promoter of social work as a profession, supported immigration restrictions. She objected in particular to the entry of the feeble-minded.

It seemed only the Roman Catholic Church was opposed to immigration restrictions and sterilization. But the church was formidable. An estimated 48 per cent of the Canadian population was Catholic and the bishops mounted aggressive opposition throughout Eastern Canada and Manitoba. There were fewer Catholics in Alberta and British Columbia, where they faced strong opposition, particularly from women's organizations. MacEachran, Hincks, and their supporters were making progress. "Mental defectives," Hincks advised the politicians, "contribute out of all proportion to their numbers to such problems as delinquency, illegitimacy, spread of venereal, and other diseases."

For many families of retarded children, the proposed law made sense. Mental retardation was usually inherited, they believed, but even if it wasn't, how could children who were unable to care for themselves possibly raise others? And once they reached adolescence, intercourse was inevitable and pregnancy was the likely consequence. How else could parents protect their children?

Health Minister George Hoadley and Premier John E. Brownlee's United Farmers were convinced that the public was now supportive. In 1922, former Health Minister R.G. Reid had said that the government was supportive of sterilization legislation but needed public

opinion to catch up. The Liberals, Conservatives, and Catholic Church remained in opposition, but the United Farmers Women, the Local Council of Women, the Imperial Order of the Daughters of the Empire, the Women's Christian Temperance Union, and the National Committee for Mental Hygiene all helped swing public opinion and push the legislation through.

The *Alberta Sexual Sterilization Act* was passed on March 7, 1928.

Dr. J.M. MacEachran would serve as Chairman of the Eugenics Board, a position he held from 1929 until 1965—just two years before Annie Smith's case was sent to the board. A group of four confidential political appointees, without expertise in eugenics and working in complete privacy outside of any court or appeal mechanism, would decide which Albertans would be sterilized. The group of four, who remained on the board for between 10 and 20 years each, decided who might cause the transmission of a mental disease or create a risk of mental injury to themselves and others. In summary, anyone could be sterilized in a manner determined by the unanimous consent of the board if they were "in danger of transmitting a mental deficiency to their children, or incapable of intelligent parenthood." Only in the case of a psychotic person was consent needed from the person or from a relative.

Following Alberta's law, proposals for eugenics laws swept the western provinces. Only Ontario and Nova Scotia in the East had proposed such laws, but they did not pass. The British Columbia government had in 1925 considered a law to restrict immigration and to use sterilization. Ellen Smith, the first woman cabinet minister in the British Empire, proposed a law so that "the English-speaking people would maintain their position of supremacy on which the peace and prosperity of the world depended." She failed in her effort, but the government would try again eight years later.

The results of a survey by the National Committee for Mental Hygiene, which stated that feeble-mindedness was a primary cause of poverty, crime, and prostitution—and the publicity given to the report by the Women's Council of Vancouver—was generating strong public support. Emily Murphy, a vocal supporter of the Alberta legislation, wrote in the Vancouver Sun about the need for sterilization of the insane in order to protect women and children from sexual attack. "Human thoroughbreds" were needed, she said, but the nation is "burdened by 25,000 lunatics." A disproportionate number lived in Catholic Quebec, she argued, where religion and politics opposed important laws.

The bill was passed in British Columbia in April of 1933, the same year the Manitoba government rejected similar legislation.

It was also in 1933 that the Nazis began their campaign for racial hygiene in Germany. That same year, a 29-year-old Prairie boy was about to receive a Masters Degree from McMaster University for his thesis on eugenics. He proposed four remedies for the burden of taxes that were unfortunately needed to care for the "unfit." These were the restriction of marriage to those with certificates of health, the segregation of the unfit to state farms, liberal access to birth control, and sterilization of the insane and feeble-minded. The research was done at the asylum in Weyburn, Saskatchewan by Tommy Douglas, who would later serve as Premier of that province.

But in 1936, Douglas was frightened by a trip he took to Germany. By the time he served as Health Minister in Saskatchewan in 1944, he had firmly rejected two reports recommending sterilization, along with a lobbying effort by Clare Hincks. The former Liberal government's Public Health Minister, Dr. J.M. Urich, had been a vigorous opponent of sterilization. Hincks had great hope in Douglas, and he was disappointed at the government's apparent change of heart. Douglas now agreed with Urich.

In Ontario, a second attempt to enact legislation was stopped in its tracks by Deputy Health Minister Dr. B.T. McGhie. The Minister had reviewed 1937 research which revealed that the alleged growth in numbers and the reported high fertility rates among the feeble-minded were, in fact, both myths. The opposition of the Catholic Church to the legislation helped McGhie convince the legislators to kill the bill. While no law was ever passed to allow sterilization in Ontario, physicians went about sterilizing hundreds of young people until 1978. After all, there was also no law explicitly prohibiting sterilization—and none of the children seemed to object.

In spite of legislative rejection in most parts of Canada, Alberta academics and politicians remained staunch in their support of Alberta's sterilization law. Addressing the Canadian Medical Association in Calgary, President Wallace of the University of Alberta pressed his associates with religious zeal. "While science has done very much to raise the quality of the stock in domesticated animals which man has reared for his service, he has done virtually nothing to raise the quality of the human stock." Wallace then instructed the physicians "to make eugenics not only a scientific philosophy but in very truth a religion."

Sterilization may not have become a religion, but it was most certainly a way of life in Alberta. Amendments to the Act in 1937 by the new Social Credit government had made decisions even more efficient. Consent of the mentally ill was no longer required.

Annie Smith's case was heard, and a decision made within minutes. When the Eugenics Board had first been appointed in 1928, the members laboured for hours over decisions and only a few inmates were ordered to submit their sexual organs to a surgeon's scalpel. The process now took the form of rubber stamping. Almost 100 people would join Annie's "sterilization class" in 1967 alone.

One of those people was Annie's hospital roommate, Nancy Park. Only 17 years of age, Nancy had been diagnosed, she said, as a high-grade moron. "How dare they!" she exclaimed. "I may have a 'damn you' attitude, but I'm no retard." The first years of Nancy's life were spent travelling from town to town while her mother tried to find work. She was considered cheerful and talkative, but she had some sexual experience and was now in open rebellion against her mother. She was determined to run away on her 18th birthday in order to live her own life in her own way. The Eugenics Board's decision to sterilize was written in plain language: "Uncontrolled sex interest and activities."

Nancy was escorted to the tiny hospital operating room along with Annie who would be next; Annie was anxious. She had agreed to this, but now it didn't seem right. The surgeon assured her it was the proper thing to do and comforted her. "The operation is a simple tubal cut," he said, "and probably reversible if things change for you in the future." Annie's mind shifted. "This room is dirty," she thought. "I will get an infection." Panic and confusion began to set in. "I must trust—no, this is a mistake!" The room went black.

Both Annie and Nancy awoke in extreme pain. The Eugenics Board surgeons were permitted to use one of two methods: a salpingectomy, which involved a minor incision in the abdomen in order to cut or remove the fallopian tubes, or an oophorectomy, which meant the complete surgical removal of the ovaries—a kind of female castration. The advantage to the removal of ovaries, said the surgeon, was a reduced sex drive. Neither Annie nor Nancy had been given a "minor incision."

Similar techniques were used with men. The simplest process was a vasectomy, which involved the cutting or removal of a duct connecting the testicles to the ejaculatory duct. The alternative was an orchidectomy, the surgical removal of the male sex organs. With the level of male hormone reduced, or even eliminated, sexually aggressive behaviour in men was believed to be drastically reduced. In Red Deer, the Superintendent of the School Hospital, Dr. L.J. LeVann, also believed that there was a genetic cellular difference between "normal" and retarded people—and that the testicles were a much-needed part of his research. LeVann apparently preferred the orchidectomy.

Annie Smith was discharged in the care of her mother after two weeks. She was severely depressed, could barely walk, and had trouble with her memory. She remembered, however, that she had five children to care for and a husband she had decided to divorce.

Annie never really understood why she had been sterilized. Neither did her roommate Nancy. For that matter, most of the 2,472 women and men sterilized as a result of Eugenics Board decisions probably never fully grasped why this had happened to them. The official records just didn't tell their personal stories. The Eugenics Board files read:

"Poor family history."

"Epileptic."

"Risk of mental injury."

"Incapable of intelligent parenthood."

"Goes home where there is a possibility of pregnancy."

"Physically handicapped."

"Was sexually assaulted by a soldier when she was 14."

And on...

Perhaps, thought Annie, the surgeons were well-intentioned, wanting to intervene in her troubled life. Doctors she thought, are usually compassionate and considerate. But the way the statistics were skewed was troubling—more women than men were sterilized, more Roman Catholics than Protestants. In the last years of the board's activities, Indian and Métis, who represented 2.5 per cent of the population, accounted for more than 25 per cent of those sterilized.

Annie knew she had to try to fix things. Back home with her mother, she regained custody of her children, divorced her husband, and returned to school. Things didn't always go smoothly for Annie; she married three more times, and on one occasion when she couldn't cope, she left her children in a Grey Nuns convent. But Annie did not give up. Study was difficult. Annie's memory problems continued and her once strong mathematical skills had somehow been lost. Reading was slow and laborious. But she persevered and, in six years, obtained an education degree while holding down a job, caring for her children, and moving men through her life.

Annie Smith, who describes herself as "half a woman with no memory and no skills" and someone who "can't do anything people tell me I can," has raised five children—a homemaker, a lawyer, a doctor of forestry, a computer specialist, and a labourer. Like many other "defective" Albertans, Annie Smith had normal children.

In 1972, Premier Peter Lougheed and his newly elected Conservative government repealed the sterilization law and abolished the Eugenics Board. Lougheed would later put his mind to reforming mental hospitals and their decades of over-crowding and under- funding.

References

Abt, Mary. Ponoka, AB. Interview with author, 1998.

Anonymous. Family member of sterilized patient—interview with author, 1998.

Anonymous. Former psychiatric nurse—interview with author, 1998.

Anonymous. Psychiatrist—interview with author, 1998.

Anonymous. Second sterilization victim—interview with author, 1998.

Anonymous. Sterilization victim—interview with author, 1998.

Blair, W.R.N. *Mental Health in Alberta: A Report on the Alberta Mental Health Study 1968*. Edmonton, AB: Human Resource Research and Development Executive Council, Government of Alberta, 1969.

Christian, Timothy J. *The Mentally Ill and Human Rights in Alberta: A Study of the Alberta Sexual Sterilization Act*. Faculty of Law, University of Alberta, 1973.

Cooke, E.H. *Annual Report*. Provincial Mental Hospital, Department of Public Health. Alberta: Provincial Archives, 1928-29.

Cooke, E.H. *Annual Report*. Provincial Mental Hospital, Department of Public Health. Alberta: Provincial Archives, 1930-31.

Dickinson, Harley D. *The Two Psychiatries: The Transformation of Psychiatric Work in Saskatchewan, 1905-1984*. Regina: Canadian Plains Research Center, University of Regina, 1989.

Faulds, P. Jonathan. Edmonton, AB. Interview with author, 1998.

Garber, Allan. Edmonton, AB. Interview with author, 1998.

Goffman, Erving. *Asylums: Essays on the Social Situation of Mental Patients and Other Inmates.* Garden City, NY: Doubleday, 1961.

Hincks, Clarence M. *Mental Hygiene Survey of the Province of Alberta.* Canadian National Committee for Mental Hygiene, 1921.

Hincks, Clarence M. and Farrar, C.B. *Report of Commissioners Appointed to Investigate the Provincial Training School at Red Deer, Provincial Mental Institute at Oliver, Provincial Mental Hospital at Ponoka.* Edmonton, AB: Government of Alberta, Provincial Archives, 1929.

Johnson, J.O., *et.al. A History of Dedication and Caring 1911-1986.* Ponoka: Alberta Hospital Ponoka, 1986.

Johnson, J. O. Ponoka, AB. Interview with author, 1998.

Lougheed, Peter. Calgary, AB. Interview with author, 1998.

McLaren, Angus *Our Own Master Race: Eugenics in Canada*, 1885-1945. Don Mills, Ontario: Oxford University Press, 1990.

Park, Deborah C. and Radfor, John P. "From the Case Files: Reconstructing a History of Involuntary Sterilisation," *Disability & Society* 13(3): 317-342, 1998.

Peel, Robert A. (ed.). *Essays in the History of Eugenics.* London: The Galton Institute, 1998.

Slater, R. *Ponoka Panorama.* Ponoka: Ponoka and District Historical Society, 1973.

Wahlsten, Douglas. "Leilani Muir versus the Philosopher King: Eugenics on Trial in Alberta," *Genetica* 99: 185-198. Netherlands: Kluwer Academic Publishers, 1997.

107

Chapter 7
Sixty Beds to a Room—
and Liking It

Chapter 7
—Sixty Beds to a Room—
and Liking It

Sixty Beds to a Room—and Liking It

1932

As he walked the dusty road, he looked like the farmer he was.
He wore an old hat, bib overalls, khaki work shirt, and boots. He
chewed tobacco and spat along the road. He had a pick-up truck, but
fuel was expensive and the weathered Ford sat idle on the family
farm near Lac La Biche. Times were tough. The price of wheat had
dropped again on the Winnipeg Grain Exchange. It was now 54
cents a bushel, an all-time low. Ten years earlier, Leo Parent's father
had received $2.15 a bushel. Worse yet, Leo's farm had suffered
such a bad year that there was little crop to harvest; the low prices
were practically irrelevant to his problems.

It was late August, and Leo had spent much of the week walking,
sometimes hitchhiking when he got lucky. The stocky young farmer
hoped he might find work in Edmonton, which had grown to about
80,000 people and would surely hold some opportunities—perhaps
shelter and food, enough to get him through the winter. Maybe he
could even earn enough to send something home to his folks. But
finding a job would be a challenge; Alberta's population stood at
171,000, and a good portion of that number were unemployed.

As Leo lumbered down the road from Fort Saskatchewan, he could
see Edmonton in the distance. He also noticed several looming
buildings just over the next bluff and wondered if that was the mental institute. Leo Parent knew about mental institutes because his
neighbour, "Little Joe," had been taken by the RCMP to the Ponoka
Hospital for the Insane when Leo was just a tyke.

The Ponoka Hospital admitted people from throughout Alberta, and Little Joe could have been sent to the mental institute if the Ponoka doctors found his condition incurable. Hospitals for the insane were scary enough, thought Leo. If the worst people come to this one, what on earth must go on inside those walls? Leo was curious about the place, but he was more interested in what kind of jobs they might have. He noticed a large farm near the institute and wondered if they could use a hand. Leo was a large, healthy boy with thick hands and a strong back. He knew farming. He would ask. Near the small community of Oliver, Leo turned off the Fort Saskatchewan Trail onto a narrow road leading to the site. The town was named after Frank Oliver, the founder of the Edmonton Bulletin newspaper and a minister in the former Liberal government. The Mental Institute itself was referred to as "Oliver."

Leo walked across the CNR tracks and up the narrow dirt pathway to the site. The grounds looked rather sparse by northern Alberta standards, cleared of native poplar and willow and replanted with "more desirable" shrubs, sapling trees, and rockeries. This was obviously meant to be a showpiece, as well as a means of providing work and activity for the inmates. Leo later learned that 290 trees, 300 shrubs, 700 perennials, and more than 750 feet of spruce hedge had been planted. On his left was a beautiful two-storey house, more than twice the size of any Leo had ever seen. It was a veritable mansion by Parent family standards: stucco finish, large windows surrounded by neatly manicured shrubs, and three nearby cinder tennis courts. The sidewalk and freshly painted white front door seemed very inviting. To the right of the home, some distance away, Leo saw the large water tower he had first seen from the trail. To the north were three additional cottages and to the east were two large three-storey buildings and a smaller dormitory, which Leo assumed provided living quarters for patients. The dormitory was connected to smaller buildings that, Leo would later learn, contained a kitchen, bakery, and dining area. A power plant, garage, and cluster of farm buildings were visible in the distance.

The unemployed farmer rapped his leathery knuckles against the white door. He was greeted by a middle-aged woman who smiled and told him that this was the residence of Superintendent McAlister. Unfortunately, the woman explained, the doctor was not available at this time. Leo could see through the porch to the finely furnished living room with its throw carpets and soft furniture, its

The Edmonton Institute shown here in 1923. (Reproduced from public documents published by Alberta Hospital, Edmonton)

paintings on the walls, and crown mouldings at the ceiling. He stared briefly, and then meekly explained the purpose of his visit. The woman suggested that he talk to the head attendant, Frank Wrigby, who lived in the service building. Leo thanked her politely and started across the grounds, where a number of men were wandering aimlessly or weeding plants and shrubs. From the two large buildings, he heard occasional screams. Perhaps this is not a good idea, he thought. But the possibility of a job was a strong motivator. Entering the service building, he asked directions of an older man whom he thought was probably a patient. Leo was ill at ease, a feeling he assumed was caused by being unsure of what to expect from these people in this strange place.

Head Attendant Frank Wrigby was a big, tough man with a gruff voice and an intimidating manner. Frank, it was rumoured, had been placed at the Institute with "authority right from the Department of Health." Under the former superintendent, Dr. Charles Fitzpatrick, the daily cost per patient had been rising, from 69 cents a day at the end of 1928 to 86 cents in 1930. Since 1923, the institution's annual payroll had increased from $15,419 to almost $34,000.

The increase caught the attention of Premier Brownlee and his Health Minister, George Hoadley, was quick to act. Hoadley preferred the Institute's previous superintendent, Dr. David Dyck, a highly militaristic man who had taken pride in squeezing value from every penny. Dyck reduced daily costs from 86 cents in 1923, when the Institute first opened, to 69 cents in 1929. Fitzpatrick had brought it right back up, though it was still less than the daily cost of one dollar that Manitoba had charged 20 years earlier. But the Government of Alberta was broke, and costs would have to come down.

Head attendant Wrigby was ruthlessly efficient. He worked and lived in the service building with his valet, who waited on him 24 hours a day. He ruled with an iron hand, was disliked intensely, and was distrustful of everyone. Wrigby rarely took people at their word and was known to check staff lunch buckets for stolen food. He wired the old radio in Unit One into his suite and then ordered it tuned to KSL in Salt Lake City. This particularly offended the staff, who wanted to listen to hockey games.

When Leo entered the office, Wrigby intimidated him at once. Who was he and what was his business? Leo explained that he had been sent from the superintendent's house and that he was looking for work. He described his good health and his willingness to do an honest day's work. He would prefer, he explained, to work on the farm. Wrigby looked the young man over and liked what he saw— an honest rural boy with good muscles, desperate for work, and Wrigby did have work. The Depression had forced many people to approach the Institute looking for employment, but Leo's timing was good. The farm, however, was out of the question. It was managed by the Department of Agriculture, and Wrigby had no authority there. The job, Wrigby explained, would be ward attendant. Leo would be paid $52 per month, plus room and board. A job with poor pay was better than none, Leo reasoned—especially one that included food and heat!

The farm boy from Lac La Biche was to join about 50 other men, caring for more than 315 inmates. Apart from the medical staff, other workers consisted of a cook, a baker, a gardener, a laundry man, two maintenance workers, and the ward attendants. All were male, none had more than a grade school education and not one of them was trained in medicine, let alone psychiatry. Until jobs had become scarce, the average stay for new staff had been less than a year.

Conditions at the Institute had, until very recently, been steadily improving. Following the 1928 report prepared by Dr. Clare Hincks, a new superintendent, Dr. Charles Fitzpatrick, had been appointed. Unfortunately, he stayed for only two short years. Fitzpatrick had been transferred from the Provincial Hospital for the Insane at Ponoka, and he had immediately been popular with staff and patients. A young man with white starched shirts and a pleasant smile, he was easy to like. Fitzpatrick was described by the staff as having a warm personality, a keen intellect, and a driving passion to improve standards of care for both the insane and the feeble-minded.

Dr. Fitzpatrick did not like the atmosphere at Oliver and began immediately to change it. He created four new staff positions and working hours were reduced from 62 to 55 per week. A 16-car parking garage was erected to provide cover from the harsh Edmonton winters. Through a contract with the University of Alberta medical school, arrangements were made for medical interns to work as consultants to staff. Morale rose. With staff support ensured, Fitzpatrick set about to change living conditions in the wards. The concrete floors were covered with "battleship" linoleum, pictures were hung to create a homier look, and singing birds were placed in the day rooms.

The new superintendent also experimented with a dining room. The long, impersonal tables were replaced by circular ones that seated only six. On each of the tables, he placed knives, forks, spoons, and paper serviettes. A small centrepiece of fresh flowers or a potted plant completed the softer effect. And the changes were more than visual. Allowing the patients to eat with knives and forks gave them a much greater range of food. The staff were nervous and the cutlery count became an important task, but if Fitzpatrick wanted it, they made sure he got it.

The superintendent was a strong believer in the value of work, and he looked for year-round opportunities for the inmates. In two years, he increased the number of patients who worked by 50 per cent with the addition of facilities such as a sewing room for the repair of clothing and bedding. The colourful grounds, with their shrubs, expansive lawns, flowers, rockeries, and small golf course, became the centre of activity. People from Edmonton would take a Sunday drive to Oliver to enjoy nature, and sometimes to gawk at the insane and feeble-minded, as they had centuries earlier at English hospitals.

Fitzpatrick oversaw the construction of a dormitory, a service building, and a bakery to facilitate his dining room innovations. Patient

The Edmonton Institute dining room shown around 1929. (Reproduced from public documents published by Alberta Hospital, Edmonton)

activities were improved. The installation of a projection booth for silent movies and regular concerts by Edmonton groups such as the Salvation Army Citadel Band gave patients much-needed diversion. Fitzpatrick heard about the value of weaving and basket making at the Mental Institute in Manitoba and he sent an attendant to Brandon to learn the trade. Basket work and wooden toys were then sold at the annual Edmonton Exhibition.

Throughout 1930, whatever spare time Fitzpatrick had was spent working in the newly formed Mental Hygiene Clinic at the University of Alberta Hospital. The clinic, modeled after one in Toronto, was the brainstorm of Alberta's Mental Health Commissioner, Dr. C.A. Baragar. Its purpose was to provide public information about "mental defectives" and "mental disorders," to train social workers and teachers, and to "advise on the home treatment and management of disorders." It proved to be popular, and the staff was overextended shortly after it opened. Problem cases were referred by schools, physicians, hospitals, and by frustrated parents.

Baragar had hoped that the clinic might relieve some of the overcrowding at the Oliver Institute, and he expressed frustration that 80 per cent of the inmates were "idiots" and "imbeciles" who, while socially urgent, were "not the most important cases for whom hopeful work is possible." With almost 200 more applicants awaiting admission to the provincial institutes and "350 reported suspects," Baragar saw no option but to construct more buildings. But Superintendent Fitzpatrick saw early care in the community as the future of psychiatry and in July of 1931, he was granted leave in order to receive a New York-based foundation scholarship to study in England. Not surprisingly, Fitzpatrick eventually ended up working in Rhode Island. The scholarship was not entirely altruistic. The American foundation was recruiting the best Canadian psychiatric minds, and Dr. C.P. Fitzpatrick's was one of them.

Fitzpatrick's replacement, William George McAlister, was a doctor of some reputation. Fifty-two years of age, with an M.D. from McGill University, McAlister had worked as the Director of Edmonton's Home for Mentally Deficient Children and Director of Red Deer's Training School for the Mentally Defective. Neither Superintendent McAlister nor Attendant Leo Parent could have foreseen the tough times ahead.

Leo's first day of work was a Monday. His orientation consisted primarily of cautions about the consequences of theft and the need for loyalty and obedience to superiors. Frank Wrigby showed the new attendant a memo which outlined his duties. The memo described the long working hours each day, the all-too-brief time off, the absence of any sick leave—and little else. These were difficult working conditions, but it was a job. Leo was given only general information about the inmates. All were chronically insane or feeble-minded. Most had been admitted before the age of 35 and almost all had been transferred in as "hopeless cases" from the Ponoka Hospital. Few of them would ever leave. Some 70 per cent were from the country, and 80 per cent were destitute. Their families shunned them. It was believed that their mental condition was caused by poverty and the difficulty of rural life. Hearing this, Leo was "darn glad" he had left the farm and that he would soon have some money. The strapping farm boy was given a uniform consisting of black pants, a white lab jacket, and a bow tie; he would also carry a large metal ring laden with long, heavy keys.

The concrete steps and metal stairs made loud hollow sounds as Leo cautiously climbed each step to the third floor of Number One building. It was 6:45 on the morning of his first day on the job, and his keys clanked loudly when he inserted them into the large metal lock. As the door creaked open, Leo was introduced to a ward that was the permanent home for many of the 50 occupants.

The inmates were just getting up. The wake-up call consisted of a loud shout of "up and ready" as the dorm's harsh overhead lights interrupted the patients' sleep. They wore loose-fitting khaki coveralls and sat, sprawled, or lay in wooden chairs and benches crowded around the perimeter of a day room. A few shuffled about; most stared blankly at the walls. They would soon be ushered into a tiny dining area. Another attendant greeted Leo warmly, glad to have the help. He gave Leo an introductory tour of the ward office, the day room and dormitory, the dining room, and the 12 single side rooms used to control aggressive inmates. For 50 men, the ward provided five toilets, five wash basins, and a single shower. There were no partitions. There was no privacy.

All but one of the side rooms was full, yet the dormitory was completely empty. The dorm, Leo was advised, was now off-limits to inmates until bedtime. The sleeping quarters were large but crowded, with the heavy steel beds and their thin sagging mattresses situated less than a foot apart. There were no side tables, no lamps, no pictures, no calendars, no clocks, and no personal belongings. The institute had strict routines. Inmates were to be up promptly and waiting in line for the washrooms. Some were assigned to make the beds. Most just waited. Breakfast was Sunny Boy cereal, toast, and coffee. Some inmates gobbled their food; others had to be helped or encouraged to eat. After breakfast, they helped with the cleanup and then waited. Some waited to go to jobs on the farm, in the kitchen, or in the laundry. Some waited to be taken to the "airing courts." Some just waited.

The morning moved quickly for Leo; he was busy. At 11 a.m. he went for lunch, returning in time for the inmates' 11:30 lunch of turnips, potatoes, meat loaf, bread pudding and more coffee. Leo was friendly but he had little time to socialize. He was given a shovel, a broom, and some disinfectant and told to clean the side rooms. The finger paintings done with feces stretched as high as the patients could reach and the odour was overpowering. Cleanliness was the hospital's top priority, and it was hard work keeping the ward sparkling and the patients presentable. It was dunk, rinse, and dry as patients moved through a bathing assembly line. The same bath water was used for a dozen patients. Then it was time to shave with a straight razor—another assembly line using the same blade for everyone, with no disinfectant. Scrubbing and polishing the floor came next, but the patients did most of that. After mopping and drying, heavy concrete blocks were dragged across the floor to bring out a shine. Supervising these tasks and passing out small amounts of tobacco were Leo's favourite duties.

For ward residents, the day was long. The ward was bare and depressing and for some, the only activity was to walk up and down the halls pushing heavy polishing blocks. At 4:30, supper arrived—soup and a piece of bread. After supper, Leo did the "sharp count," making sure that every knife, fork, and spoon was accounted for. Patients could enter the dormitories at 7 p.m.; they were required to be in their bunks by 9 o'clock, but most were already shuffling off to bed as Leo went off duty just after the dorms opened. A tough first day, he thought, but the inmates seemed happy enough.

Three years went by and Leo's routine remained much the same as it had been on that first day—except that coping seemed to become tougher. Few inmates left the Edmonton Institute, with the exception of those who left in coffin boxes. The condition of those who remained was chronic, and most of their families had given up. The hospital at Ponoka continued to admit and screen people for the entire province; as it became increasingly overcrowded, it sent still more severely troubled patients to the Oliver Institute.

The doctors complained that the Institute was being used as a "common jail," and all but Superintendent McAlister left to take positions elsewhere. The new experimental treatments being tried at the Ponoka Mental Hospital were not being used at Oliver, and the physicians were frustrated. The government of the United Farmers of Alberta was in debt by more than $160 million, and money for unproven treatments or for replacing doctors at an institute filled with patients thought to have little or no hope of recovery was certainly not a top priority.

Leo was now placing mattresses on the floor. No one could be refused admission. And the new inmates seemed more aggressive. Conditions became more crowded, and privacy became nonexistent. Fights broke out so often that the ward was virtually unmanageable. Rarely did a day go by when the big farm boy was unable to avoid a wrestling match. Inmates would urinate, spit, and throw feces at the attendants.

The side rooms were constantly filled to overflowing, and an increasing number of the residents had to be bathed with hoses, fed with spoons and paper plates, held in straitjackets, and completely "locked down" for periods of up to 24 hours. Attendants constantly had to be alert and they too, became increasingly aggressive. To Leo and the rest of the staff, beating a man who had taken the first punch was not only justified, it was necessary to prevent future transgressions. Leo didn't feel good about the cruelty, but that's just the way it was. There were, of course, inmates who were quiet, who sat in the corner or against a wall and did nothing. Leo didn't have time to be bothered with them. In any event, the staff was too busy attending to the fighters. Besides, few of the inmates ever complained. Many had come from shacks with leaky roofs, hovels where they woke up to ice in the water pail, perhaps with empty stomachs. At the Institute they were warm and dry, with a mattress, food, and a bit of tobacco. Surely this was better, Leo thought.

There were 60 beds to a room and the patients apparently "liked it."

Superintendent McAlister didn't like it. He was frustrated by what he saw as the gradual deterioration of the Edmonton Institute. Shock-therapy treatment had been tried in the early 1930s, but there had been no real attempts at treatment recently. His only weapon against insanity and feeble-mindedness was sexual sterilization. The problems were hereditary, thought McAlister, and sterilization would help future generations by "carrying on the fight against the root cause [of] defective stock and its propagation." But what about the poor souls he had to look after in the here and now? The superintendent again appealed to the health minister for help, but the government had no money.

McAlister became increasingly concerned about the safety of the attendants and inmates. He continued to live on the grounds with his wife and had taken to walking around after dark, peering in windows and sneaking onto the wards. He was a short man who walked with a bit of a shuffle. He often wore baggy pants, a torn brown sweater and soft slippers in order to slip into the wards unnoticed. The staff joked about being careful not to mistake McAlister for an inmate, but Leo wondered how anyone could be fooled. The superintendent's key ring was nearly a foot in diameter.

Doctors were difficult to find, but McAlister was finally able to recruit the Institute's first graduate nurse, Francis Cook. A small infirmary was set up in a portion of the dormitory in Number Two building. Except for a government dentist and a private specialist who examined eyes, ears and noses, Miss Cook was responsible for all of the medical care for the entire patient population, which had now grown to more than 500 men. She had few days off and no relief. In an attempt to ease her burden, she began teaching attendants from a text book on "mental nursing."

Leo Parent was finally getting some formal education in his chosen profession, and he was being taught by an attractive woman. Francis was only the third woman to work in the asylum, the others being a secretary and a seamstress. Leo was pleased with the gender addition. Education aside, life became less tolerable every day. The staff was small, doctors were unavailable, and the number of inmates continued to increase.

The government then implemented yet more cutbacks and took away the reduced work hours introduced by Superintendent Fitzpatrick five years earlier. Leo now worked 72 hours a week, his salary was frozen, he paid for his own uniforms, and he was expected to work "voluntary" overtime. The Institute's movie projector was useless; silent films were no longer available, and there was no money to buy a new projector for "talkies." Inmate and staff recreation was limited to seasonal ball games. Even the tennis court had been plowed under. But Leo knew there were hundreds of people on the outside who would gladly accept his frustrations if they could have his job.

The frustration in the Institute was mirrored in the farms, villages, and cities across Alberta. The province was entering an election year and people were seeking any solution that might relieve them of the intolerable conditions of the Depression. The government of the United Farmers appeared to have lost touch with the people; seven months before the election, people were starving without work while their government talked about a health care scheme. On August 25, 1935, Leo read the front page of *The Edmonton Journal*, "Wiping out the UFA in a whirlwind landslide, Social Credit forces in this province have elected 20 members and also led in 38 seats when returns were compiled at 10:30 p.m. on Thursday." The turnout for the election was 73 per cent. William Aberhart's weekly commentary on the radio's "Back to the Bible Hour" had promised economic prosperity and a way out of the horrors of the Depression. Perhaps the promise would extend to a way out of the horrors at Oliver.

A year went by, and Premier Aberhart had yet to deliver on Social Credit promises. In fact, the government still hadn't coughed up the $25 dividend promised to every adult Albertan. Leo was disappointed; he had planned to send his dividend home to his parents.

There were, however, a few signs of change in the Institute. A salary of $137 a month was found to hire a new graduate of the University of Alberta Medical School, and the Department of Agriculture, which had been managing the farm at an annual loss, turned it over to the Department of Health. The farm became a program of the Institute and was placed under the supervision of a farmer and his wife. The appointment of the new medical graduate seemed to make little difference on the wards. He and Superintendent McAlister were the only two physicians, and most of McAlister's time was taken up with administrative duties. His assistant would serve as the resident physician whose job it was to hold "sick parade" each morning for a half hour at the most. He was to write a two-line progress report on each patient every six months. That was it. No treatments. After weeks of boredom, the physician resigned and McAlister was alone again. And so were the inmates.

In spite of his frustration, McAlister would stay on as superintendent for another decade. Leo couldn't wait for better conditions, and he wondered if changes at the farm might create a new opportunity. The young farmer from Lac La Biche hit it off with the new farm manager. Leo was, of course, the perfect candidate—a farming background, three years' experience as an Institute attendant, and excellent health. He joined the farm team as one of two assistants. Job benefits included a house on the farm, and his responsibilities included supervising the 14 men and 25 inmates who tended to 900 acres, 90 cows, and assorted pigs, poultry and vegetable gardens.

Local farmers expressed concern to the government that the farm had an unfair advantage and was costing them the opportunity to sell their produce to the Institute. The health minister reviewed their concerns but concluded that the farm was a financial benefit and would stay. After a single year under the management of the practical farmer and his assistants, the farm turned a profit and provided most of the food for the Oliver Institute—and some for Ponoka. The yearly production of 750,000 gallons of milk, 548,000 pounds of potatoes, and 20,000 pounds of beef was "nothing to sneer at," said the health minister.

The farm also provided activity for the inmates. But they were restricted to menial tasks such as hoeing and weeding, and were kept away from the "hygienic" tasks such as milking cows. They were taught few new skills and were repeatedly assigned to the jobs they were best at. They worked hard and were not paid. But they ate well, kept busy, and enjoyed a degree of freedom unknown to most of their wardmates. Relatively speaking, they had it good. And so did Leo. He had found a good job on a modern farm with good housing and a fair salary.

For most people in the Institute, staff and inmates, the conditions weren't nearly as good. The hospital's 10th anniversary report detailed difficult but tolerable staff conditions. It also described how inmates slept 60 to a room—and "liked it." If that indeed continued to be true, that was good. For it would take another 20 years for any hope of a different life.

References

Abercrombie, Sheila. *Alberta Hospital Edmonton 1923 to 1983—An Outline of History to Commemorate the 60th Anniversary.* Edmonton, Alberta: Alberta Hospital Edmonton, 1983.

Abt, Mary Frances McHugh. *Adaptive Change and Leadership in a Psychiatric Hospital.* Edmonton, Alberta: Ph.D. Thesis, University of Alberta, 1992.

Abt, Mary Frances McHugh. Ponoka, AB. Interview with author, 1998.

Anonymous. Family member of patient—interview with author, 1998.

Anonymous. Former hospital attendant—interview with author, 1998.

Anonymous. Former psychiatric nurse—interview with author, 1998.

Anonymous. Former registered nurse—interview with author, 1998.

"Connecting the Past to the Present: The History of Psychiatric Mental Health Nursing in Alberta," *On Our Minds: Mental Health—Research and Scholarly Activities Report 1996-1997.* Alberta: University of Alberta Faculty of Nursing, 1998.

Cooke, E.H. *Annual Report.* Provincial Mental Hospital, Department of Public Health. Alberta: Provincial Archives, 1928-29.

Cooke, E.H. *Annual Report.* Provincial Mental Hospital, Department of Public Health. Alberta: Provincial Archives, 1930-31.

Dickinson, Harley D. *The Two Psychiatries: The Transformation of Psychiatric Work in Saskatchewan, 1905-1984.* Regina: Canadian Plains Research Center, University of Regina, 1989.

Goffman, Erving. *Asylums: Essays on the Social Situation of Mental Patients and Other Inmates*. Garden City, NY: Doubleday, 1961.

Jones, Maxwell. *The Therapeutic Community: A New Treatment Method in Psychiatry*. New York: Basic Books, 1953.

Stanton, Alfred H. and Schwartz, Morris S. *The Mental Hospital: A Study of Institutional Participation in Psychiatric Illness and Treatment*. New York: Basic Books, 1954.

124

Chapter 8
Pills and Possibilities

Chapter 8
Pills and Possibilities

Pills and Possibilities

1954

She walked to the toilet for the first time in three years. Jennifer Small suffered from schizophrenia, a severe group of illnesses that cause thoughts, feelings, and actions to become disconnected. Three years ago, Jenny had slipped into a catatonic stupor, unresponsive to everything and everybody. She laid, stood, or sat in a fixed position until someone moved her to another. She had to be dressed and bathed. She was tube-fed and tied to a post to keep her upright; otherwise she would lie on the floor and smear her feces. She did not talk and her eyes reminded the Ponoka nurses of the "living dead."

Or so it was until Jenny was given the drug chlorpromazine. Feeling as if she had awakened from a deep sleep, Jenny walked to the bathroom unaided and relieved herself. She then washed herself and continued on to the kitchen to ask for food. The nurses were astonished. Jenny began to speak incessantly, as though years of thoughts and feelings needed to break free. Her speech was intelligible and detailed, perhaps too much so. She proceeded to vividly describe every nurse who had treated her kindly—and those who hadn't.

A skinny, pale-faced woman of 26, Jennifer Small was one of the first patients at the Ponoka hospital to be given the new experimental drugs known as neuroleptics, named by French psychiatrists for their ability to reduce "nervous activity." The drugs were introduced in Alberta by Dr. Randall MacLean, the Acting Director of the Public Health Department's Mental Health Division and a former superintendent in Ponoka. MacLean had been told of the new drugs at an American convention in 1953 and was enthusiastic about their potential. But other psychiatrists were skeptical, and Health Minister Dr. Warren Wallace Cross was concerned about the costs.

Cross had served as public health minister since 1935. He described himself as a "silent country lover" and made headlines for his views on insanity. Cross wanted to empty the asylums through preventive work. His plan was to have a psychiatrist visit every school, every year, to pick out the "weak children" and give them special training. The effort, he thought, would "save them from becoming wards of the state"—and would alleviate the chronic overcrowding in the province's mental institutions.

Although the scheme was never implemented, Cross remained interested in emptying the asylums and MacLean would sell him on another way to do it—with drugs. Costs would be lower, promised MacLean, people could finally be discharged, patient numbers would drop, and damage to the buildings and their contents by aggressive patients would be reduced. Cross was convinced and agreed to a trial. But the Alberta treasury was strained, and money would have to be found in existing budgets. Patient clothing allowances would be reduced to help fund the experiment.

Hailed as a miracle of modern science, the new medication chlorpromazine, known commercially as Thorazine and Largactil, could not have come at a better time. Only months before the drugs were introduced in 1954, the governors of every American State had gathered at a Governors' Conference on Mental Health. They agreed that their states would almost certainly go bankrupt if they didn't find a solution to the growing numbers of the "chronically mentally ill in state hospitals." The Canadian premiers could have held a conference with similar conclusions. The situation was just as dire in Canada and budget pressures were just as extreme in most provinces.

This apparent but unproven "cure" for mental illness had not only arrived at a great time, but it came in the form of a pill—easy to administer, not as controversial as electro-shock and lobotomies, and relatively cheap. First discovered in Germany in 1883, chlorpromazine was rediscovered in the 1930s and tried in treatments of various disorders from allergies to malaria. Then, in 1951, a French Navy surgeon used the drug for pain relief when he ran out of morphine. He reported its tranquilizing effects as "a veritable medicinal lobotomy." In 1952, two French psychiatrists published reports on the drug's usefulness in affecting mood, thinking, and behaviour of the insane.

A small French company originally held the patent but sold it to an American pharmaceutical company, Smith Kline French. They did not immediately see the drug's full potential and initially thought it might have some value in relaxing patients and controlling nausea during surgery. Use with the mentally ill was a secondary consideration—psychiatrists did not typically support pharmaceutical treatments, so it was assumed there would be no percentage in marketing the drug to them. Although the reports from the French psychiatrists looked promising, discussions between the drug company representatives and the American doctors had not gone well.

Most of the psychiatrists appeared committed to electro-shock or psychoanalysis. Analysis took years of training to master and the psychiatrists were not about to abandon it quickly. So the Smith Kline French (SKF) sales force hit the publicly funded mental hospitals. The superintendents were interested, but anything that increased their daily cost of about $2.50 per patient was out of the question. Besides, the drugs were unproven. Of all the doctors SKF contacted in the first year, only New York's Deputy Commissioner of Mental Hygiene, Dr. Henry Brill, was prepared to take the risk.

Undaunted, the drug company put together a larger task force to sell physicians on the drug's potential. More importantly, they would try to convince politicians that they could "save money by spending money." It wasn't easy. Politicians were already concerned about the high cost of treating mental illness, and the salesmen couldn't guarantee results. The drug company needed to take drastic action. In one state, Smith Kline French convinced the governor to hold a special legislative session in a mental hospital. They then arranged for television coverage by the "Today" show. This proved to be the breakthrough that committed the legislature.

The lobbying efforts worked in most states and, by 1957, the use of Thorazine had taken off across North America. In a few years, more than two million patients would be receiving the drug. This was just about the time that researchers in 113 of 348 published studies expressed concern about "Parkinson-like" side effects such as tremors, muscular weakness, drooling, and a peculiar walk—none of which slowed the sales of the product.

In Canada, most psychiatrists had strong views about what worked and what didn't, and they were pretty much committed to water, weaving, work, shock therapy, and surgery. But in Alberta, the

Mental Health Division Director, Dr. Randall MacLean, was an innovator. His minister was also interested in emptying mental hospitals. Alberta would lead the pack in using the new medications, despite resistance from the physicians. Ponoka Superintendent T.C. Michie, for example, wondered if the 1954 introduction of new and largely untested drugs would prove to be like 1889, the year the Bayer drug company introduced a new "non-addicting" cough suppressant called heroin. Hospital staff in Ponoka were initially as skeptical as their physicians and described the medication as a "passing fad."

Most of the nurses received very little information about the new drugs, except for what side effects they needed to report. They were suspicious of the drug's dangers, particularly when a number of them developed skin allergies from touching the tablets. Known as Largactil, Serpasil, Raudixin, Equanil, and Trilafon, each of the different drugs had different effects and some experimentation was required. It was difficult to set the proper dose and some patients didn't settle down until the recommended dosage had been increased as much as tenfold.

In some cases there was almost complete secrecy, and staff became even more suspicious. One drug, code named 78-43-RP, was given to a select group of patients for three days. Its effect, according to the staff, was "about as subtle as a nine-iron." Patients became violently ill and one fell dead. The test was terminated. Staff would never know what drug they had dispensed. Another group of patients were given an unnamed drug that turned their skin purple—and it stayed that way.

Some staff members expressed concern about drug studies which were done without patients' consent—and often without their knowledge. Patients drooled, others walked "sloping forward," some trembled, and others became rigid. And for many, the drugs did very little good. Tim Yu from Lethbridge was a tiny "compulsive" man. He couldn't seem to control his behaviour and walked in circles all day. The new tranquillizers merely reduced the circumference of his circle.

But it soon became clear that medicated patients were quieter patients; "better patients." Audrey Killop became one of those better patients. A muscular woman in her early 30s, she would attack staff without provocation. She refused to cooperate; even bathing her was a wrestling match that often saw Audrey prevailing against four staff. Shortly after starting on the tranquillizers, she settled down. She expressed concerns verbally rather than by fighting and even voluntarily attended occupational therapy. She was eventually discharged and returned to her home in Edmonton.

Steven Donald was also now one of the better patients. Known as "Big Steve," he was a large, angry, and aggressive man. Big Steve had been locked in a side room on Male 12, the refractory ward, for 18 years. He had no clothing, only a blanket clad in heavy canvas. He never shaved and no one made him—he got only an occasional "clipping." At meal time, the big man would be slipped two metal bowls, one with food and the other with tea. Big Steve trusted no one, so dispensing pills to him was out of the question. The staff used liquid Largactil and slipped it into his tea. Within a few weeks, Steve settled down. He asked for a paper and pencil to write his sister. "I have been here for a few weeks," he wrote. "I am doing fine." To everyone's amazement, Big Steve was also soon discharged.

The discovery that the wards were quieter and that some patients could be discharged virtually guaranteed ongoing use of the medication. The hospital became a much more comfortable place to work and by 1956, 60 per cent of the Ponoka patients would spend less than three months in hospital before being discharged. Staff, patients, and families were beginning to have hope. Hospital Superintendent T.C. Michie, the man who had originally expressed skepticism, reported "a decreased need for seclusion" and "a marked improvement in behaviour."

At the Oliver Institute in Edmonton, staff had been less skeptical. The Institute opened its new admissions building in 1965 in order to provide "active treatment" for the northern half of the province. Oliver was poised to finally become a hospital in its own right, and Superintendent A.D. MacPherson was "keen to enter the 20th century." His personal philosophy of "tender loving care" needed some help from science. In their first year of use, new drugs were given to more than 400 people. New admissions seemed to benefit little, but many of the more chronic patients exhibited dramatic change. There was less fighting and less damage to property. Most of the aggressive patients were removed from seclusion, and other withdrawn patients began to speak. Even the use of shock therapy was reduced.

Within a decade, the whole environment began to change. An open door policy, whereby some doors were left unlocked, was implemented and on some wards, men and women were integrated into the same living areas. Behaviour improved even more dramatically as men and women were placed in one another's company. Except for the "refractory" wards, which held patients who were most resistant to ordinary treatment, freedoms were increased. Trips to Edmonton were more frequent, and visiting groups from the Canadian Legion, the United Church, the Canadian Mental Health Association, the Student's Christian Movement and other community organizations provided a host of activities from teas to dances.

Recreational activities were increased whenever equipment could be found. CMHA and the Legions donated some sporting goods and on other occasions, the staff improvised. Toni Perusini of the hospital's recreation department filled old jam cans with concrete and stuck a sawed-off wooden broom handle in each one so they could be thrown like curling rocks. He then flooded the tunnel from Number One building to the kitchen and—voila!—an indoor curling rink. Like Toni, many staff put heart and soul into their work. Pastor Emil Walker, for example, sat closely with patients on the narrow beds and ward benches, much closer than most would have cared to. He was not afraid to touch patients physically, emotionally, and spiritually. He even spent many of his Christmas holidays with the patients. Psychiatrists at Oliver said Pastor Walker truly "understood the pain and loneliness of each man there."

As patients responded to the drug treatment, occupational therapy was expanded, the hospital's first psychologist was hired, and an outpatient department was formed. Some of the patients were given trial home visits, and foster and group homes even became a more realistic option as more and more patients were discharged. But a huge percentage of the patients also returned. Five years after the use of tranquillizers began, hospital discharges jumped from 730 to 1,271 in a single year. Unfortunately, admissions and readmissions stood at 1,269—a difference of only two souls.

The drugs that were designed to make patients more responsive to treatment became the treatment. Once the patients were out of hospital, many of them chose not to continue taking the drugs regularly, if at all. The hospital was beginning to experience the "revolving-door syndrome"—admission, drugs, discharge, abandonment and then readmission. Staff, patients, families, and communities had to learn the hard way that if the patients' overall needs were not addressed—as is often the case when medication is the sole treatment—that in the long run, even the best of medication would be useless.

For some it was worse than useless. Patients who took the new tranquilizers over a long period risked an irreversible side effect called tardive-dyskinesia, a horribly disfiguring condition that caused involuntary muscle jerking in the tongue, arms, and legs. In the 1500s people with leprosy had bells tied to them so that the public could hear them approaching. The modern lepers, the poor souls with a severe mental illness, would have a "chemical bell." The public was sure to know they were coming.

The number of available anti-psychotic drugs grew to more than 30. The same drugs were marketed under several different names such as Stelazine, Flouanxal, and Modecate, so patients and their families often mistakenly assumed there were hundreds of different products on the market. Each variant of the drugs came with a different set of side effects. The most common were drowsiness, blurred vision, muscle spasm, restlessness, a shuffling walk, weight gain, and on occasion, the dreaded tardive-dyskinesia.

Many patients found the side effects too disabling, so psychiatrists frequently prescribed other drugs to counter them. Doctors also advised patients to concentrate on the benefits of the drugs, not the "relatively minor" disadvantages of the side effects. But patients often disagreed, and treatment compliance became a major problem. The hazy, mind-numbing effects of the drugs got in the way of daily living, so many patients chose instead to live with the terror of their bizarre thoughts and visions.

131

Tranquilizers were, of course, only one of many weapons in the psychiatrists' chemical arsenal. Sedatives like Dalmane and Halcion were used to help people sleep. Anxiolytics, also known as "minor tranquillizers," with such names as Ativan, Librium, and Valium were prescribed to help relieve distress and tension.

The "growth drugs," though, were the antidepressants. Useful for stabilizing moods and occasionally reducing anxiety, the medications were in great demand. There were several different kinds, and the product names became more numerous than those of tranquillizers. "Tricyclic" antidepressants like Elavil, Surmontil, and Tofranil became widely used, even though they carried a caution for people with heart conditions. Monoamine Oxidase Inhibitors (or MAO inhibitors) like Nardil and Parnate caused dangerous reactions with foods and other drugs, so were usually only used if other antidepressants failed to work. Lithium, a drug that affected nerve conduction in the brain, was considered highly effective for treatment of manic depression, a fluctuating mood disorder with euphoric highs and suicidal lows.

Mind-altering drugs were also in broader use in the community during the 1960s as women became increasingly frustrated with the social pressure to accept their role as "housewives." Psychiatrists began prescribing antidepressants by the millions. Drug company advertisements promised women they could now fly through their housework. The Canadian Medical Association expressed concern that drugs that had value in the treatment of mental illness were being taken "frivolously by healthy Canadians trying to escape the normal tensions of everyday life."

Antidepressants also had side effects, many of them—such as drowsiness, blurred vision, muscular weakness, and dry mouth—resembling those associated with tranquilizers. They also affected body function and memory in unpredictable ways. Still, many patients felt that the side effects were worth the improvement in mood, although psychiatrists still found compliance with treatment to be a problem.

Clozapine, a new anti-psychotic drug useful for symptoms of treatment-resistant schizophrenia—such as hallucinations, delusions, and hostility—was discovered in Switzerland in the mid-1960s. Unlike first generation anti-psychotic drugs, Clozapine and its derivatives were subjected to rigorous testing before being made widely available in North America in the 1990s, when it was marketed under the name Clozaril. The maker of Clozapine, Sandoz Pharmaceuticals, claimed the drug did not appear to cause the dreaded tardive-dyskinesia, although, in 1 or 2 per cent of users, it affected bone marrow cells and even caused death. Careful monitoring through blood testing was required for Clozapine users and the cost of equipment, staffing and the drug itself was more than $1,000 per patient per year. While this was an impossible cost for many patients, for the health system, it represented only the cost of a couple of days in hospital.

The effects of Clozapine were dramatic. Community nurses and social workers reported previously lethargic patients getting out of bed, making meals, improving their personal hygiene and, in some cases, finding jobs and developing relationships. Psychiatrists reported that more patients were taking medication earlier—and staying on it. The wild, aggressive behaviour seen in mental hospitals during previous decades had virtually vanished. The new anti-psychotics weren't a magic bullet, but they were getting closer.

Along with the anti-psychotics, a whole new generation of antidepressants was introduced to Albertans during the 1990s. These drugs affected the levels of serotonin in precise areas of the brain, and their side effects were not as intense nor were they considered to be as dangerous as those caused by earlier medications. They were safer and more "pleasant" drugs—less sedating, less mind-dulling. Names like Prozac, Paxil, Zoloft, and Serzone became commonly known by the public and were soon the most-prescribed group of medications in the country.

By the year 2001, the Alberta Health Care Insurance Plan reported the antidepressant Paxil as the seventh most prescribed drug in Alberta, with 53,506 prescriptions written in the previous year. Then the Canadian government's health department, Health Canada, reported that an estimated 650,000 Canadians were taking Serzone, another of the anti-depressants introduced eight years earlier.

But almost all medications seem to carry some risk. Many doctors, pharmacists, and patients expressed fear that even the modern generation of "safe" drugs would, in time, bring unknown problems. In July 2001, Health Canada issued an "advisory" that while only four cases had been reported in the country, Serzone had been associated with reports of jaundice, hepatitis, and liver failure resulting in hospitalization, liver transplantation, or death elsewhere in the world. The drug showed none of these problems in extensive clinical trials prior to its approval for use in Canada.

Almost 50 years earlier, in 1954, psychiatrist Dr. Randall MacLean had argued that the then-new tranquilizers were the reason the mentally ill could be "de-institutionalized." Mrs. Dorothy Cameron, the newly elected and first president of the Canadian Mental Health Association in Alberta, urged caution. The new drugs were as yet unproven and they could have serious side effects. In addition, the notion of providing community follow-up implied that these people would have somewhere to go, said Cameron. She had toured the mental hospital and institute and knew that many patients and inmates would not have the luxury of family and community support. The advent of the drugs was "exciting," she said, but they might be a "coincidental and fortunate" occurrence to be exploited by politicians who simply "want to reduce costs." Mental health care costs had indeed taxed the treasury, Cameron said, but caution was in order.

Cameron may have underestimated the potential of medication, but she was right to exercise caution. Many of the Albertans with mental illness were about to receive little or nothing in the way of treatment, except for medications. The discharged patients would, in many cases, have no suitable place to live and community follow-up would be available only to a fortunate few.

A decade later, as de-institutionalization began in earnest, things would only get worse.

References

Abercrombie, Sheila. Alberta Hospital Edmonton 1923 to 1983—An Outline of History to Commemorate the 60th Anniversary. Edmonton, Alberta: Alberta Hospital Edmonton, 1983.

Abt, Mary Frances McHugh. *Adaptive Change and Leadership in a Psychiatric Hospital*. Edmonton, Alberta: Ph.D. Thesis, University of Alberta, 1992.

Abt, Mary Frances McHugh. Ponoka, AB. Interview with author, 1998.

"Addicts Can Help Addicts: Expert," *The Albertan*, January 21, 1970.

Alberta Health Care Insurance Plan. *Statistical Supplement*. Service Years March 31, 1996 to 2000. 2001.

Anonymous, Former civil servant—interview with author, 1998.

Anonymous, Former psychiatric nurse—interview with author, 1998.

Anonymous, Family member of former patient—interview with author, 1998.

Blair, W.R.N. *Mental Health in Alberta: A Report on the Alberta Mental Health Study 1968*. Edmonton, AB: Human Resource Research and Development Executive Council, Government of Alberta, 1969.

Bland, Roger. Edmonton, AB. Interview with author, 1998.

Cancrow, Robert, "The Introduction of Neuroleptics: A Psychiatric Revolution," *Psychiatric Services*, Volume 51, No.3. March 2000.

Carling, Paul J. *Return to Community: Building Support Systems for People with Psychiatric Disabilities*. New York: The Guilford Press, 1995.

"Denunciation of Drugs draws Pharmacology Chief's Rebuttal," *The Edmonton Journal,* December 5, 1969.

"Doctor Urges: 'Use Ex-Addicts to Curb Drugs,'" *The Calgary Herald*, January 21, 1970.

Goffman, Erving. *Asylums: Essays on the Social Situation of Mental Patients and Other Inmates*. Garden City, NY: Doubleday, 1961.

Guild, J. "Modern Concepts of Mental Illness". Paper presented at the seminar on Mental Health, of the Alberta Division of the Canadian Mental Health Association, held at St. Stephens College, Edmonton, May, 1960.

Health Canada. Advisory: Risk of Severe Liver Injury Associated with Use of the Antidepressant Nefazodone. Ottawa: Health Canada, July 9, 2001.

Humphrey, Edythe. "Report on Ponoka Hospital cites Lack of Funds, Staff," *The Albertan*, May 8, 1970.

Issac, Rael Jean and Armat, Virginia C. *Madness in the Streets: How Psychiatry and the Law Abandoned the Mentally Ill.* New York: The Free Press, 1990.

Johnson, Ann Braden. *Out of Bedlam: The Truth about Deinstitutionalization.* New York: Basic Books, 1990.

Johnson, J.O., *et.al. A History of Dedication and Caring 1911-1986*. Ponoka: Alberta Hospital Ponoka, 1986.

Johnson, J.O. Ponoka, AB. Interview with author, 1998.

Jones, Maxwell. *The Therapeutic Community: A New Treatment Method in Psychiatry*. New York: Basic Books, 1953.

Keonig, Jean. "Geriatric Infirmary Opening at Oliver," *The Edmonton Journal*, February 17, 1971.

"Mental Health Group Blasted as 'Hindrance,'" *The Edmonton Journal*, November 30, 1956.

"Mental Health Group Denies It's Hindering,"
The Edmonton Journal, November 30, 1956.

Michie, T.C. *Annual Report.* Provincial Mental Hospital,
Department of Public Health. Alberta:
Provincial Archives, 1954.

"Prozac Takeover Could Hurt Generic Companies,"
The Edmonton Journal, December 8, 1998.

"Psychiatrists Offer Varying Suggestions on Drug
Problem," *The Edmonton Journal,* March 11, 1970.

Simmons, Harvey G. *Unbalanced: Mental Health Policy
in Ontario, 1930-1989.* Toronto: Wall & Thompson,
1990.

Slater, R. *Ponoka Panorama.* Ponoka: Ponoka and
District Historical Society, 1973.

Smith, Graham. "Alta. Mental Health Pamphlet
'Inaccurate and Misleading,'" *The Edmonton Journal,*
November 29, 1956.

Stanton, Alfred H. and Schwartz, Morris S. *The Mental
Hospital: A Study of Institutional Participation in
Psychiatric Illness and Treatment.* New York: Basic
Books, 1954.

Szasz, Thomas S. *The Myth of Mental Illness:
Foundations of a Theory of Personal Conduct.* New
York: Harper and Row, 1961.

"To Spend $4,150,000 on Mental Hospital," *The
Edmonton Journal,* September 3, 1957.

"They Should be in Hospital," *The Edmonton Journal,*
March 15, 1957.

*'Treatment or the Treadmill'—A Case for a New
Approach to the Problem of Mental Health in Alberta.*
Edmonton, Alberta: The Alberta Division of the Canadian
Mental Health Association. Undated (Circa 1955).

"We Average 9 Prescriptions: Depression,"
The National Post, March 29, 2001.

Weil, Robert. "Psychiatry's 'Power Elite,'"
The Medical Post, October 10, 2000.

Chapter 9
Backwards from
Back-wards

Chapter 9
Backwards from
Back-wards

Backwards from Back-wards

1967

First you hate it, then you get used to it. If you stay long enough, you come to depend on it. The words summarized the experience of Beardsley Cleghorn and hundreds like him who spent months and years as patients in Alberta institutions. Beardsley was 41 years old in 1967, and he had been in hospital since he was 22. As a young man, he had been a friendly, outgoing, average student who enjoyed mechanical things. He seemed to like his life in the town of Vermilion. He loved automobiles and dreamed of owning a 1945 Ford "straight eight." After high school, Beardsley got a job at the local garage, where he pumped gas, fixed cars, and saved money for that prized Ford.

Then his behaviour began to change. He would sit and stare for hours. Sometimes his eyes would roll into his head so that only the whites showed. He began talking foolishly, and even his walk seemed to change. He had trouble rising in the morning and he could no longer handle his responsibilities at the garage. Beardsley's parents took him to the family doctor, who sent him to Edmonton to see a specialist. The young mechanic, it seemed, had schizophrenia and needed to be admitted to the provincial hospital at Ponoka.

Beardsley Cleghorn wanted to go home, but he respected his parents—and they thought going to hospital was best. He hated it, but as the years went by and contact with his family became less frequent, he began to get used to it. He enjoyed working on the hospital's farm machinery, and the staff treated him well. Three meals a day, a warm bed, the odd game, a bit of tobacco. If life mattered at all, Beardsley thought this was a decent way to spend it. Even his

139

transfer to the Institute at Oliver was okay. A different building and a different farm, but life would be much the same. Some people thought that the closing of the Institute farm in 1963 would be a major blow, but it wasn't really. Beardsley still had the security of the ward.

The young mechanic from Vermilion was beginning to experience a condition that would worsen the already difficult problem of schizophrenia. By the late 1960s, staff at the institutions were becoming increasingly aware of a phenomenon known as "institutionalization." Many studies were being reported in medical journals and Alberta physicians, many of whom were from the United Kingdom, were particularly interested in a study by an eminent British psychiatrist, Dr. R. Barton, who examined the long-term effect of institutions in England, Europe, and America. Barton concluded that, although perhaps unintentionally, life in an institution caused "apathy, loss of interest, loss of initiative," and perhaps even the "characteristic posture and gait" which was typical of many patients as they walked through the wards.

Barton identified a number of factors that took away "all hope of a life outside the hospital." These included lost contact with the outside world (including family, friends, and personal items), enforced idleness, drugs, an authoritarian atmosphere, and loneliness. Beardsley Cleghorn had experienced them all. After 20 years in institutions, he had moved well past any hope of a life in the community. In fact, he feared such a life.

Cleghorn now depended on the institution and didn't want to go anywhere else. The staff urged him to move to a foster home, but he wouldn't hear of it. "You put me in here, and I'm going to stay here till hell freezes over," he declared. But in 1968, the Oliver hospital still had 996 patients and a new deinstitutionalization plan called for 45 patients to be discharged every week. Beardsley asked about returning to Ponoka, but it still had 882 patients and its discharge plans were just as ambitious. Cleghorn would have to find another home.

The increasing depopulation of mental hospitals was driven by many factors. Bulging hospitals were outstripping their budgets and a cheaper approach was needed. New drugs made the movement feasible and in Alberta, political pressure created by the Official Opposition, with help from the Canadian Mental Health Association and newspaper reporters, had created a sense of urgency.

There were also options which had not existed in previous years. Volunteer organizations like the CMHA were providing residential housing and local communities were building lodges and other long-term care facilities for seniors. More importantly, local general hospitals were developing psychiatric units and mental health clinics were expanding across the province. The government, influenced by Mental Health Division Director Dr. A.R. Schragg, thought that the services, working together, could reduce mental hospital admissions and help provide follow-up.

Psychiatric units in general hospitals, like those expanding across Alberta, had their origins in Europe and North America in the 19th century, when the notion of mental illness being associated with religion and morality was first abandoned. At the same time, the physician became the dominant treatment authority. More and more psychiatrists wished to work with their medical colleagues in general hospitals, and as early as the 1930s, progressive physicians began to see the future of psychiatry in the communities. The growth of the mental hygiene movement and its interest in prevention, along with more medical education, combined to fuel interest in expanding psychiatric units. In theory at least, the mentally ill could and should be treated in the same institution as those with physical illnesses.

Money and status were also factors. In the late 19th century, in both England and the United States, separate institutions were built to treat those who were "more fortunate in circumstance." Superintendents had observed that most people in the publicly funded asylums were poor. They thought that separate and more attractive wards for paying patients would "prompt reluctant relatives to seek cures at an earlier stage." The separate wards were attached to mental hospitals, but that still failed to attract the middle class.

At the turn of the century, Dr. Walter Channing opened America's first psychiatric unit at the Albany Hospital in upstate New York. The "psychopathic unit" was intended to attract the monied classes. Secondary goals were to reduce the pressure on the overcrowded mental hospitals and provide an opportunity for medical students to learn more about psychiatry. The plan worked, in that the patients came. According to psychiatrists, the new patients "were not afraid of being locked up there or specially labeled." And the patients paid; economics had generated an entirely new way of treating the mentally ill.

Canada's first psychiatric unit, the "Toronto Nervous Ward," opened in the Toronto General Hospital in 1906. Bending to pressure from Dr. Hincks and the Canadian National Committee for Mental Hygiene, the Manitoba government opened a psychopathic ward in the Winnipeg General Hospital in 1919. Then, four years later, North America's first "integrated" psychiatric unit was opened at the Henry Ford Hospital in Detroit, Michigan. It had no locked doors, no barred windows and no segregation from patients who were physically ill. Not even the sexes were to be separated.

Alberta's first "psychopathic ward" opened at the University of Alberta in 1933. But other general hospitals were slow to follow. In 1945, all the provincial directors of mental health met in Ottawa, and Alberta Director Dr. Randall MacLean pushed hard for expansion of the number of psychopathic units across Canada. He believed a national movement would also encourage the Alberta government to act more decisively. He recommended that 10 per cent of the beds in all general hospitals of over 200 beds should be set aside for psychiatry. No decisions could be made by the directors, but the seed was planted.

The idea received strong support from Clare Hincks of the Canadian National Committee for Mental Hygiene who, after surveying most of the province's hospitals and institutes, had declared that "the mental hospital as we have known it in the past is more or less obsolete." In addition to the criticism leveled at the provinces by Hincks, there were inducements by the national government that endorsed the 10 per cent formula. In the mid-1950s, Ottawa offered cost-sharing arrangements on both new buildings and renovations, if programs were part of general-hospital facilities. Even some operating expenses could be covered. But the federal government's cost-sharing plan called for the provincial and city governments to each pay a third. The civic governments refused, fearing they would set a dangerous precedent. The plan failed.

The expansion of psychiatric units across Canada faltered until 1959, when the federal government agreed to fund them through the Hospital Insurance and Diagnostic Services Act. Mental hospitals would continue to be funded solely by the provinces.

Psychiatric units then gained unexpected public interest in the early 1960s when United States President John F. Kennedy took a personal interest in mental health reform after an experience with the treatment of a family member. Kennedy publicly recommended mental health centres in general hospitals. Shortly afterwards, the United States Joint Commission on Mental Health and Illness recommended that every community hospital of 100 or more beds establish a psychiatric unit. In 1962, the Canadian Psychiatric Association at last endorsed the plan MacLean had proposed to other provincial mental health directors 17 years earlier.

Then, in 1963, the Canadian Mental Health Association published its landmark report, More for the Mind, prepared by a team of five psychiatrists led by British Columbian Dr. J.S. Tyhurst. The plan emphasized community care, but the focus was medical. Community care was defined as "a large range of psychiatric services at the local level." Beyond psychiatric units and physicians, the report was vague on what constituted the remainder of community care. "In all instances," it said, "mental illness is regarded as a disorder or breakdown of living requiring psychiatric intervention." In this field, the report concluded, "the psychiatrist is the acknowledged senior authority."

The report was criticized by academics and psychologists who viewed it as too medically oriented. The detractors preferred to see mental health clinics and public-health services as the centre of a community-based system. Many psychiatrists, on the other hand, seemed to agree with the proposals in "More for the Mind" which emphasized community hospitals and physicians. The doctors saw the possibility of significantly improved services for their patients. They also hoped that working closer with the community and with other physicians would help raise the prestige of psychiatry and therefore of psychiatrists. That, in turn, could lead to more comparable salaries. Pay to physicians working in mental hospitals had been historically much lower than that paid to physicians in other specialties.

143

As for the membership of the Canadian Mental Health Association who produced the report, their general director was a nationally respected psychiatrist, Dr. John D. Griffin, and the report made good common sense. In its simplest form, the report called for programs to be decentralized, regionalized, integrated, coordinated, and equipped to provide continuity of care. The rest was incidental. The CMHA was a lay organization, and its members were not about to get involved in professional turf wars.

The report had significant influence and a general plan for the future appeared to be agreed upon by most of the key stakeholders. Physicians would be in charge, Federal money would be made available, and advocates were apparently supportive. Mental hospitals would continue to be funded entirely by the province and would be limited in size with no new stand-alone facilities to be built. Psychiatric units would serve as the core of the community mental health system with out-patient services serving a specific "catchment" area.

By 1968, Alberta would have more than 200 beds in Edmonton and Calgary general hospitals. The province's population was growing, and the public was responding well to the new units. Services were located closer to home, psychiatric units were better staffed than mental hospitals, and patients remained in a familiar environment with less stigma attached. The mentally ill and their families had become somewhat less reluctant to admit to emotional problems and seemed to search for help earlier. A greater range of less chronic illness was now being treated—and the general hospitals were soon overwhelmed.

As psychiatric units in general hospitals assumed their role as the centre of the community system, Alberta's mental health clinics began to carve out a preventive role by working with children and their families. First established in 1929 as "mental hygiene clinics" by Commissioner Baragar, their initial purpose was "prevention through education." The clinics were structured around information provided by Dr. Clare Hincks and Ontario's Mental Health Director, Dr. G.T. McPhie, after a trip to Boston, Massachusetts. The state had established 33 outpatient "child guidance" clinics, each serving a geographic area. The clinics did mental hygiene promotion, family care, and after-care of patients leaving the hospital. Hincks and McPhie were impressed and while McPhie encouraged his government in Ontario to take similar action, Hincks promoted the information throughout the nation by way of a newsletter and local volunteers.

Ontario, often the leader in Canadian health innovations, this time followed Alberta's lead by a full year. Initially located at the University Hospital in Edmonton and at the Department of Health in Calgary, each of the new clinics was made up of a staff psychiatrist from the mental hospital and a combined psychologist/social worker/secretary. After operating for two years as mental hygiene clinics, Baragar wanted a more publicly acceptable name and re-named them "guidance clinics," after the Boston centres. The clinics expanded into Lethbridge, Medicine Hat, High River, Drumheller, and Ponoka. By the end of the decade, travelling clinics toured most of the populated areas in the north of the province.

In the mid-1960s, the federal government announced the Canada Assistance Plan to help fund community clinics and, by 1968, permanent stand-alone clinics existed in all the major cities in the province, with travelling teams covering most rural areas. Just as the general hospitals had generated a whole new group of patients, so did the clinics. The major focus remained the guidance and treatment of children and their families, but the mental hospitals had difficulty arranging follow-up services. In frustration, both the Ponoka and Edmonton mental hospitals organized separate follow-up teams of doctors, social workers, and nurses who would work with patients in their home communities, an idea borrowed from Alberta's neighbours to the east.

The "Saskatchewan Plan" of depopulating the mental hospitals had begun in 1963, almost four years before Alberta began rapidly discharging patients in large numbers. Saskatchewan's original plan called for the development of psychiatric units in and near general hospitals and the reduction of mental hospital populations in Weyburn and North Battleford where each of the hospitals held more than 1,200 patients. The push by physicians and bureaucrats was for the hospitals to be reduced to their rated bed capacities—950 at Weyburn and 1,000 at Battleford. Premier Tommy Douglas was from Weyburn, and he certainly had no intention of closing the large mental hospital in his constituency.

But two important developments occurred in 1964. The first was the opening of an innovative new 148-bed psychiatric centre on the grounds of the Yorkton Union General Hospital. Made up of a cluster of five cottages, the buildings provided private rooms, an atrium with palm trees, and the same choice of meals as the general hospital. Domestic work was done by hired staff, and patients received intensive therapy through personal encounters. Discharges were quick and teams including a psychiatrist, a social worker, and a - community psychiatric nurse provided follow-up.

By 1966, it was found that each team, arranging for boarding homes, medication, and personal support, could keep the patients in the community. The Yorkton beds were not all needed. Two units were converted to other use and the "psych unit" bed capacity was reduced to 60. The community nurses were proving their value as more than "cheap social workers," a term used by the deputy minister of health.

The use of psychiatric nurses in the community, as practised in Yorkton, was originally developed in the United Kingdom and carefully modeled in Yorkton. The strategy, however, had been used by the Weyburn Hospital before the Yorkton experiment, but the scheme was based less on British theory and more on practicality. As more patients began to be discharged, "surplus nurses," according to administrators, were found to be "sitting on their asses." The government of the Co-operative Commonwealth Federation (CCF) was nearing an election and since the unions had been their partners, they did not want to cut civil service jobs. The deputy minister advised the hospital administrators to "give those nurses a car and tell them to go visit some of those chronics out there." To everyone's surprise, the nurses played a major role in keeping the patients "out there" and the scheme, supported by the Yorkton experience, was later expanded across the province.

The second 1964 development was the defeat of Tommy Douglas and his socialist government, ending 20 years of CCF rule. The new Liberal Premier, Ross Thatcher, was an autocratic leader with conservative ideas. Saskatchewan had Canada's only unionized civil service, and Thatcher had no loyalty to them. His goal was to provide services at the lowest cost, and Yorkton had proven patients could be kept in the community for only a few dollars a day. In contrast, daily costs at the Weyburn hospital had crept above $20 per patient. By 1966, when the federal government announced funds for community programs, Thatcher and his Liberals drew the only logical "low-cost" conclusion—reduce the size of the Battleford hospital and close Weyburn. Tommy Douglas could no longer defend his constituency.

The "Saskatchewan Plan" of closing the mental hospitals was not considered a good idea for Alberta. The psychiatric units were already busy and the daily bed cost in general hospitals had crept above 10 times the bed cost in mental hospitals—much more than originally expected. Unlike Saskatchewan with its daily costs of over $20, Alberta's mental hospital costs had been kept to near $7 per day. There was no apparent economic value in community care if you factored in the cost of general hospitals.

In summary, the Saskatchewan plan was not wanted in Alberta—except for the "cheap social workers." Alberta's new community nurses were perceived to have prestigious jobs, and they liked the newfound freedoms and challenges of working outside the institutions. As a rule, the nurses were more enthusiastic about community placement than the social workers, who viewed themselves as therapists who would rather be counseling than searching for housing. Discharges were frequent, but the conditions for patients on the outside were often questionable—dingy rooms, little money, and few human contacts.

In Ponoka, Superintendent Dr. J.M. Byers oversaw bed reductions of more than 240 patients between 1968 and 1972. When Dr. Roger Bland was appointed superintendent that year, his reputation as a strong supporter of the "Blair Report," a 1968 government study of mental health service deficiencies and its recommendations for community care led staff to believe that the pressure for discharges would be even greater. Instead, discharges actually slowed under Bland's leadership, as he demanded that his staff work harder in order to find better placements and to provide better follow-up. In spite of the modest slow down, Bland would oversee bed reductions of just under 200 persons in four years.

At the Oliver Hospital, superintendents Dr. John Patterson, Dr. Charles Hellon, and then Dr. David Cornish oversaw the downsizing. The bed reductions between 1968 and 1972 totaled more than 500. In spite of the superintendents' declared commitments and best intentions to build community supports, most of their energy went into the internal demands of running the hospitals. Reorganizations, construction, initiating the accreditation of programs, and other general improvements all demanded time.

Meanwhile, the community nurses drowned in the demands of their many placements. In 1969 alone, the program's first year, two committed nurses, Karen Dobranski and Shirley Capp, logged more than 4,700 contacts in the community. There were simply too few staff and too few resources. Housing was limited, jobs were nonexistent, welfare payments were low, and opportunities for recreation and friendship were few. It would take another seven years for the community nursing and child-guidance services to be coordinated and restructured into three regions serving the entire province, an initiative that helped many of the chronic patients find help as they struggled to fit in. On the other hand, the decision pulled resources away from children and their families. Every action had a reaction.

In spite of the dedicated effort of many staff, help for the chronically ill remained woefully limited. While the five previous decades were dubbed "the shame of the hospitals," the late 1960s and early 1970s became the "shame of the streets." When Londoners had watched the antics of the mad at the Bedlam asylum, they jeered from a distance and provoked the poor souls to even more bizarre behaviour. Beardsley Cleghorn experienced the same conditions in Edmonton. When Philippe Pinel unshackled the chains of the mad at the Paris Bicetre asylum, he described "beards and hair matted and infested, tattered clothing, nails grown long like claws" and bodies "encrusted with dirt and filth." Beardsley Cleghorn experienced the same conditions in Edmonton.

Not everyone was like Beardsley, of course. Many patients returned to their homes and others found clean, safe housing in foster homes, apartments, and houses run by volunteer nonprofit organizations. But there were far too many that were discharged to no home at all, or whose attempts at fitting into new homes ended in dismal failure.

Patients were sent out in one of four ways. They were either discharged, placed on trial leave, boarded out, or referred to nonprofit group homes. The preference was to discharge the patients outright. That way the health department had no further financial responsibility—maintenance was passed on to the families or to the Department of Social Development.

After his discharge in 1968, Beardsley was driven by a community nurse to a small, homey-looking bungalow on 54th Street in northeast Edmonton. Cleghorn's parents had died, the neighbours said, of broken hearts. He had no family and no friends, and a direct discharge would not work. A middle-aged couple agreed to provide room and board for a fee.

Timid and withdrawn, the former patient stared at the floor as he was introduced to his "new family." He was shown his tiny but neat room in the corner of the basement, and as the nurse bid farewell, he timidly settled in, listening to a small radio. Beardsley refused supper, which was finally brought to him after the foster family failed to coax him to the table. At about 10 p.m., he crawled onto his bed and stared at the ceiling. He heard his "new parents" lock the door between the basement and main floor.

The next morning, Beardsley got out of bed and spent most of the day staring at the wall. He was afraid. He wanted to go back to the hospital. After several days of this routine, he was advised that in future, he would have to get up by 8 a.m. and leave the house by 9 a.m. The foster parents seemed kindly enough, but languishing in a basement room was no good for anyone. With nowhere to go, Beardsley wandered the streets.

At night, he returned, ate supper, and rolled up in the security of his bed. He quit taking his medication and some days he forgot to wash and comb his hair. He began talking to himself. His new family, fearing the strange behaviour, phoned the nurse to return him to hospital. By the time the nurse could find a minute to respond, Cleghorn wasn't there. And he didn't return. The streets of Edmonton were now his home. A bearded, insect-infested, half-starved derelict, he lived in hostels or found filthy rooming houses where he could spend most of the day staring at the walls. Hallucinations were a sometimes pleasant relief from his reality.

Over the next decade, Beardsley Cleghorn would be joined by hundreds of others who would gather throughout the inner city in both Edmonton and Calgary. Storefront social-service agencies like Edmonton's Boyle Street Co-op tried to help, but, by 1983, they were swamped and appealing for help themselves.

In a report entitled "Backwards from Back-wards," Boyle Street Co-op Assistant Director Jon Murphy, a casual and somewhat disheveled young man with extraordinary sensitivity and skill with street people, detailed a range of problems and suggested some common-sense solutions.

He described community care as a broken promise. The haste with which hospital populations were reduced had placed an "unreasonable expectation on drug therapy," said Murphy, and "other aspects of community service tended to be forgotten." Drugs, Murphy said, were helpful for some but not for others. For many, he said, the benefits were restricted to the time in hospital. In fact, some ex-patients operated better without the drugs, "in spite of the dire warnings of their doctors." The tranquilized person, said Murphy, had problems with memory, was unable to transpose the things he learned in hospital for use in the community, and was in some ways less able to cope.

Murphy then cited studies to support the conclusions that he and his staff had reached. The answer was not to stop the deinstitutionalization plan, which Murphy supported. The answer was to provide community resources—such as a reasonable place to live and some personal support. There were so few opportunities. Mental health clinics, said the report, served only a small percentage of clients. "Intimidating offices" located in high-rise buildings, with scheduled appointments and an emphasis on taking drugs, were "effective barriers."

The emphasis was on seeing psychiatrists and other professionals, but the clients' need was for money, housing, and friendship. The mental health budget, the report concluded, was being spent incorrectly. As for general hospital psychiatric units, Murphy stated, they had little interest in the chronically ill, and they would not generally deal with patients who were uncooperative. People who had been admitted even once to Alberta's mental hospitals were most likely to be returned to them—so the psychiatric units, with more staff and better facilities than the mental hospitals, were often not available to the sickest of the sick.

Murphy said the remainder of the community's resources were uncoordinated and difficult to access. If the patient left hospital or a foster home against the advice of a doctor, social workers were reluctant to approve any financial assistance. People like Beardsley Cleghorn would wander from office to office looking for money, food and a safe place to sleep. He would spend many nights in the Single Men's Hostel, on the streets, or with the Boyle Street Co-op. Murphy noted that an increasing number of people were leaving the hospital with instructions to find community follow-up at the Co-op.

The Co-op was simply not equipped to provide it. The street agency of last resort was rapidly becoming the first resort for many of Northern Alberta's de-institutionalized.

Most of the available money for mental health care was spent in the institutions and that irked Murphy. "On a human level," he wrote, "the daily experience of co-op outreach workers endorses this scenario: hugely expensive hospital facilities prepare patients for discharge into an environment providing almost no supports." Murphy's proposed solutions were not complex. They included a redistribution of funds from hospitals to community service organizations and self-help programs, an emphasis on the creation of work opportunities and housing options and a coordinated effort between the hospitals and community groups. Most everyone Murphy talked to seemed to agree.

Beardsley Cleghorn only agreed that he had moved backwards from the back-wards of the Ponoka and Edmonton hospitals. But many of Beardsley's friends did not agree with him. No matter how vile the conditions they lived in, the freedom and friendship of the street was preferable to life in an institution. They had not moved backwards from the back-wards, but they had most certainly moved from the back-wards to the back-streets.

Homeless former patient camps on a city bench. (Reproduced courtesy of Edmonton's Boyle Street Co-op)

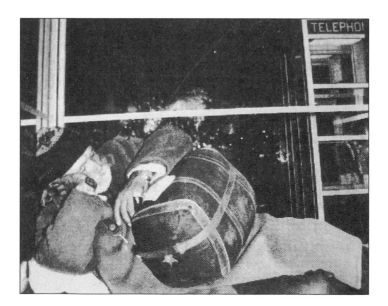

References

Anonymous. Family member of former patient—interview with author, 1998.

Anonymous. Former patient—interview with author, 1998.

Anonymous. Former Social Worker—interview with author, 1998.

Anonymous. Former home operator—interview with author, 1998.

Bachrach, L.L. *Deinstitutionalization: An Analytical Review and Sociological Perspective.* Rockville, MD: National Institute of Mental Health, 1976.

Byers, J.M. *Annual Report.* Alberta Hospital Ponoka, Department of Health. Alberta: Provincial Archives, 1967.

Byers, J.M. *Annual Report.* Alberta Hospital Ponoka, Department of Health. Alberta: Provincial Archives, 1968.

Byers, J.M. *Annual Report.* Alberta Hospital Ponoka, Department of Health. Alberta: Provincial Archives, 1969.

Byers, J.M. *Annual Report.* Alberta Hospital Ponoka, Department of Health. Alberta: Provincial Archives, 1970.

Carling, Paul J. *Return to Community: Building Support Systems for People with Psychiatric Disabilities.* New York: The Guilford Press, 1995.

Dickinson, Harley D. *The Two Psychiatries: The Transformation of Psychiatric Work in Saskatchewan, 1905-1984.* Regina: Canadian Plains Research Center, University of Regina, 1989.

Ducie, Rose. "Saskatchewan May Lead the Way," *The Western Producer*, January 17, 1957.

Goffman, Erving. *Asylums: Essays on the Social Situation of Mental Patients and Other Inmates*. Garden City, NY: Doubleday, 1961.

"Hospital 'Warehousing' of Mentally Ill is Branded as Backwards," *The Edmonton Journal*, October 14, 1990.

Government of Canada. Royal Commission on Health Services. 1964.

Issac, Rael Jean and Armat, Virginia C. *Madness in the Streets: How Psychiatry and the Law Abandoned the Mentally Ill*. New York: The Free Press, 1990.

Johnson, Ann Braden. *Out of Bedlam: The Truth about Deinstitutionalization*. New York: Basic Books, 1990.

Leighton, Alexander H. *Caring for Mentally Ill People: Psychological and Social Barriers in Historical Context*. London: Cambridge University Press, 1982.

Murphy, Jon. *Backwards from Back-Wards: The Unmet Needs of Recovering Psychiatric Patients in Edmonton*. Edmonton: Boyle Street Community Services Co-op, 1983.

National Health and Welfare. "Mental Health for Canadians". Ottawa: Government of Canada, 1988.

Psychiatric Services. "Whatever Happened to Community Mental Health? A Look Back." *Journal of the APA*. May 2000.

Stanton, Alfred H. and Schwartz, Morris S. *The Mental Hospital: A Study of Institutional Participation in Psychiatric Illness and Treatment*. New York: Basic Books, 1954.

Szasz, Thomas S. *The Myth of Mental Illness: Foundations of a Theory of Personal Conduct*. New York: Harper and Row, 1961.

Szasz, Thomas S. New York, NY. Interview with author, 1978.

Toews, John and Barnes, Gordon. *Chronic Mental Disorders in Canada.* Ottawa: Health and Welfare Canada, 1982.

Tuck, D. Hack. *The Insane in the United States and Canada.* Arno Press, New York. 1973.

Chapter 10
Hospital as Newsroom

Chapter 10
Hospital as Newsroom

Hospital
as Newsroom

1968

She had been admitted to a back-ward. "Surrounded by a sea of faces, I lie on my 30-inch, coffin-sized bed, separated by less than a hand's width from the sleepers on either side. I'm drenched in perspiration, and I'm trying to insulate myself against the insistent snores, and the intense heat coming from the wall less than a foot away. At that I am fortunate; the heads of six of the beds lining the wall have been pushed directly against the radiators." The words appeared in a lead story in *Canadian Magazine*, a weekend insert in the local newspapers.

On a cold February 24th in 1968, more than a million Canadians sat in the warmth of their kitchens and living rooms reading in disbelief. Journalist G. Tori Salter had faked schizophrenia and been admitted to the Alberta Hospital in Edmonton. In the magazine, she described in graphic terms her "Five Days of Degradation."

"I am lying on what seems to be a number of small rocks, but proves to be a knotty 3-inch mattress, foul-smelling and supported by a single sheet of plaited steel that serves as a spring. The bright beam of light from the nurses' office looks directly into my eyes. Sleep is impossible, and around 2 a.m. I slip out of bed and sit in the cool darkness of the empty day room until a nurse approaches with a sleeping pill. Accepting it, I return to the dormitory and fall into a soggy sleep, only to awaken minutes (or so it seems) later, to find the overhead lights blazing and the room a blur of activity, with the loud voice of a nurse calling, 'Ladies it is 6:30. OUT OF BED! EVERYONE UP.'"

Behind these walls men and women sleep in dormitories that are either freezing or suffocating. They eat their unappetizing meals from dirty dishes. They have nothing to do and they move like robots through their endless days. Are they in prison? No, they're in one of Canada's mental hospitals. Writer Tori Salter faked schizophrenia to get herself admitted, and nobody knew she wasn't the suicidally depressed woman she pretended to be. Here she reports on her

FIVE DAYS OF DEGRADATION

By G. Tori Salter

author (right) says every one of her senses had been bruised and battered by the time she left the ria Hospital for mental diseases (far right) in Edmonton.

"G. Tori Salter experienced five days of degradation" at the Oliver mental hospital. (Reproduced from the *Canadian Magazine*, Feb, 1968)

Salter went on to describe how she had been coached by a psychiatrist and then, in November of 1967, as Canada was winding down its centennial celebrations, arrived at the hospital posing as a depressed and suicidal woman with schizophrenia—"a role that Bette Davis would have loved to get her teeth into." Salter had no difficulty. She told the admitting doctor that faces formed on the wallpaper, that she heard voices, that she couldn't sleep, and that she sometimes "felt like committing suicide." She needed to be admitted, said the doctor, but not for long, because Tori had a very clear understanding of her condition. Insight was very important.

Ushered through a maze of corridors and locked doors, the journalist was taken to a nursing station which overlooked a day room for 64 patients that "would have been crowded with half that number." Salter described how her senses were assaulted with the "odor of floor polish, the smell of bodies in a poorly vented room and an eye-stinging haze of cigarette smoke." Light filtered into the ward from several small windows "heavily reinforced with steel." She was then taken to a dormitory where the "beds sagged like hammocks." Her suitcase, clothing, and purse were taken away to be placed into secure storage, and she was issued "a faded gingham house dress, a cotton vest, bloomers, and yellowish-brown cotton stockings with holes in the heels."

Oliver Mental Hospital's crowded sleeping dormitories showing sagging mattresses in 1968. (Reproduced with permission of *The Edmonton Journal*)

Salter reported that most of the patients passed the time in idleness. "Patients not on the work or therapy lists went from their beds to sit in the dayroom. The chairs were placed armrest to armrest, in three long rows and on two walls." The only recreational tools were a television set, a piano, puzzles, and decks of cards. "Many patients spent their days sitting, chin in hand, uncommunicative, and sunk in deep depression," she wrote. "Some paced the floor, stopping to press their foreheads against the small cool window panes. Others would go lie on their uncomfortable beds after all their ward-cleaning chores were done, pulling their threadbare blankets over them."

The scenes Tori Salter painted were depressing and dehumanized. Doors were locked and patients could only make two phone calls a week, provided the name and relationship of the person to be called was posted on a bulletin board. Permission had to be obtained from a doctor, and nurses listened in on the conversations. Nurses gave orders to patients, and the side rooms and eating areas were cold and stuffy. Breakfast was eaten with no cutlery.

Most occupational therapy, according to Salter, "came in the form of a strong invitation to do domestic work in such areas as the laundry, kitchen and dining room." The ward had only four tubs and six toilets for the 64 patients, and the bathrooms were "open to the gaze of all." Paper towels were not supplied and hands were wiped on a "community towel." Even access to the doctors was difficult. They held weekday "rounds" and walked through the tense ward between 9 and 10 a.m., "managing to at least look at our 64 patients as well the additional 20 in the ward extension." The doctors were understaffed and underpaid, sympathized Salter, and they had little time for therapy. As a result, they relied on shock therapy and pills.

The remainder of the article in Canadian Magazine dealt with second-hand information. Patients reported information about people who were kept naked on mattresses in side rooms, about an alcoholic who was taunted by whiskey poured under the door, and about an attractive female patient who was stripped by attendants who "kept coming back to look through a small barred window." When Salter signed herself out of the hospital, giving the required three days' notice, a nurse told her disapprovingly that she was going to miss the "security and support that we have provided you here." The author replied, "No, I don't think I will." Never in her life would she be so sure of anything.

In a related sidebar article, Salter compared the conditions at the Edmonton hospital to the Brandon Hospital where she found the "same sordid, spirit-numbing, overcrowded wards where people who are stripped of both dignity and identity functioned as a mindless mass at their keepers' direction." The writer then contrasted the two hospitals to Saskatchewan's Yorkton Psychiatric Centre, a new and small 150-bed unit located on the grounds of a general hospital. It was, she said, providing a modern approach to treatment and care "on the same basis as the physically ill." Following her five days at the Alberta Hospital, Tori Salter contacted hospital Superintendent Dr. James L Patterson, who admitted to problems. But she also quoted him as explaining that it was "utterly impossible to make any pretense of providing optimum care on our allotted $8.75 per day, per patient—impossible!"

Albertans were outraged, including many who worked in the Edmonton hospital or sat in the provincial legislature. Dr. J. Donovan Ross, the large, tough-talking physician who was health minister, had been given an advance copy of the article and was one of the first to respond.

It was true that the hospital was overcrowded, he admitted, but several items in the story were "completely false." Several more, he grumbled, "were a matter of her personal opinion." The minister gave examples: The writer said she signed a voluntary admission form, but the hospital had stopped using those forms in 1965. "What she signed was a diagnostic and treatment consent form," said Ross. What the difference was, he didn't explain. He also denied there were bathtubs in the open. "There is a screen alongside the tubs— although they are open at the ends," he admitted.

As to the physicians being underpaid, Ross claimed that "they pay more in Newfoundland and Nova Scotia, but that's because you have to pay people to move there." The complaint by Salter that she did not have a single personal interview with her physician in five days in hospital was given a quick dismissal: "Personal interviews are going out. We use group therapy." Ross said. He went on to deny that a male staff member would have anything to do with removing a female patient's clothing. As to eating with hands, Ross sputtered that Salter's readers should have been told "what a weapon a fork is in the hands of a patient who is suicidal."

In the legislature, the Conservative opposition members under Peter Lougheed couldn't believe their ears. Lougheed demanded that the elected members tour the hospital, and his colleague, Dr. Hugh Horner, blasted the health minister. In a loud voice, he threatened that if the minister refused to arrange a tour, he would exercise his own right as a physician and go by himself. Horner, a former member of Ottawa's House of Commons, noted that more than half of the patients were elderly and their needs demanded a "crash program" of building new nursing homes. Mental hospitals should be phased out because "gigantic hospitals are a gigantic evil," he boomed. "If local hospitals were crowded like this hospital, people would have been up in arms long ago."

Many people agreed with the Conservative physician, and *the Edmonton Journal* was deluged with letters and calls. Marion Schacter, a university student who had worked at the hospital the previous summer, wrote that Salter's analysis was not exaggerated. "It is time such facts as these are being made known to the public," she said, expressing hope that the controversy would have the desired effect in producing the required drastic improvements. "It certainly takes great dedication and devotion to work there for any length of time," she added. An Edmonton psychiatrist who wrote to the *Journal* anonymously predicted the collapse of mental health services in the province unless the government supported "the integration of all psychiatric services with other medical services and within the same hospitals."

Hospital staff contacted reporters and shared information in confidence. The hospital was in the midst of a "spit-and-polish campaign," they confided, in preparation for a tour by members of the legislature. Bed linen was being replaced and new table cloths issued. The employees reported that most of the staff welcomed the inspection because it would help "both employees and patients in the long run." They also issued cautions: "Be sure to pay special attention to wards A, B and C, the sick ward in Number Eight building, and Ward 4-A. They are a disgrace."

But not all hospital staff agreed. Some thought the story by Salter was one-sided, misleading, and superficial. They denied that abuse ever occurred and noted that physical conditions in some parts of the institution were much better than in others. Salter, they said, was unfortunately in an older ward and had refused to accept an offer to come back and tour a new "open ward." Employee Edmond Greene was particularly offended and wrote an impassioned letter to *the Edmonton Journal*, saying he "was tired of remaining silent." The Journal published the letter, along with pictures, on a half page with a banner headline. Salter's statements, Greene wrote, "injure through ignorance or design." He said that he, his children, and other hospital employees had endured snide remarks since the publication of the story.

In his rebuttal, Greene quoted statement after statement from the article in Canadian Magazine and then provided an "answer." Salter's criticism that only six, open, filthy toilets existed for 64 patients and that they had no towels were dismissed outright. The number of toilets was correct, Greene admitted, "but does she seriously suggest the toilets were frequently filthy?" The hospital, he pointed out, "launders several thousand towels a week [and] it's not for decoration." Salter exaggerated many things, he wrote. For example, her statement that beds were two inches apart was disputed with a picture of a dormitory with beds crowded side by side less than a foot apart. As to reports of abuse, Edmund Greene maintained that it was all hearsay. "The loser in the end is the patient," he concluded, "because when staff become discouraged over attacks such as this one, they leave."

The Canadian Mental Health Association in Alberta agreed with Edmond Greene's concern about the effect the controversy might have on patients and their families. But the story needed to be told, they said. "One of the unhappy, but unfortunately necessary, aspects of exposing conditions to the public view," said President Glen Brant, "is the stress and anxiety it may cause patients, former patients, and their relatives." And Brant had a greater fear, which was the "attitude on the part of government to prefer to maintain the status quo." Mental institutions, added the CMHA's Executive Secretary Walter Coombs, "cling to the idea they are protecting society from a special kind of people." In other centres, said Coombs, "smaller groups of patients have been treated within the framework of general hospitals and communities with far better results."

In support of its arguments, the CMHA cited the 1964 report of the Canadian government's Royal Commission on Health Services. The study described mental hospitals as "the storage bin philosophy of treatment." It recommended that psychiatric services receive federal dollars, but that no funds be provided for the construction of any mental hospital with more than 300 beds. The report further proposed that "henceforth all the discriminations in the distinction between physical and mental health in the organization and provision of services for their treatment and the attitudes upon which these discriminations are based be disavowed for all times as unworthy and unscientific."

The controversy dominated media reports for weeks. But it was not as if the information was new. *Edmonton Journal* reporter Karen Harding had produced an earlier series of articles entitled "The One in Ten," named for the Canadian statistic on the percentage of people who could expect to be admitted to a mental hospital in their lifetime. In fact, Harding's reports had begun a year before Salter's article in *Canadian Magazine*.

Harding had taken several months to research her findings. People seemed to succumb to her charm quickly, and she had no difficulty finding and interviewing more than 100 sources—patients, former patients, family members, professionals, advocates, and government officials. She travelled to British Columbia to witness firsthand the programs that appeared to be working. Her conclusions were presented in a series of full-page stories in the daily Journal. Hard-hitting and critical, the series began on January 24, 1967 with a front page lead article entitled "Mental Health—Our Province's Stepchild."

Writing in editorial form, Harding complained about public apathy, government disinterest, and staff insensitivity. "Until those involved in mental-hospital administration can place themselves in the position of the patient, little can be done," she wrote. Patients know and care about what needs to be done, explained Harding, but they are not listened to. The attitude of staff seemed to be, "What could they possibly know? After all, they're insane."

Reporting the views of patients and families and quoting local and international experts, Harding detailed the necessity for innovative community mental health clinics, psychiatric units in general hospitals, and programs to help "mental patients over the hump when they are discharged." Listing 16 recommendations—from the need for citizen boards and patient rights to better funding and training of staff—the reporter then laid out a blueprint for mental health reform in the province.

Harding's second article dealt with the lack of resources at the mental hospitals in both Edmonton and Ponoka. She gave praise to staff who were working under difficult conditions. People like Howard Clifford, Director of the Social Work Department in the Edmonton hospital, who had "spearheaded the establishment of the hospital's foster-home program, through which more than 200 former patients have been placed in homes in Edmonton." But his was the only local initiative the journalist liked, and Clifford had announced he would soon be leaving the hospital. Harding lamented the government's problems in attracting and keeping staff. A psychiatrist confided in her that "nobody who is any good or who tries to work towards change stays very long."

At Ponoka, however, the writer found some innovations. Clinical Director Dr. David Phillips was, according to Harding, a "human dynamo" with a burning empathy for his patients. He rushed through the day seeing as many patients as possible, introducing new medications, leading group therapy and helping to form ward patient councils. He also ensured that people were treated humanely. Harding viewed the Ponoka Hospital as far more advanced than the Edmonton hospital and gave the credit to Dr. Phillips and to the efforts of Dr. Randall McLean, the former superintendent.

The contrasts were startling. The Edmonton hospital, reported Harding, had open bathrooms where men were lined up and pushed along under the watchful eye of a nurse who "may not hesitate to use the broom on them." In Ponoka, the bathrooms had doors. In Ponoka, the wards also had pictures on the walls, plants, and other homey touches. Edmonton's wards were cold and institutional. But neither hospital was appropriate, suggested Harding. "Years ago it was thought best to build mental hospitals away from the population, because of fear and ignorance," she wrote. In Alberta, patients had to leave their homes in Lethbridge or Fort McLeod, and later their families would have to make the same trek to visit. "Because of this," Harding concluded, "patients have been neglected and even forgotten."

The articles and the criticism continued. The Canadian Mental Health Association issued a news release stating that the Harding articles were "a true and accurate account of the situation in Alberta." The association appealed for citizen support, predicting that "only massive public demand will be effective in stirring the government to action." Its president, Glen Brant, requested a meeting with the Premier but was rebuffed. The association's relationship with government became severely strained, but Brant would not back down. The problems with government were an unfortunate risk of taking a firm stand on the issues, he said. The organization then detailed a plan of action that would attempt to recruit other organizations, including city governments. Lastly, more than 50,000 individual Albertans were asked to sign a petition.

Community organizations like the Alberta Association of Registered Nurses, the Alberta Farm Women's Association, and the Catholic Women's League quickly joined the chorus to demand action. Letters to the editor from former staff and patients questioned policies and demanded changes. Former patient Jane Sawyer, who had lived in the hospital for almost two years, asked why family contact was discouraged: "Why are letters incoming and outgoing withheld at the staff's pleasure? Why is it so very difficult to phone one's relative when a familiar voice and a friendly word could make a difference? Why are visitors turned away without a logical explanation?" She added with sadness, "I was not allowed to see my infant son—my dearest possession."

Calgary's second major daily paper, *the Albertan*, assigned reporters to the topic and a flurry of articles was published. The major theme was "a system in crisis." The cause was considered to be "far-off, short-staffed, and outmoded institutions." But not all newspaper editors agreed. The Red Deer Advocate described the Canadian Mental Health Association as "getting too cocky." The Association was suffering from "a cliché it had oversold: that mental illness is just like any other illness." The editor was convinced the problem was not the mental hospitals, but rather the lack of professional staff. That being the case, CMHA's idea of small community hospitals was "out of touch with reality." The necessary staff, of course, could never be found.

Premier Manning and Health Minister J. Donovan Ross also were not influenced. As with most media issues, public interest would soon wane, and the concern would pass. It always did. Mental health staff were instructed to bar Harding from entering the hospital grounds and from talking to staff. It only made her more tenacious. She continued her articles, but changed the tone and approach—she would now be less technical, with fewer editorial comments and no recommendations, but with much more emotion.

"I Must Be In Hell," screamed the next headline. Describing terrible physical conditions, inadequate treatment and days spent in numbing idleness, Harding detailed her informants' reported experience in hospital. But the patients held no animosity to staff. "The hospital is so short-staffed, they have to act more like jailers than nurses," she explained. Harding reported stories of naked patients, sterilizations, predatory homosexuality—"little boys are mixed in with older men"—and censorship. The premier and health minister had to take notice. The Journal reporter, assisted by the CMHA and other organizations and individuals, was being supported in the legislature by Lougheed and his opposition members. Perhaps the matter would not go away after all.

In November of 1967, the same month reporter Tori Salter was arranging to be admitted to the Alberta Hospital and more than 11 months after Karen Harding had begun her quest, Premier Manning announced a major study of mental health services. It would be conducted by Dr. W.R.N. Blair from the University of Calgary.

Although the government had hoped the announcement would kill the controversy, Salter's article in Canadian Magazine stimulated renewed public and political interest. The nationwide press the government received was embarrassing enough, but now the article inspired a flurry of additional mental health reports by other provincial journalists. In an editorial, *the Edmonton Journal* said the time was long overdue for drastic action. "The situation is a disgrace," the paper charged, but the editors pleaded for hospital staff not to be blamed and concluded with a challenge for the legislature and the government to "face up to their responsibility."

In the same week, *the Albertan* in Calgary called for the "emergence within the legislature of concern for the mentally ill." Governments are notorious, it advised, "for hesitating to initiate action which is not being urged upon them ... Publicity and public interest together constitute the key to public action." But according to government, Manning was acting. The Blair study was underway and, following its completion, the government would decide what action, if any, should be initiated.

The Albertan posed the theory in an editorial that the key to reform was "publicity and public interest" and that had seemed to be a truism over much of Alberta's history. Governments only commissioned studies after a public controversy over a major crisis such as abuse or a death. Most newspapers searched for these crises, and *The Edmonton Journal* was the most aggressive in the province. The least aggressive was the *Ponoka Herald*.

In 1928, *The Edmonton Journal* reported the death of a Ponoka patient with a bold headline which read, "Patient Dead; Eight Arrests At Ponoka Asylum." The *Ponoka Herald* headline read simply, "Ponoka Hospital Attendant." It tried to explain the problem by describing a patient who had been at the hospital for some time and was "continually under the delusion that some person was trying to poison him." When the attendant was convicted, the Journal headline read, "Ponoka Attendant Is Given 5 Years." The Herald ignored the matter and reported on the success of the hospital's football team.

Following the release of the Blair report in March of 1969, *The Edmonton Journal* devoted two full pages to its findings. A major recommendation was the decentralization of the mental hospitals. *The Ponoka Herald* ignored the report, but later invited area residents to hear Dr. Blair report on his findings. The invitation was accompanied by glowing reports on the "remarkable, active and effective" programs at the hospital. The paper did not report the results of Dr. Blair's visit or his call for mental hospital downsizing. Later in the year, a community meeting was organized by the Ponoka Chamber of Commerce in order to express concern to the health minister. It was attended by more than 400 citizens. The next *Ponoka Herald* headline read, "Ponoka Decries Decentralization of Hospitals." The article predicted that mental illness would receive a "fatal blow" if specialized centres were downsized. The same day that the *Ponoka Herald* reported the hospital's value, a group of Alberta Service Corps volunteers, university students who had worked the previous summer at the Ponoka Hospital, released a report which described adverse conditions and recommended a government investigation. The *Ponoka Herald* dismissed the claims, saying the criticisms were "ill founded to say the least." Their sources for the reassurance were not disclosed.

Some newspapers did seem to make a difference.

In the early 1980s, when mental health reform initiatives began to lose momentum again, *Edmonton Journal* reporter Wendy Koenig picked up the torch and with Karen Harding's zeal, wrote story after story of inadequacies in social services and atrocities at the Alberta mental hospitals. The stories, combined with lobbying efforts by citizens and organizations led to a change of minister, some new policies, new funding, and innovations like Alberta's Suicide Prevention Program. The training program and its electronic reference library made Alberta into "a leader in North America in efforts to combat this frightening social problem," Koenig wrote. It also saved many lives.

In January, 1999, *Edmonton Journal* reporter Allyson Jeffs received front page coverage for her story, "Oberg Plans to Scrap AISH." Dr. Lyle Oberg, a young conservative physician from Brooks, Alberta, was minister of family and social services. Jeffs received a leaked copy of a memo from Oberg to other members of the Alberta Cabinet in which Oberg recommended shutting down Lougheed's Assured Income for the Severely Handicapped program. It would be replaced with a new Open Doors program which would "limit access, reduce benefits, and promote employment."

More than 23,000 people would be affected—and members of the disabled community were scared and angry. Changing the program to improve its flexibility for people with "transitional disabilities" such as a recurring mental illness or to improve work opportunities was broadly supported, but reducing benefits was not. Many disabled people and their families didn't trust the government, and the public outrage was immediate and strong. The Journal reported on rallies, protests on the steps of the legislature and the existence of growing discontent among individuals and advocacy organizations. Headlines persisted and an increasing number of people wrote letters to the editor describing the callousness of government in its dealings with the "most vulnerable of citizens."

Not everyone agreed, of course. Terry Boyko, of Cherhill, Alberta, wrote the Journal to say that "we all know" of people who found the program to be a "soft touch." He questioned the definition of severely handicapped, pointing out that hundreds were able to attend a rally in the middle of a harsh winter and that ability, he said, "speaks for itself." Terry hoped that the authorities had attended the rally to collect names so that "benefits would immediately be cancelled." But Boyko seemed to be in the minority, and the pressure on government continued. Premier Klein was asked difficult questions by reporters who were covering his Mexican visit. Oberg returned from holidays to find that MLAs across the province were being lobbied.

On January 27, 1999, reporter Jeffs again received front-page coverage with a story entitled "Province Scraps Leaked Plan."

There were of course other reporters who influenced change. *The Calgary Herald's* Robert Walker wrote a series of hard-hitting stories spanning more than two years, in which he repeatedly reported on that city's shortage of psychiatric beds. In the year 2000, the Calgary Health Authority announced plans for new beds while admitting they were long overdue.

The Edmonton Journal's Liane Faulder wrote a number of columns over the same period, her focus being the lack of adequate housing for those leaving psychiatric hospitals. In the Journal's February 13 "Sunday Reader," several full pages chronicled the plight of "society's most vulnerable citizens (who) often must fend for themselves in their search for safe shelter." The stories helped influence the addition of several million more dollars into community programming for mentally ill people, but little, if any, new housing materialized. As Faulder had so astutely reported, responsibility for housing was a "political hot potato," and no government department would commit to addressing the problem systematically.

Salter, Harding, Koenig, Jeffs, Walker, and Faulder all made a difference by motivating public and political action. Their efforts, though, had to be persistent and sustained—and they obviously needed editorial support to keep going. Editorial support, according to Koenig, usually follows the editors' perception of whether or not the public is interested in the issues. In the closing paragraph of her 1968 sidebar in *Canadian Magazine*, Salter described two major obstacles standing in the way of the reforms needed for proper treatment. "First, officials who tend to view changes—however urgently needed—with alarm, favouring an 'all-in-good-time' philosophy." "Secondly," she wrote, "the indifference of both the public and the medical profession to existing neglect and abuses." That group, she added, "includes most of the people who are reading this article."

References

Brant, Glenn S. "Government Fails in Modern Methods." President, Alberta Division, Canadian Mental Health Association. Canadian Mental Health Association (Alberta Division) Press Release, January 30, 1967.

Greene, Edmund. "This Controversy is Hurting Oliver Patients," *The Edmonton Journal*, March 5, 1968.

Gregoire, Lisa "Nothing Easy About AISH—Recipient Doubts Mildly Disabled are Qualifying for Subsidy,"*The Edmonton Journal*, January 27, 1999.

Faulder, Liane. "Finding a place in society for the mentally ill." *Edmonton Journal*. February 13, 2000.

Harding, Karen. "Mental Health—Province's Stepchild," *The Edmonton Journal*, January 24, 1967.

Harding, Karen. "One in Ten: Doctor-to-Patient Percentage Startlingly Low in Province," *The Edmonton Journal*, January 25, 1967.

Harding, Karen. "The One in Ten: Critical Professional Shortage in Alberta Mental Institutions is Not Being Dealt with as Urgently as the Situation Demands," *The Edmonton Journal*, January 26, 1967.

Harding, Karen . "The One in Ten: B.C. Mental Health Services Constantly Seeking Betterment," *The Edmonton Journal,* January 27, 1967.

Harding, Karen. "The One in Ten: Provincial Government Blamed for Mental Hospital Conditions," *The Edmonton Journal*, January 28, 1967.

Harding, Karen. "'I Must be in Hell'—Crowding, Boredom, Censorship Recalled by Former Patient at Alberta Hospital," *The Edmonton Journal*, May 1967.

Harding, Karen. "Hospital Tour Provides Little Chance to Probe," *The Edmonton Journal,* March 2, 1968.

169

Howitt, Eaton. "Tory Wants Nursing Homes Built to Ease Overcrowding at Oliver," *The Edmonton Journal*, March 2, 1968.

Jeffs, Allyson. "Oberg Plans to Scrap AISH: Disabled will have to Meet Tougher Financial Restrictions to Qualify for Aid—Memo," *The Edmonton Journal*, January 15, 1999.

Jeffs, Allyson. "Benefits to Disabled get Boost—Province Scraps Leaked Plan," *The Edmonton Journal*, January 27, 1999.

Koenig, Wendy. "Alberta to be Leader in Suicide-Prevention," *The Edmonton Journal*, January 18, 1982.

Koenig, Wendy. "Staff Shortage Blamed for Ponoka Patient's Injury," *The Edmonton Journal*, October 6, 1982.

Krieken, Chris Van and Koenig, Wendy. "Ombudsman to Investigate Youth's Suicide in Hospital," *The Edmonton Journal*, October 6, 1982.

Lougheed, Peter. Calgary, AB. Interview with author, 1998

Martindale, Carolyn. "Patient care suffering from shortage of qualified psychiatrists— Problems at Ponoka." *The Advocate*, June 17, 1982

"Mental patients dread '91st day.'" *The Albertan*, February 6, 1967

"MLAs and Mental Health." *The Albertan*, (Editorial Page), February 29, 1968

"MLAs Will Not See 'True Picture,'" *The Edmonton Journal*, February 29, 1968.

"Open Oliver." Letters to the Editor *The Edmonton Journal*. *The Edmonton Journal*, March 29, 1969

"Peter Lougheed Visits Alberta Hospital; Tours Facilities, Meets with Staff!" *The Ponoka Herald*, February 9, 1971

"Ponoka Hospital Attendant." *The Ponoka Herald*, 1928

"Ponoka's Problems." *The Advocate*, June 16, 1982

Robinson, Art. "Alberta Hospital Crowded but Clean, ML As Agree," *The Edmonton Journal*, March 1, 1968.

Royal Commission on Health Services. Government of Canada. 1964.

"Ross Rejects New 'Expose,'" *The Canadian Magazine*, 1968.

Salter, G. Tori. "Five Days of Degradation," *The Canadian Magazine*, February 1968.

Schachter, Marion. "Oliver Hospital," Letters to The Journal, *The Edmonton Journal*, February 28, 1968.

Sellar, Don. "Mental Hospital Tour Offered MLAs," *The Calgary Herald*, February 27, 1968.

Szasz, Thomas S. *The Myth of Mental Illness: Foundations of a Theory of Personal Conduct*. New York: Harper and Row, 1961.

"Well! Just What did Reporter Howitt Expect at Oliver?—Inquires Edmontonian Anne Jarvis—A Medieval Asylum or a Modern Hospital?" *The Edmonton Journal*, June 2, 1966.

172

Chapter 11
The Premiers and
the Professor

Chapter 11
The Premiers and
the Professor

The Premiers and the Professor

1971

"This is the field of priority that I put at the very top." They were the last 13 words of a lengthy and passionate presentation by Opposition Leader Peter Lougheed in the Alberta Legislature on February 25, 1971. The speech had special meaning for Lougheed, who stood to second a motion by his "shadow" Minister of Health and Social Services, Len Werry.

Werry had set the stage for Lougheed and he did it well. Werry had a reputation for charm and sensitivity. He was straightforward with no guile, and he captured the attention of the legislature with his genuineness. In his speech, he made frequent references to the Canadian Mental Health Association's 1963 publication "More For The Mind," which called for a mental health system which was "integrated, regionalized, decentralized, coordinated" and provided "continuity of care." The plan made good sense to Werry.

It was now eight years since the Canadian Mental Health Association report and three years after the release of the government's own study, the Blair report on mental health care in Alberta. The CMHA, Werry reported, had told him that "individual and piecemeal undertakings have given the impression of progress, but Alberta's mental health programs operate on no sounder a basis now than in the years before the submission of the study." The situation had become a major problem for the province, he said, adding that the government is "looking right down the barrel." Unfortunately, they have "difficulty in terminating obsolete programs to make resources available for new programs."

The staff in the mental hospitals live with great uncertainty, he complained. It is time for action. Werry then described the reduction in patient numbers in the provincial mental hospitals, noting that community resources were unable to cope with the influx of ex-patients. "But mind you," he added, when hospitals are needed, "the community is where the patient should be—in the local general hospitals, in nursing homes, and in auxiliary hospitals." Werry then attacked the lack of "follow-up" for patients leaving hospital and demanded better outpatient care.

Lougheed was next. An athletic lawyer of 43, he had a keen intellect, a good memory for everything and everyone, and very strong ideas about what constituted good government. He was highly critical of the Social Credit government for its lack of creativity and change. He particularly objected to leaving cabinet ministers in the same departments over long periods. "What happens is, you're defending your past decisions and having made them, you don't reverse them." He had publicly characterized the Socreds as "old worn shoes" and with an impending election, Health Minister James Henderson and his boss, Premier Harry Strom, were concerned about Lougheed's ability to make political points in the legislature.

"Mr. Speaker," Lougheed began in the traditional way, "members in this House should be deeply concerned." Lougheed had brought the matter of mental health services to the attention of the House two years previously in debate on his motion about "the urgent need to improve mental health facilities in Alberta" and the need for government to give it first priority. He was not satisfied with progress. One of the Opposition Leader's biggest concerns was the lack of a "clear statement and future direction" for the Alberta mental hospitals.

Lougheed believed the role of hospitals would have to change and that this decision was necessary before any other plans could be put into place. He was not unfamiliar with the hospitals, having toured Oliver three years earlier. At that time, he had demanded that MLAs undertake a complete inspection following the story "Five Days of Degradation" by Tori Salter in the Canadian Magazine. Days later, the government's own Board of Visitors, a group charged with providing reports on the quality of institutions, tabled a highly critical report.

The minister, Dr. J. Donovan Ross, agreed to a "surprise inspection"—and then arranged for it to be conducted as a photo opportunity for 40 MLAs and media representatives. Nursing staff contacted the MLAs and cautioned they would not see the true picture. When the legislators arrived, most of the patients were outside or in activities, halls were gleaming, flowers were displayed on tables, and beds were neatly made—though still lined up side by side, 30 to a room. When the visitors asked where the patients' clothes were, Superintendent Patterson replied that they were "kept upstairs, because there is not sufficient room here." While walking through a corridor, a female patient asked an MLA what he thought of the hospital. "Very nice," the MLA answered. "Bullshit," she replied.

At the end of the tour, Socred and Liberal members described the conditions as crowded but clean. "There's no evidence of neglect," said one MLA. "I'm convinced a lot of the criticism was unjustified," said another, referring to Salter's report. Lougheed was sickened.

Peter Lougheed had also recently toured the Ponoka Hospital, stopping for media photos while conditions were better than in Edmonton. Once again he saw large dehumanizing wards, wall-to-wall beds, few personal effects, drafty windows, and communal bathrooms. The reporters and staff who toured with him were moved by his obviously emotional response to the experience. The tour had special meaning for Peter Lougheed and in the legislature he appealed to the government to "move with urgency, Mr. Speaker, to make up for the past."

Opposition leader Peter Lougheed tours Ponoka Hospital with administrators in 1970. (Reproduced from the former *Ponoka Herald*.)

The past for Edgar Peter Lougheed began in Calgary. The grandson of a senator and the son of Edgar Lougheed and Edna Bauld, Peter was, by most standards, born privileged. The people considered the Lougheed family wealthy, largely because Sir Edgar Lougheed owned a number of buildings, each named after one of his four sons. But much of the estate had to be sold in order to pay taxes following the senator's death in 1925, and the family home was taken by the city for back taxes a year later.

Then came the Great Depression. Rental revenue from the properties came to a trickle. Edgar and Edna moved from home to home and like other Prairie families, struggled to keep dust off the table and food on it. Displaced from her native Halifax, with two young sons at home and a husband who rarely was, life for Edna Bauld was far removed from her idyllic youth. She found it increasingly difficult to cope and slipped into a deep and dark depression. Edgar and his two sons were devastated when mother was taken to the Provincial Mental Hospital at Ponoka.

But life had to go on. Mother would recover, and Peter would attend the University of Alberta, where he excelled at academics and football. He served as president of the student union, earned two degrees, achieved the second highest standard in his law class and met his future wife. Peter also found two years in 1949 and 1950 to play football with the Edmonton Eskimos. His father died when he was only 23 and although deeply saddened, Peter would not be deterred. In 1952, he obtained his law degree and married. He then obtained a third degree in Business Administration from Harvard. After time in the United States and Europe, Peter and his wife returned to Calgary to build a family, a business, and a political career.

The Tories were shut out of the 1963 election and they went looking for a new leader. Lougheed was approached, but he cautioned his suitors, "I'm not sure I'm even a Conservative." He saw himself as "fiscally conservative" to be sure, but he wanted it known that on social issues he was a "progressive." Peter Lougheed was elected to the provincial legislature in May, 1967 by the largest majority of any candidate. He and only five other Conservatives would line up in opposition, in a one-to-10 ratio against the members of the re-elected Social Credit government—the government of Premier Ernest Manning, the acknowledged master politician of the West.

Although Ernest Manning was re-elected seven times and although his provincial treasury was bulging after the 1947 discovery of the giant Leduc oil field, social reform would not make it to the top of his agenda until his last term in office. In 1947, he commissioned a survey of the mental hygiene clinics and institutions by the Canadian National Committee for Mental Hygiene, and when the report came back relatively favourable, he moved on to other matters.

Even a proposal from the national government for a medicare plan had been opposed by the Social Credit government. Manning had his own ideas, and he was not easily influenced. The legislature met only a half a dozen weeks every year, and there were very few meetings with his MLAs. Backbenchers had no offices and no staff. Their only seats were at "schoolroom" desks in the legislative chamber. Their "offices" consisted of coat hooks with their names neatly printed above them. Decisions were apparently made by Ernest Manning, sometimes with advice from his Cabinet.

Then in November of 1967, in an uncharacteristic response to public pressure, Manning announced a full probe of mental health services. The new Canada Health Plan had also been announced and funding for psychiatry was in the formula. This could be a good opportunity to capture more federal money. The study would be conducted independently by Professor W.R.N. (Buck) Blair of the University of Calgary's Department of Psychology.

When CMHA members led by Alberta president, Glen Brant, met with the premier, they submitted a 50,000-signature petition, which was also supported by the municipal governments of seven of Alberta's 10 cities. The petition had been intended to press for the probe into mental health services and now that the decision had been announced, Brant used the opportunity to congratulate the premier on his decision to appoint Blair. Brant also tabled a CMHA five-point plan for reform and asked for a role in the study—plus a commitment to making its results public. Manning refused.

Dr. Blair's appointment to undertake the probe of mental health services would be one of the biggest and most challenging of his life. He would have one year and $70,000 to complete the job. The government's concerns apparently stemmed from a series of ongoing and increasingly critical news articles from papers across the province. Particularly aggressive and frequent were reports by *Edmonton Journal* reporter Karen Harding and *Calgary Herald* reporter Walter Nagel. They wrote dozens of heart-rending stories of poor and cruel treatment, and both supported the call of advocates like Walter Coombs, the executive director of the Canadian Mental Health Association in Alberta, and Dr. Keith Pearce, the University of Calgary's new chairman of the department of psychiatry. Peter Lougheed also fuelled the discussion of mental health issues in the legislature.

Central concerns were the problems in the provincial mental hospitals, plans for a new mental health centre in Calgary, stories of family difficulties, and mentally ill people languishing in police cells. Headlines such as "I Must Be In Hell," "Mentally Ill Care Assailed," "Equality Urged for Mentally Ill," "Government Clinic Head Quits In Protest," and "Jailing of Mentally Ill Hit" were fuel for public fear and outrage.

With an election planned for mid-1967, Manning was particularly concerned about Calgary. The proposed 300- to 400-bed Calgary Mental Health Centre, which was to have been a "good-news story," was becoming a hotbed of controversy. First announced by Health Minister J. Donovan Ross in 1964, it was initially supported by the CMHA and the local medical profession. Then attitudes towards the plan began to change. By the time Ross announced that construction of the $6-million complex would begin early in 1968, people were having second thoughts.

Physicians expressed concern about difficulty in treating patients properly in a separate institution. The Alberta Medical Association formally opposed the plan, as did the Alberta Farm Women's Union. The CMHA, in its zeal for any new resources, had initially welcomed the hospital, then apparently realized that its support had violated its own principles detailed in the More for the Mind report. Walter Coombs was now calling for 10 per cent of all general hospital beds for psychiatry, with no new mental hospitals.

A frustrated Deputy Minister of Health Dr. Patrick Rose said it would be hard to change plans at this stage. "Put yourself in the position of my minister and my government," he pleaded at a meeting of the Alberta Psychiatric Association. Calgary's second major newspaper, *the Albertan*, was not sympathetic to his view. In a lead editorial, it suggested that the position of the two doctors, Ross and Rose, was not the issue. "Surely," it read, "the doctors should put themselves in the position of the people who will occupy the beds."

178

By February of 1967, a banner headline in *The Edmonton Journal* predicted "Mental Aid Probable Vote Issue." It was. Lougheed was elected to the Official Opposition in June, and Manning announced the review of mental health services five months later. A year after that, Ross announced a delay in the proposed Calgary mental hospital until after the review had been completed.

Premier Manning was searching for a cautious, practical, no-nonsense kind of man to head his proposed study. His prime candidate was University of Calgary professor W.R.N. (Buck) Blair, born in Ontario to a "railroad family." He taught school until the Second World War, when he joined the infantry. Following the war, he remained in the army's personnel division and attended university where he obtained a doctorate in psychology. He had turned to psychology because "it emphasizes making maximum use of human talent." Dr. Blair retired from the army in 1964 with the rank of colonel and was appointed head of the Psychology Department at the University of Calgary two years later. A youthful man at age 52, the pipe-smoking Blair was known for his patience, a relaxed manner, soft-spokenness and, above all, a belief in personal responsibility. He had a military history and was a team player—exactly the right philosophy and credentials for Manning.

Mental health services "are seriously inadequate and must be completely reorganized."

This and other phrases like "mental hospitals are deep, dark holes," "practices are outmoded and unfair," and "patients are not receiving a fair deal in comparison with their more-fortunate physically ill fellow citizens" reverberated from the 30-foot ornamental walls of the Alberta Legislature. It was April 11, 1969 and the "soft-spoken" Blair's hard-talking 340-page report, Mental Health in Alberta, was being tabled with MLAs. They had not been provided with advance copies, and they had to hurry through the report in search of detail.

Blair had set up 11 study groups, hired consultants, invited briefs from individuals, volunteer organizations, and professional groups, and heard presentations at six locations across the province. The study took about 17 months. Blair had heard horrible stories and received many good recommendations. He was not about to mince his words.

The professor demanded additional services to cut down on the "suffocating pressures" in mental hospitals. "Staff shortages," he argued, "have passed a critical point." Mental health and physical-health services are organized separately, he complained. Contrary to the national trend, the Department of Health "continues to maintain an illogical division of these services." This division, he wrote, was uneconomic, unscientific, and unfair. "One part is under rigid, centralized government control, with a limited scope of operation," he charged, "while the other is under community control with necessary community involvement and a much greater capacity for the provision of necessary services."

With regard to children, Blair detailed a litany of complaints regarding the lack of coordination between government departments. Hospital beds for children, he wrote, needed to be increased, especially south of Red Deer, but only for "short-term diagnosis." Special facilities such as a "residential school and treatment centres" were desperately needed. The professor also recommended that the guidance clinics should play a central role in treatment and that all programs should be regionalized and coordinated. Finally, he argued for early treatment and the involvement of the family.

The study included 189 recommendations and 13 priorities. The priorities included a new coordinated and integrated structure; taking the pressure off mental hospitals through new general, auxiliary hospital, and nursing home beds; recruiting more staff; improving standards of care; expanding research; and reducing patients in mental hospitals as community facilities were developed. The controversial Calgary Mental Health Centre, Blair wrote, "should not be built."

The only part of the mental health system to avoid scrutiny was the provincial Eugenics Board. This review had been done by a colleague and friend of Blair, Dr. David Gibson, who supported compulsory sterilization and later was appointed to the Eugenics Board. His report's conclusions were that "eugenics programs are supportable in terms of biological and social sciences" and that the board members "adequately and justly implement the Act." Membership on the board, he recommended, "should be expanded by one."

Premier Strom stood in the legislature and presented a stoic face. The Blair report, he said, was critical "of certain measures practiced in the past" and any action must be "considered carefully." Health

Minister Ross, who saw the Calgary Centre as his crown jewel, was more critical. He said angrily that he found many things in the report he wouldn't agree with and many recommendations he would object to. He said the report was written in the "context of an idealized situation." His department's plans, he said, would be "more realistic."

Conservative Dr. Hugh Horner agreed with the report's recommendations that general-hospital psychiatry should be expanded and that no mental hospitals should be built. NDP leader Grant Notley described the report as an "eloquent plea for both compassion and reason." The report, Notley said, "exposed the callous indifference of a society which has boasted about commercial exploits while ignoring the basic human problems of our people." Lougheed would save his attack for later.

At the press conference announcing his report, Blair said that if we want to "point the finger" for past mistakes, it should be pointed toward the public. "Each nation deserves the kind of service it has." he said. He then commended the Saskatchewan government for its work, noting it had reduced the province's mental hospitals by one-half. The problems won't go away, Blair predicted, "as long as we continue to stow away our mistakes, our fears, and our inadequacies in large custodial institutions." It was time, he said, for Albertans to take on their proper responsibilities and "attack the problem instead of ignoring it."

Premier Manning had been right about one thing—Blair did believe in individual responsibility. But Premier Harry Strom inherited Manning's problems just before the report was scheduled for release. At age 55, Harry Edwin Strom was a large man known for his "soft kindness." He knew the Social Credit government was losing favour with the public, and he wanted a new series of social policies to lead the way to the end of the century. A new, more positive report, he reasoned, might counter the criticisms of his government detailed in the Blair report and then provide a sort of blueprint to explain the problems of the future, along with his government's plans to address the problems.

In 1970, Strom published what many considered to be a very progressive social-policy paper entitled "Social Futures for Alberta 1970-2000." Even the health minister now seemed more conciliatory. He admitted there were about 600 people in the Edmonton and

Ponoka hospitals who were harmless but had nowhere else to go. He said there were no other facilities, and "no one is prepared to take responsibility for them." He complained that the government had the tough job of trying to drag public opinion along as it implemented its reform plans. The new Social Credit philosophy was privately supported by the Conservatives, who would use it as a foundation paper for Peter Lougheed's own policies as they met in Banff in December of 1970. Packaged as "NOW—New Directions for Albertans in the 1970s," the platform contained the central policies which Lougheed would use to defeat Harry Strom. Lougheed would turn the Social Credit report against the government that commissioned it.

The chair of Lougheed's policy committee was MLA Merv Leitch, a private, compassionate man known for his empathy towards others. Leitch had experienced extreme poverty during the Depression, and his wife had tragically killed herself following her own fight with mental depression. His values were instrumental in the writing of the policy paper, which placed a heavy emphasis on mental health services. He had helped give Lougheed a cause and provided ammunition to go with it.

In a powerful speech in response to the government's February 1971 Speech from the Throne, Lougheed cited the many problems expected in Strom's "Social Futures" report. He accepted the report's conclusions but laid blame on the government, claiming it had "certainly contributed towards the trends forecast." The only question to be decided, he said, was whether the necessary changes would be provided by "an old government or a new one."

Lougheed then laid out most of his election platform. In the area of mental health, Lougheed blasted Health Minister Ross, who, he said "gave a rather enlarged talk about what little action has been taken." He referred to Blair's criticisms and described his own three goals.

"First," he said, a Tory government would "make a clear-cut policy declaration as to the essential need and objectives of the provincial mental hospitals." This would improve staff morale, he added, something he found was badly needed. Secondly, he would implement the most "urgent recommendations of the Blair report," and finally, he promised, "I will use the Premier's office to create public support and encouragement for mental health reform." Members of the Social Credit Party listened politely. Premier Strom took lengthy notes.

In August of 1971, Peter Lougheed was swept into office with 49 of the 75 seats. The "mental health crusader" was finally in charge. His election campaign platform, which placed a high priority on mental health, gave new hope to thousands of patients and their families. Workers in mental hospitals and community clinics were optimistic. Advocates like the CMHA were ecstatic.

It was now 29 months since Dr. Blair had released his report, and he was growing increasingly skeptical. Only days before Lougheed's response to the Throne speech, Blair attended a CMHA conference in Banff and announced he had resigned his position as "unpaid chief mental health adviser to the government." He was protesting the lack of action on his report. His major concern was the increased number of mental-hospital discharges without the benefit of any help when patients returned home. The pressure on mental hospitals had been relieved by transferring patients to unprepared families and communities, he said. The professor said it would be disloyal of him to speak out publicly if he were "presumed to be a government consultant."

Perhaps with Lougheed things would change, Blair hoped. The first Conservative government in the history of the province was sworn in at Government House in Edmonton September 10, 1971. During the ceremony, Peter Lougheed's son held his father's hand. Looking up, he asked innocently, "What do we do now, Dad?"

What indeed. The first few days were utter and complete chaos. There was so much to learn and so much to do. Lougheed had made many promises and the government's cupboard was bare. The province's debt stood at $146 million and Lougheed faced a record deficit of an additional $100 million.

There were also many competing priorities, but Lougheed demonstrated his concern for social issues with his first legislation, the *Alberta Bill of Rights*. His second piece of legislation, The *Individual Rights Protection Act*, provided minorities with protection from discrimination. While the physically ill were included, the mentally ill were not. Advocates were upset, but Lougheed and his cabinet refused to budge. Labour Minister Bert Hohol said the concern came from the business community. They felt that "mental disability" was too difficult to define and that vagueness would create problems when trying to deal with unproductive employees.

Then Lougheed began to make good on his promises to people with mental illness. The *Sexual Sterilization Act* was abolished, the departments of health and social development were combined, and in May of 1972 a new *Mental Health Act* promoted community services, an expanded role for "non-medical" professionals, and improved rights for patients. The Act supported most of the priorities outlined in Blair's 1969 report. Dr. Charles Hellon, a highly regarded psychiatrist, was appointed Director of the Health Department's Mental Health Division, and programs to provide housing, recreation, counseling, and support were funded through voluntary agencies across the province. Budgets for community programs were more than doubled, totalling $1.8 million within five years.

The proposed Calgary mental hospital was cancelled in favour of expanding units in general and auxiliary hospitals and nursing homes. Psychiatric unit beds jumped from under 200 to 381. Admission practices for mental hospitals were changed to recognize the need for consent and appeal. Community mental health clinics tripled to 30 in number, and each was accredited. Staff salaries were improved, a $1.8 million mental health research fund was established, and a new suicide-prevention program was begun. Spending in the field had increased by over 300 per cent in the first decade of Lougheed's term.

The Conservatives also introduced the country's most generous disability benefits, the Assured Income for the Severely Handicapped (AISH). The chronically mentally ill who were unable to hold down jobs would finally have a chance to live outside of hospitals with their own income—and the final cost to government would be lower than keeping them institutionalized.

Peter Lougheed became the first and only Canadian premier to receive an award from the national organization of the Canadian Mental Health Association. In 1980, in the ballroom of the Banff Springs Hotel, more than 600 delegates from across Canada congratulated Lougheed with a standing ovation as he received a national Special Recognition Award for his "leadership in developing a comprehensive mental health program in Alberta."

But Lougheed had not addressed the tough question of the future role for mental hospitals. He had earlier claimed that defining this role was a prerequisite to reform, but now he recognized the full extent of the political and economic consequences associated with phasing the hospitals out, as other provinces, like Saskatchewan, had done. Some attempts were made to carve out a new role, but the Ponoka Hospital was particularly difficult to change because of its rural location. Plans for a new 200-bed Brain Rehabilitation Unit at Ponoka were opposed by academics, advocates, and government civil servants. An expansion of forensic service to treat the criminally insane at the Edmonton hospital seemed to make sense, but what else could be done?

In 1976, Lougheed's government had contracted the Rockliff Partners, Architects and Planners, to do a confidential review of the hospitals, with the intent of developing a master plan. The report was damning. "Seven ward buildings at Alberta Hospital in Ponoka are unsafe and in a state of severe physical decay." At the Alberta Hospital in Edmonton, "four ward buildings are functionally obsolete and have severe physical deficiencies." Programs, the report charged, "are undermined by their poor physical circumstances." The report went on to criticize the uncoordinated children's programs run by the Mental Health Division and by the Department of Social Welfare and the uncoordinated alcoholism programs run by the Alcohol and Drug Abuse Commission and by the Ponoka Hospital. The geriatric patients could be better cared for in nursing homes, it recommended. It then complained that "retarded people are still found in mental hospitals."

The Rockliff Partners also had a few solutions. Alberta Hospital in Edmonton could increase its forensic services for dangerous patients to 150 beds and provide "long-term rehabilitation for the province with a maximum of 250 beds." All other acute care, children's programs, and housing for the elderly should be transferred to community settings. The obsolete buildings, according to the report, should be demolished.

As for the future of the Ponoka Hospital, the report was less optimistic: "AHP will not be needed as a mental hospital." The buildings were obsolete and unsafe, the facility was not well-located, and the "perpetuation of the hospital in its present form would be a service liability." It called for transferring, phasing out, and "scaling down" all services. The report went on to explicitly describe expanded community-based services and their projected cost of about $30 million annually. It concluded with nine recommendations, two dealing with forensic services in Edmonton and Calgary and four dealing with children's programs, food services, sheltered workshops, and renovations.

The Rockliff report and its recommendations would not be seen by the government caucus. The health department would ensure it remained confidential—indefinitely. The three recommendations to scale Ponoka to a 200-bed facility, to allocate 252 additional acute general-hospital psychiatric beds, and to redeploy resources to the community were too controversial and too costly and would have to wait. The recommendations would be tough for a premier committed to decentralizing government services and wishing to build strong relationships with rural Albertans—not to mention the opposition of the Tory MLA from Ponoka.

The wait would be even longer than mental health director Dr. Charles Hellon could have possibly imagined when he was appointed in 1972. By the end of the 1970s, one of the government's strongest advocates, Len Werry, had died in an automobile accident, and Merv Leitch and Peter Lougheed were preoccupied with the federal government's National Energy Policy. Health Minister David Russell who, as a student architect in Manitoba, had done a design project on Ponoka, had a personal interest in the hospital, but responsibility for the institutions was about to be transferred to the Department of Social Services. Dr. Hellon would move to warmer and less stressful surroundings on Vancouver Island.

Public interest in mental health reform had waned, the media had lost interest, the province's economic future looked bleak and the Honourable Bob Bogle was in charge. Even the strongly opposed 1979 government commitment to the 200-bed brain injury unit at Ponoka would be scaled down. Eighty beds were all the government could afford.

Although progress appeared to be stalled, the CMHA stood by its 1980 award to Lougheed, describing him as the "strongest political advocate for mental health reform in the history of the nation." The public, however, quickly forgets history.

By 1982, an editorial in *The Edmonton Journal* described Lougheed's commitment to mental health reform as a "shocking failure." The paper described "drift, confusion and maladministration." After Lougheed retired in 1985, he admitted frankly that his government had been preoccupied with energy, economic issues, and the Constitution in its last few years. Although proud of his many achievements, he conceded with regret, "We have not given as much attention to developing social programs as we should have."

References

Anonymous. Former Psychiatric Nurse—interview with author, 1998.

Anonymous. Former provincial MLA—interview with author, 1998.

Blair, W.R.N. Mental Health in Alberta: *A Report on the Alberta Mental Health Study 1968*. Edmonton, AB: Human Resource Research and Development Executive Council, Government of Alberta, 1969.

Blair, W.R. N. Calgary, AB. Interview with author, 1982.

Cavanagh, J.C., Allison, F.J., and McCoy, E.E. *The Child Welfare System*. Edmonton, AB: Court of Queen's Bench of Alberta, 1983.

Government of Canada. Royal Commission on Health Services. 1964.

Howse, John. "City Mental Hospital Promised," *The Albertan*, February 10, 1967.

Issac, Rael Jean and Armat, Virginia C. *Madness in the Streets: How Psychiatry and the Law Abandoned the Mentally Ill*. New York: The Free Press, 1990.

Johnson, Ann Braden. *Out of Bedlam: The Truth about Deinstitutionalization*. New York: Basic Books, 1990.

Lougheed, Peter. Calgary, AB. Interview with author, 1998.

Leighton, Alexander H. *Caring for Mentally Ill People: Psychological and Social Barriers in Historical Context*. London: Cambridge University Press, 1982.

Manning, Ernest C. A *White Paper on Human Resource Development*. Alberta: Provincial Archives, 1967.

Simmons, Harvey G. *Unbalanced: Mental Health Policy in Ontario, 1930-1989*. Toronto: Wall & Thompson, 1990.

Toews, J. and Barnes, G. *Chronic Mental Disorders in Canada. Ottawa:* Health and Welfare Canada, 1982.

Tyhurst, *et. al. More for the Mind.* Toronto: Canadian Mental Health Association, 1963.

Wood, David G. *The Lougheed Legacy.* Toronto: Key Porter Books, 1985.

190

Chapter 12
So, Who Gives a Damn

Chapter 12
So, Who Gives a Damn

So, Who gives a Damn

1972

His client got a year and a half. The lawyer got life. The judge's decision was a very important one for the young prisoner and extremely gratifying for the lawyer.

The story actually began a year-and-a-half earlier in 1970 when, with a look of professional confidence, the young lawyer from Calgary slid into the back seat of a cab. Suddenly he was face-to-face with an agitated man brandishing a large knife. Aleck Trawick had been assigned by a senior partner with the Macleod Dixon law firm to assist the Canadian Mental Health Association. Trawick was told he would be picked up by cab in front of the Bentall Building in 10 minutes. He had been given no other information by his employer.

When the cab pulled up, Trawick saw two men in the rear seat. The taxi squeezed to the curb and the rear door swung open. A large, disheveled man of about 35 crowded to the centre seat. With a little less confidence, the lawyer calmly introduced himself. Raising his trembling hands, Harvey Inger showed Aleck the large knife and told him he had attacked someone. Inger had been assured by a mental health worker that he would receive medical and legal help if he turned himself in. Inger looked somberly at the young lawyer. "You better be good," he said, sizing Aleck up. Harvey would hang on to the knife for insurance.

An hour earlier, the man had walked into the CMHA's second floor offices on 12th Avenue demanding to see a counsellor. As Harvey sat across the desk from the staff member, he explained he was a "compulsive man" who occasionally received "messages I cannot control." He told the worker he had sexually assaulted a young woman in Central Park the night before and now he couldn't sleep. He then stopped talking and with intense, bleary eyes abruptly stated: "I feel like I should throw you through that window. What do you think of that?" The CMHA worker remained calm. "It would hurt," he said. "And then I wouldn't be able to help you. You obviously came in here for a reason." The troubled man agreed.

Harvey Inger and the knife were turned over to police, and Trawick represented the man in court. The young lawyer pleaded the defendant "not guilty by reason of insanity." At the trial, during the evidence of the defence, a psychologist described the death of Harvey's mother while giving birth to him. The event resulted in his father continuously beating Harvey over the years, accusing him of killing his mother.

Inger couldn't handle the testimony and burst through the oak prisoners' box, running towards the judge. He was grabbed by vigilant constables and wrestled from the room. The irrational behaviour required the court to consider if Inger was mentally fit to continue his trial. When the judge asked Crown psychiatrist Dr. Morris Carnat for his opinion, he stood slowly, circled his index finger around his temple and declared, "He's crazy." Harvey was quickly found unfit to stand trial and was transferred to the Alberta Hospital Edmonton's forensic unit. He was to be locked up until he regained fitness to stand trial—which in a true sense meant indefinitely.

But Harvey responded well to drugs and after a year and a half, he phoned Trawick to ask if the lawyer would again represent him—at the same fee of course—"pro bono." Inger wanted to plead guilty in order to escape the open-ended incarceration he had been given when found unfit to stand trial, along with any future indefinite sentence he might be given if he returned to court and was found not guilty by reason of insanity. Trawick negotiated with Crown prosecutors and a judge agreed to the guilty plea and an 18-month sentence. Harvey served it at "Spy Hill," just outside of Calgary.

Upon release, Harvey found a job at the 4 & 20 Car Wash, where Trawick would visit while indulging his own obsession for shiny automobiles. Trawick was hooked. Helping people with mental illness would become a lifelong passion. His family would need to share his time with the "voluntary sector."

Voluntary action was not new. It could be traced back to 16th-century Britain, although it began to really come into its own in the 1800s. One of the earliest records was made by a Mr. A. Esquiros from France while visiting England in 1861. He wrote: "This tendency of the English to form groups deserves our attention....In France, men like to meet for the sake of meeting; the Englishman is perhaps less sociable: he requires an object, a community of tastes, a peculiar tie which draws him nearer his fellowmen." Esquiros concluded that the voluntary association was the "counterpoise of British personality."

Alberta had a strong "British personality," and volunteerism in the province has been part of the culture since 1910. But after World War II, governments began to take greater responsibility for social problems. Charities and other organizations that had spearheaded almost every health and welfare initiative in the province would be shoved aside. Their demise was considered by many church and charity leaders to be imminent.

Then, during the 1960s and 1970s, the sector gained fresh vitality. A new generation of volunteers formed organizations to tackle health and welfare inadequacies. By the beginning of the new millennium, the province would have more than 100 societies of volunteer citizens working in the health and welfare sectors alone. Hundreds of additional "special interest groups" would deal with sport, cultural, and business concerns. Across Canada there were more than 78,000 registered charities and an estimated 100,000 other nonprofit organizations who raised $90 billion in annual revenues, managed $109 billion in assets, and provided the equivalent of 549,000 full-time workers in 2000.

Volunteers with an interest in helping the mentally ill had organized a bit ahead of the pack. American reformer Clifford Beers was involved as far back as 1908, and Canadian advocate Dr. Clare Hincks began his crusade in 1918. In 1954, volunteers began organizing in Alberta. With the leadership of 15 citizens encouraged by George Gooderham and guided by Dorothy Cameron of Calgary and Dr. S.C.T. Clarke of Edmonton, they formed the Alberta Division of the Canadian Mental Health Association.

The group hoped to support, encourage and supplement official efforts to combat mental illness. Its official aims were "to promote popular education in mental health principles, to promote research into the methods of preventing mental ill-health, and to help those with mental illness." Within just a few years, hundreds of citizens—generally from the "privileged class," often wives of professionals or businessmen, and sometimes professionals like Aleck Trawick—would be involved in the work.

While Albertans who had made outstanding voluntary contributions could be found throughout the province, few would have the same intense involvement as the young Calgary lawyer. Born in Regina and educated at the University of Saskatchewan, Trawick was ambitious. He described his tastes as "simple—only the best will do." But from the beginning, he developed what friends described as "a natural sense of justice mixed with social outrage." Put simply, he believed in fairness.

Impressed by Trawick's legal work, the CMHA recruited him to serve on the board of its Calgary branch. Within five years, he was elected vice-president. Along with his service as a founding member of the newly legislated Regional Mental Health Advisory Council and an appointment as chairman of one of two review panels under the 1972 Mental Health Act, the young lawyer stayed busy. If his involvement with Harvey Inger had enticed Trawick to the mental health system, his work with the review panel had confirmed it as his life's work.

The purpose of the review panels was to consider the condition of all involuntary patients in the province in order to see if they should be released from hospitals. Trawick's panel interviewed most of the patients in Ponoka plus a few in Oliver and Claresholm. They interviewed many very disturbed individuals, but all too frequently found people whose involuntary status, in the panel's judgement, needed to be removed. One such woman was the daughter of a prominent Calgary family—a family who had abandoned her when she had first been admitted to the mental hospital. She had spent years in Ponoka without any family contact, and she remained withdrawn and timid. Staff said they could no longer find evidence of a mental illness but that she was frightened to leave the hospital. Indeed, she cried at Trawick's suggestion of discharge. Her legal status was changed, but she remained in the hospital.

Another woman was described by her doctor as "uncommunicative." She then proceeded to speak freely and at some length with the panel members, who were later advised by nurses that she had been talking for years. The doctor was apparently unaware of the dramatic change in the woman's condition. Her involuntary status was lifted—as it was for almost 40 per cent of the patients the panel interviewed.

Subsequently, the crusading lawyer was contacted by the Swedish Consul to represent a complaint by a Sten E.H. Gyllenram, who had written the King of Sweden to protest that he had been wrongly held in a mental hospital since the late 1930s. He wanted his freedom and the return of his honour. Gyllenram, Trawick discovered, was a Swedish immigrant who had come to Canada to make his fortune at farming. The drought and poverty of the 1930s took its toll, and neighbours finally contacted the police to assist the man who was starving and freezing in his shack. The young Swede was committed to Ponoka.

Gyllenram attempted over the years to write his family in Sweden, but the letters were intercepted by hospital staff. The new *Mental Health Act of 1972* prohibited the censoring of mail and a letter finally made it through to the King of Sweden. Gyllenram was, just as he claimed; "The Right Honourable Sten E.H. Gyllenram, a heredity member of the Swedish House of Nobles," and a cousin to the King—a "delusion" that kept him locked in hospital for decades. Armed with a formal letter resplendent with gold braid and a Royal Seal, Trawick was able to arrange freedom for Gyllenram, along with a small settlement and a formal apology from Alberta's Lieutenant-Governor and Premier, published in the *Alberta Gazette*. Aleck framed the letter and presented it to the old gentleman, who was ecstatic. His honour had been returned.

After serving 14 years on the CMHA's Calgary Board, Trawick was elected divisional president in 1982. Social Services Minister Bob Bogle was in the fourth year of his appointment, and the mental health system was rife with controversy. On Christmas Day in 1981, a 17-year-old, Grant Lee Phillips of Calgary, hung himself from a clothes-rod in a hardwood cupboard at the Ponoka hospital. The suicide was followed by the resignation of the hospital's executive director. Numerous newspaper stories, family complaints about conditions at the hospital, and staff discontent led Trawick to order a study of conditions. The Social Services Department, which oversaw the hospital, refused to cooperate, but hospital staff were helpful and informative, as were patients and their families. Ever since Dr. Roger Bland left the superintendent's job in 1976, hospital staff seemed to be working under increasingly difficult circumstances—and they wanted improvements.

In April, the Ombudsman for Alberta, Dr. Randall Ivany also announced an investigation of the death of Grant Lee Phillips. Dr. Ivany was just completing a second special report on conditions at the Alberta Hospital Edmonton, following complaints about that facility. Following extensive media attention and formal complaints about Ponoka, the Ombudsman concluded that an investigation into Phillips death was "appropriate."

The CMHA study group, chaired by Dr. James Browne of Edmonton, concluded in a July 1982 report that conditions at the hospital were " little short of scandalous." The report made 25 recommendations for improvement, including the transfer of responsibility for the hospital to the Department of Hospitals and Medical Care, the appointment of a Board of Governors and the movement of Gary Rykee, a high-ranking civil servant in the Social Services Department, to other responsibilities.

Minister Bob Bogle was quick to respond to the report—he refuted the allegations and therefore needed to propose no solutions. In Ponoka, Director of Nursing Mary Abt, received word that she had been fired. She would not even be allowed to attend the nursing graduation exercises at the hospital to be held the next day. The event was always a special time for Mary and the young graduates. During the ceremonies, government dignitaries ignored the controversy and Abt's absence was not mentioned until the new Provincial Mental Health Director and former Ponoka Superintendent Dr. Bland spoke. He broached the topic directly, commenting on nurse Abt's many efforts to improve the hospital. It was a gutsy action on behalf of a gutsy lady. Bland received loud and sustained applause.

Back in Edmonton, the Communications Director for the Social Services Department joined Rykee at a news conference in order to announce a $1.5-million defamation lawsuit. The action against the CMHA volunteers also included former director of nursing Mary Abt, whose employment was also terminated. The suit also named the CMHA's study chairman, Dr. Jim Browne, their executive director, Ron LaJeunesse, and President Trawick. Volunteer Browne, a University of Alberta psychology professor, received information about the lawsuit on a Saturday morning over coffee in his kitchen. As he opened the front page of *The Edmonton Journal*, he was con-

CMHA lawsuit appears on the front page of *The Edmonton Journal* in headline, July, 1982. (Photo courtesy CMHA).

fronted with one-inch bold print announcing, "$1.5-million suit by government official." He choked on his coffee.

Trawick and Abt had been informed by CMHA staff in advance, but Trawick's initial calm turned to rage as he watched television news. Minister Bogle's communications man, Jim Dau, was posed quietly in the background as administrator Gary Rykee, on the steps of a government building, announced his civil suit. Rykee could be a volatile man and he appeared angry. So was Trawick. While his relationship with the social services minister was strained, he was readily able to contact Attorney General Merv Leitch, a man whom Aleck had supported politically. "I certainly can't apologize for the suit," said Leitch, "That is Mr. Rykee's right. But you have this government's apology for any use of government staff or property during a civil proceeding."

Was this just clumsy politics or was it calculated intimidation, Trawick wondered. If so, it wouldn't work. Letters from Trawick were forwarded to every MLA in the province. Each included a copy of the report on Ponoka. While most of the elected members responded, they either expressed a simple "thank you for the report" or referred to Bogle's blistering four-page letter of rebuttal, which denied that service at Ponoka was "lower than similar urban services."

Exceptions to the vague responses were from Health Minister David Russell, who talked about his "complementary" programs of psychiatry at general hospitals. Another was from MLA Dennis Anderson, who promised to "raise the issues in a government caucus meeting," and another from MLA Gerry Amerongen, who apparently reviewed the report in detail and noted that "as a catalogue or litany of complaints, it is outstanding." He congratulated the CMHA on the report but concluded "that from a political point of view, it may be totally unwise for me to be so forthright."

The media pressure continued unabated, some of it at the national level. Not the least of the criticism was a wholly unflattering *Edmonton Journal* cartoon of Bogle guarding the steps of the Ponoka institution, followed by a Journal editorial demanding that Bogle be held politically responsible. "It is his lack of leadership," the editorial read, "that has contributed to the mess known as the Department of Social Services and Community Health. He should pay for it with his job."

Then a *Calgary Herald* editorial said Bogle was "a man who surely would have caused the word incompetent to be coined." Even the *Alberta Report* predicted that the Premier might soon give Mr. Bogle "shallower waters in which to tread."

By February of 1983, when the Ombudsman issued his "Special Report" on Grant Lee Phillips, responsibility for the Ponoka hospital had been transferred out of the Department of Social Services and Community Health and a Board of Governors was appointed as recommended by the CMHA. The Ombudsman's report focused on recommendations relating to internal hospital procedures dealing with bed availability, observation levels, and administrative reviews. All were acted on.

The lawsuits against the CMHA volunteers eventually were withdrawn, and Browne continued his volunteer involvement with the association for decades. After serving a term as president of the Alberta division, he moved to British Columbia, where he was eventually elected divisional president—the only Canadian ever to serve as president of two provincial divisions of the CMHA. Mary Abt returned to university, obtained a Ph.D. in nursing, and began a new career teaching the young nursing students she so admired.

Although Harvey Inger, Trawick's first mental health client, had received an 18-month sentence, the young lawyer did indeed get "life." He couldn't seem to get away from volunteerism with the CMHA. In addition to serving as president of the Calgary local and then as the organization's 15th divisional president, he served as national vice-president for several years. His career in volunteerism was interrupted between 1987 and 1989 when he was appointed Alberta's Ombudsman, a position that allowed him to work full-time assisting disadvantaged people.

When Trawick returned to private practice, he was appointed the CMHA's honorary solicitor, a role in which he and his law firm, Blake Cassels & Graydon, contributed hundreds of thousands of dollars in free legal work over almost a decade. In 1999, he was re-elected by the Association's membership to the divisional Board of Directors and, in 2001, was elected by the Board to serve as executive vice-president. The seasoned lawyer seemed to be back on his way to the top CMHA volunteer job in Alberta.

Mental health advocate Aleck Trawick, as Provincial Ombudsman in front of the Alberta Legislature, with Premier Getty in the background, 1988. (Reproduced with permission of *The Calgary Herald*.)

Trawick's many contributions earned him more than a dozen awards, including a Commemorative Medal from the Government of Canada, presented by the Governor General. The medal was in recognition of "a significant contribution to Canada." Then CMHA's National Board instituted a new annual award for "legal advocacy" named the Aleck H. Trawick Q.C. award in his honour. People like Harvey Inger knew that the recognition was for "giving a damn." Aleck Trawick, QC, like hundreds of Albertans before and after him, really did care.

Caring comes in many forms. For some it is more personal. Jim Hunter was a crusty, irreverent, chain-smoking staff sergeant with the Royal Canadian Mounted Police. He joined the force in 1954 and spent 20 years working in various detachments, then as a trainer for officers in the new Canadian Security Service. The Mountie had been trained as a political analyst, and he thought of himself as a good problem-solver. Married, he had two loving sons, a final posting in his beloved Edmonton, a retirement pension while he was still in his mid-40s, and an offer of a new position with the Alberta government. Life was good.

Then the unthinkable happened. It was 1976 and two months past one of his sons' 16th birthday when Jim and his wife, Bobbie, noticed unusual changes in the boy's behaviour. A previously thoughtful, caring child with a strong interest in football, he began to withdraw. His sleeping patterns became erratic, and he seemed unusually suspicious. The police had threatened him, he said, because he had information about illegal drug sales. Using his police contacts, Jim determined that there hadn't been any threats and that no investigation was pending. The Hunters thought their son would be relieved to hear the information, but instead, discovered they had challenged the young man's delusion—and that made him even angrier. They found a psychologist, but the boy wouldn't accept that he had a problem and he refused to communicate. Other efforts to find help were no more successful.

After two years, the situation became unbearable. Jim arranged a "warrant" to have his son apprehended under the *Mental Health Act*. He had become dangerous, Jim said. In truth, the "boy was never considered dangerous," said Jim. I had to "lie" because the boy "needed to be dangerous in order to get help." Admissions should be based on "illness and not dangerousness," he complained. Jim was neither embarrassed nor apologetic about the deceit. Only his son's health mattered. The son spent the next 30 days in the Alberta Hospital. The family received neither information nor support. They didn't know what to do. "You spend years thinking you're competent," said Hunter. "Then you find out you're not." Jim suffered the first of five heart attacks.

For the next five years, the Hunters' son would live on the streets. He lived "under the stars," in rented rooms and boarding houses, in shelters and in group homes. "The People in Need House was good," said Jim. Most places were not. The young Hunter found odd jobs, but oftentimes he wouldn't be paid at the end of the day. He travelled to the Northwest Territories and back. He wandered. He searched for a place where his internal torment would stop. He occasionally went home, but his presence inevitably brought chaos to the Hunter household, and Jim would have to ask him to leave.

The family's biggest frustration was not knowing what to do. In 1983, that frustration led them to the Alberta Friends of Schizophrenics. Branches of the group had been formed in both Edmonton and Calgary three years earlier, following a visit by national founder, William Jefferies of Oakville, Ontario. Jefferies himself had two brothers and a son with forms of schizophrenia, and his passion was to build a national organization dedicated to addressing the illnesses. Friends of Schizophrenics was initially planned as a family-support group, but the volunteers soon found that public education and advocacy were also badly needed.

The Alberta organization, under the voluntary leadership of Jagan Wani in Calgary and Mary Fitzgerald in Edmonton, grew slowly but with dedication. By the time the Hunters arrived, dozens of volunteers were educating themselves, speaking in public and publishing a newsletter. Psychiatrists like William Dewhurst and Roger Bland were providing volunteer support in Edmonton, while Doctors Peter Roxburgh and Keith Pearce helped out in the south.

201

The Hunters learned all they could about the illnesses and developed their own form of "tough love" with their son. "If you do all that you can do, we will always be there for you," they said. The inference, of course, was that he needed to cooperate with treatment. They now knew that schizophrenia had a biological origin and that their son's illness was not their fault. But as Jim grew stronger with their newfound knowledge and support, their son's delusions grew worse.

One day, the troubled young man wandered into a strange home and settled into an easy chair to watch TV. When the owners arrived, they demanded to know what he was doing in their house. Most of the time, he hung around Jasper Avenue where one evening he jumped on the back of a "seven-foot cop" he believed to be "the devil in disguise." The assault resulted in two years on probation, which turned out to be good news for the Hunters. Their son was ordered to live in a group home and to take his medication. For once, he complied. At the end of his probation, the young Hunter approached his dad and said he would be willing to agree to continuing treatment if his father approved of the psychiatrist. Jim was proud of him.

Jim's son would spend the next 12 years seeing the same doctor. His delusions were under control and with the Lougheed-initiated AISH disability pension, he was able to eke out a relatively normal life in the community. For 13 years, he did all that he could to hang on. "He is one of the bravest men I know," said the elder Hunter. "But it makes me cry to see what he has lost."

In late 1997 Jim's son admitted himself to the Alberta Hospital to participate in a new volunteer drug study, saying he wanted to improve his condition and "contribute to the knowledge of schizophrenia." The new drugs did have an effect. Unfortunately as the symptoms of schizophrenia lessened, mental depression increased. He began to "recognize his losses," said Jim. The thought was also a sobering one. Jim had long prayed for a "magic bullet" that might cure his son's illness. Now he wasn't so sure. "We could have even more suicides," he predicted, with a sadness that sometimes follows insight. "I am tired of moms and dads phoning to say their sons or daughters have died."

A year later, Jim's son was still in hospital—and Jim was still visiting him almost every day, despite the fact that 20 years after his son's first admission, communication remained poor. But Jim still believed the mental hospital was helpful. "I understand the dangers of institutionalization," said Jim. "It may be that all the institution has over the general hospital is 'time.'" But for families, time all too often means that the institution is all there is."

In 1990, Jim was instrumental in the support group's name change from the Friends of Schizophrenics to the Schizophrenia Society of Alberta, reflecting a modern notion that people suffered schizophrenia and that they should not be defined as solely "schizophrenic." It also made it easier, the pragmatic Hunter said, for people to find us in the phone book. Jim served as the society's provincial president, then as a national board member for six years. By 1997, Jim had made an undeniable impression on the entire movement, and he was awarded the Schizophrenia Society's national Bill Jefferies Family Award for his contributions. Hunter was thankful but modest. "Each step is so incremental that it is difficult to be proud," he said. Most of the society's work was not significant, he claimed, "just overdue."

After almost 18 years of advocating rights for people with mental illness, Jim Hunter of Sherwood Park was awarded a Human Rights Award by the Alberta Human Rights and Citizenship Commission in December, 2000. In typical fashion, he said the recognition was about finding ways to make a difference. "It's not about me." Jim cared right to his soul and his efforts would not end, he said, while there were still "far too many people with schizophrenia in the hospitals, institutions, jails, and cemeteries."

Government inaction was not based on malice, he claimed, "just misinformation and stupidity." Hunter has read dozens of reports written over the past 80 years, most of them making nearly identical recommendations for changes in the mental health system. Unfortunately, he says, "there is little evidence that any of them were read by the politicians who paid for them." Family members were definitely needed in the healing and lobbying processes, and more of them. "If there is no personal experience," said Hunter, "there appears to be no will to overcome the natural inertia."

Vince Van de Pol had personal experience in spades—he was "crazy." He also had little difficulty overcoming inertia. Vince was a consumer or user of mental health services, and he certainly didn't try to hide the fact. He preferred the term "survivor," but used it rarely because it offended the professionals upon whom he relied for care.

Van de Pol was brilliant and passionate. Born in the Netherlands, he immigrated to Winnipeg at age four. The eldest of four children, Vince was an exceedingly capable young man. Like many parents who had suffered the devastation of war, the Van de Pols wanted nothing but the best for their children. His father, who worked for the CPR, recognized his son's abilities and began to groom Vince at an early age to be a physician—and a good Catholic.

After the family moved to Calgary, Vince attended Bishop Grandin High School and then enrolled at McGill University in Montreal. He earned a Bachelor of Science, graduating magna cum laude with majors in mathematics and chemistry. He won awards and scholarships at every level of his education. He was brilliant and rebellious, but with a strong sense of justice. It was the early 1970s and campus revolts for "just causes" were part of what motivated him, but Vince also admitted to an ingrained resistance to authority.

While in Montreal, Vince worked as a teacher for the Pointe St-Charles Community Project, a literacy program. He tried hard but he didn't fit into the poor neighbourhood. The volunteers were seen as "do-gooders," and their students were rebellious. After some of the students smashed glass and committed other minor acts of vandalism, there was a visit from police. The young teacher hid the truth and protected his students. His response was unplanned, but through his support, Vince had become "one of them." He saw it as a valuable lesson.

Van de Pol liked to learn. He also liked fun and travel. His parents were waiting impatiently for their "doctor," but although Vince was accepted at three medical schools, he decided to take a year off and travel Europe. The trip was troubling. Vince felt anxiety and depression and found himself preoccupied with relationships. Free love was indicative of the period, and the former altar boy became a child of the times. But when he fell in love with a first cousin while visiting the "old country," Vince's family began receiving messages from relatives who warned that he was becoming "bizarre."

The family nixed the relationship and convinced Vince to return home, where he began his medical studies at the University of Calgary. He soon found the closeness of his family stifling and asked for a transfer to the University of Alberta medical school in Edmonton. He still couldn't concentrate on his studies. Sleep was difficult and he felt depressed. He found a physician who prescribed antidepressants and the black mood lifted quickly—too quickly and too high. The young student became manic—walking, smoking, and talking uncontrollably.

Vince was admitted to the university infirmary and, later in life, he would describe it as his "best admission." Staff were friendly and supportive and they had time for him; some of the nurses even challenged him to games of chess. He felt like an individual. His friends visited. Vince also now realized he didn't want to be a doctor. His inability to rebel against his family's wishes that he become a doctor, Vince believed, was a large factor in his illness. "I didn't want to be in medical school," he said. "But I wanted to comply with my family's wishes. So I went crazy."

Van de Pol withdrew from medical school in 1973 and, although he wanted to work, he remained unemployed. He had few skills, having never been taught how to do things by his family for fear he might "hurt his doctor's hands." After a year, Vince returned to the university to study education. He enjoyed teaching literacy in Montreal and hoped to make teaching a career. His marks, however, didn't reflect his previous capability and Vince complained that the medication dulled his mind. He wanted to stop taking the drugs, but he was afraid to do so. So he persevered, first obtaining a teaching certificate and then a Bachelor of Education degree.

The young teacher then returned to McGill to study theology. He married while in Montreal, but the relationship didn't work because they "were too busy trying to save each other." Work was difficult. Entry-level jobs weren't motivating him, and his attempt at starting a tutoring business failed when the children's parents found out he had a history of mental illness.

By 1980, Vince was living back in Alberta where he began substitute teaching in Edmonton, Calgary, and the remote town of Fort Vermilion. The Fort was a mistake. The stress of teaching grades one through nine, the isolation, the lack of sunlight and "hassles with the authority structure" all took their toll. Vince was placed on medical disability. His manic and depressive episodes were becoming more frequent, and doctors were beginning to suspect physical causes. An operation to install a brain shunt was attempted in order to relieve pressure, but nothing seemed to work. Van de Pol himself now wondered if there weren't physical reasons behind his torment.

"It's like a broken governor on a car," explained Vince. "I would speed out of control, love the action, and then crash and burn." Hospital admissions increased and Vince became even more rebellious against authority. He had worked as a volunteer with the Civil Liberties Union, and he knew his rights. He also knew lawyers and a great deal about medicine. Some psychiatrists thought he knew a little too much. Vince challenged paramedics, police, and psychiatrists. Each time he would gain release from hospital, another encounter just seemed to lead him back to "longer and harder time."

Vince saw himself as attending the "University of Psychiatry," and he wasn't too impressed with the education. Nor were many of the people he met in his frequent trips to hospital—and they had company right across North America.

In the early 1970s, a small number of angry ex-patients in the San Francisco area forged a loose alliance and produced a journal, *Madness Network News*. The magazine fuelled interest across North America and, within a few years, hundreds of similar groups had sprung up. Most of the people forming these "mental patient liberation" groups were bitter as a result of personal experiences. They called themselves "consumers," "users," "survivors" or a combination of the words. The more radical people defined the terms as meaning people with illnesses had been manipulated to take products and had survived the treatment. Others saw the terms as meaning they were the most important part of any system—the customer or consumer or user—and had survived the illness.

In Canada, more radical groups emerged in the metropolitan areas of Vancouver and Toronto. While most of the initial groups were anti-psychiatry, some were also "anti-capitalism." The Boston Mental Patient Liberation Front contended that all treatments, including drugs, were "used to coerce us into conforming to the narrowly competitive, individualistic, sexist, classist roles which are deemed acceptable by capitalist society and which drove us 'crazy' in the first place." In Toronto, consumer activist Don Weitz wrote that the urgent task was to "demythologize all medical-psychiatric treatments" by publicly exposing them as "inhumane atrocities." In Vancouver, the 1978 Congress of the World Federation For Mental Health saw hundreds of demonstrators waving placards and demanding an end to "psychiatric abuse."

But radical opposition to psychiatry wasn't evident on the Prairies. Edmontonian Nadine Stirling, an "ex-patient," was doing volunteer work with the Canadian Mental Health Association where she was introduced to the idea of ex-patients, clients, or "consumers" having their own organizations and their own goals. Like many other clients of the mental health system, Nadine was angry about much of her experience, but she was not "anti-psychiatry." She understood very well the need to control her bouts of depression and anxiety with medication. Her time with her counselor was helpful. But she also believed the mental health system was inadequate and that only the consumers really could make a difference—because "only we can understand."

In 1989, with the help of CMHA at the local, provincial, and national levels, Stirling attended Toronto and Vancouver conferences and agreed to try and organize a consumer network that would operate in Alberta as part of a larger system stretching coast-to-coast. Nadine met Vince in Calgary and together, they set out to build the new organization. Both Nadine and Vince were highly sensitive to "power issues" and wanted to develop a completely democratic organization in which leaders would be elected by a broad membership at an annual conference. Even the chair would rotate so that no individual could assume control. The organization, therefore, would remain leaderless until a founding conference could be held.

The group debated the use of the term "consumer" or "user" of services and they didn't like them, but "consumer" was now in most prominent use internationally and they would accept it. As to membership, it would be open to "any person who has used the services of the formal or informal mental health system." The goals, they agreed, would be to provide an "organization through which consumers can connect with each other to reduce their isolation, share resources and support, and strengthen their collective voice."

As first steps, large numbers of members would be recruited, a newsletter called Thinking Allowed would be published and the group's aims would be promoted through the media. Town hall meetings would be held with consumers across Alberta, and policy statements such as a Patients' Bill of Rights would be developed. Van de Pol and Stirling would do most of the work.

Then the Network received a major blow—Nadine Stirling died in the spring of 1991. Officially the cause was suicide. Nadine had been preparing for another Toronto organizational meeting, and she had been upbeat but somewhat anxious. The meetings were intense and emotionally draining for Nadine and she had needed help to sleep. Stirling had developed a nasty habit of self-medicating. "If one tablet makes me sleep," she would reason, "two or maybe three will really make me sleep." Nadine died of an overdose.

The Network volunteers were devastated, but they remained determined. The job of organizing the founding conference fell to Van de Pol and Karin Kossman, who was hired to replace Stirling. Van de

Pol would continue to work for the Network as much as humanly possible, given his disability. He attended the Toronto organizational meetings with other consumers from across Canada and like Stirling before him, found the meetings intense and emotional. On one occasion, he returned to Calgary in a manic stage with no luggage, no wallet, not even his shoes. Friends arranged his admission to the Foothills Hospital.

When the "founding conference" was finally held in Red Deer in October 1993, more than 100 consumers from across Alberta attended educational workshops, shared personal experiences, and found new friends. They also voted to elect a "steering committee" that would oversee the next stages in the group's development. Vince Van de Pol was at the top of the popularity list. This was a major life event for Vince, and he confided in his closest friend, Judith McGrath, that he was afraid it might stimulate another manic episode. He was right.

Van de Pol was once again admitted to the Foothills Hospital in a hyperactive state. This time was worse than others. Vince would leave the ward to deliver Network brochures in other parts of the hospital. He phoned almost everyone he knew and demanded that they visit him. His doctor grew increasingly concerned and the treatment became more intrusive. Vince was heavily medicated, his walks were controlled, and friends were turned away. Vince needed to be "brought down." Nine days after the Red Deer conference, Vince Van de Pol's heart stopped.

His loss affected hundreds. A few contacted his friend Judith McGrath and suggested they demand an investigation. They were convinced psychiatrists had killed him in order to prevent the growth of the consumer movement. Others even questioned the death of Nadine Stirling two years earlier. A few of them would later write a newsletter referring to the government's "20 per cent solution" of causing the mentally ill to suffer and die, while 80 per cent of the population "praised the solution." Most of Vince's friends, however, seemed to eventually accept the harsh reality that mental illness is all-too-frequently fatal.

The Consumer Network would be set back, but it would pursue Van de Pol's dreams. Dreams of liberty for people with mental illnesses. Dreams of crisis programs and safe houses where the mentally ill could receive comfort and support from people who "have been there" and finally, dreams of an advocacy movement involving all of the people who really cared.

When the Congress of the World Federation For Mental Health met for the second time in Vancouver in July, 2001, had Van de Pol been alive, he might have initially been distraught by what he saw. More than 300 people dressed in black shirts emblazoned with the slogan "Hugs Not Drugs," picketed and chanted "nothing about us without us" and other slogans at a "Mad Pride" event outside the Vancouver Convention Centre. The angry "survivors" made vitriolic speeches attacking psychiatry, and they distributed materials with bold headings like "Psychiatry is the single most destructive force that has affected society within the last 50 years" and "He sought help to understand his feelings…Now he doesn't feel at all."

But inside the conference centre Van de Pol would have seen a somewhat different story. Consumers/users, family members, professionals, and volunteers socialized, sponsored information booths, and attended joint sessions that looked at issues from the latest drugs to successful consumer-run programs.

There was debate and disagreement to be sure, but there was also partnership. Van de Pol would have been proud to see the Alberta Mental Health Self Help Network—formerly the Alberta Consumer Network—distribute hundreds of pieces of information. He would have also been able to watch consumers present workshops, participate on panels and lead resolutions to the Federation's governing members. He would have witnessed the support of professionals, family members and volunteers alike. They passed a consumer-presented resolution opposing the use of electro-shock "against anyone's expressed wishes," and they endorsed continuing involvement of consumers in all of the activities that affected them—"nothing about us without us."

They all gave a damn.

References

Anonymous. Survivor of mental health services—
Interview with author, 1998.

Anonymous. User of services—Interview with author,
1998.

Anonymous. Consumer of mental health services—
Interview with author, 1998.

Blaine, Joanne. "Mental Health Care System
Overloaded," *The Calgary Herald*, September 4, 1982.

Blaine, Joanne. "Patient Care Quality Poor at Ponoka,
Employee Says," *The Calgary Herald*, June 28, 1982.

Blaine, Joanne. "Ponoka Probe Leader Plans Active Year
for Mental Health Cause," *The Calgary Herald*, June 19,
1982.

Canadian Mental Health Association—Alberta Division.
*Alberta Hospital Ponoka—Report: An Organizational
Review.* 1982.

Cope, Gordon. "Last Chance for Justice," *The Calgary
Herald Sunday Magazine*, September 25, 1988.

Garber-Conrad, Martin. *Sermons for the New Millennium.*
The Muttart Fellowships. 1999.

Helm, Richard. "Bogle Withheld Child Care Report," *The
Edmonton Journal*, October 27, 1981

Henderson, Ross. "Longtime Lobbyist for the Mentally
Ill Honoured: Sherwood Park Dad *The Edmonton
Journal*, December 11.2000

Receives Alberta Human Rights Award," *The Edmonton
Journal*, December 11, 2000.

Humphrey, Edythe. "There's Still Room for Volunteer
Aid," *The Albertan*, March 6, 1969.

Hunter, Jim. Edmonton, AB. Interview with author, 1998.

Hustak, Alan. "The Psychiatrists' Revolt—Four Quit Rather Than Report to a Social Worker," *Alberta Report,* June 28, 1982.

Introducing the Voluntary Sector Initiative. Secretariat, November, 2000.

Koenig, Wendy. "$1.5 Million Suit by Gov't Official—Gary Rykee Claims He was Defamed in Ponoka Report," *The Edmonton Journal,* June 19, 1982.

Koenig, Wendy. "All Wards are Short One Nurse and Recruiting More is Tough," *The Edmonton Journal,* June 23, 1982.

Koenig, Wendy. "Latest Ponoka Suicide Victim was Decorated Wartime Pilot," *The Edmonton Journal,* June 18, 1982.

Koenig, Wendy. "Madness Book Packs Jolt of Painful Reality," *The Edmonton Journal,* July 26, 1982.

Koenig, Wendy. "Ponoka Likely to Lose Rating," *The Edmonton Journal,* July 31, 1982.

Koenig, Wendy. "Trailers to Relieve Crowding at Ponoka Mental Hospital," *The Edmonton Journal,* June 21, 1982.

Laing, Robert David. *The Divided Self.* Toronto: Penguin Books of Canada, 1960.

Leighton, Alexander H. *Caring for Mentally Ill People: Psychological and Social Barriers in Historical Context.* London: Cambridge University Press, 1982.

Martindale, Caroline. "Bogle Pledges to Build Brain Unit in Ponoka," *The Advocate,* June 23, 1982.

Martindale, Caroline. "Lack of Leadership, Direction Leave Hospital in Limbo—Problems at Ponoka," *The Advocate,* June 18, 1982.

Martindale, Caroline. "Low Morale, Conflicting Mandates take Toll on Hospital Staff—Problems at Ponoka," *The Advocate,* June 19, 1982.

Martindale, Caroline. "Patient Care Suffering from Shortage of Qualified Psychiatrists—Problems at Ponoka," *The Advocate*, June 17, 1982.

"Mental Health Group's Oliver Work Praised," *The Edmonton Journal*, January 26, 1957.

McGrath, Judith. Calgary, AB. Interview with author, 1998.

"Ponoka's Problems," *The Advocate*, June 16, 1982.

Stirling, Nadine. Edmonton, AB. Interview with author, 1991.

The Alberta Hospital Ponoka—Report: An Organizational Review. Alberta: The Canadian Mental Health Association, Alberta Division, 1982.

Trawick, Aleck H. Calgary, AB. Interview with author, 1998

Van de Pol, Vincent. Calgary, AB. Interview with author, 1978.

Chapter 13
The Reality of Myth

Chapter 13
The Reality of Myth

The Reality of Myth

1986

She was a champion of the underdog. Elected to the Alberta Legislature in 1986 in the City of Edmonton, the diminutive MLA would serve for seven years, take a four-year hiatus for medical reasons, and then return in 1997 as leader of Alberta's New Democrat Party (ND). But the demands of a stressful personal and political life would take its toll. "It's like living through a daily barrage of meteorites."

Pam Barrett, leader of Alberta's New Democrats, was explaining the personal stress which led to her January, 1998 announcement that she needed to "step down for six weeks." She needed a break and wanted to seek counseling for personal problems. The tiny, energetic, and highly regarded MLA had suffered the loss of her mother and a bout with cancer, along with a move to a new home, a highly publicized incident involving a live-in boyfriend, and the suicide death of a close friend. All of this on top of leading a political party that was attempting to give opposition to a huge Conservative majority—with only one other socialist MLA to share the load.

Sometimes known as "Mighty Mouse," Barrett was having trouble sleeping and began to harbor thoughts of suicide. She knew she needed help and with some trepidation called a news conference to explain her decision. Her honesty and candor seemed to win over the press. In front-page coverage, *The Edmonton Journal* headline read, "Barrett steps aside as ND leader for six weeks stress leave." And the Edmonton Sun, usually known for its dramatic treatment of mental health issues, ran a headline which read, "ND Leader steps down temporarily due to stress."

The New Democrat Party president said he wanted "to see Pam get better, come back, and keep leading the New Democrats." Premier Ralph Klein expressed concern for Barrett and said she should "take the time she needs." The former Conservative health minister, Nancy Betkowski, now Liberal leader Nancy MacBeth, wished her colleague well and said it took "courage to decide to seek help—especially when the person works in public."

Kristin Kinnaird, a young Calgary secretary, understood what MacBeth meant. While Kristin did not "work in public," she understood the stigma of admitting to problems. As she read the account of Barrett's experience, she wondered how genuine the responses of her colleagues had been. They were quite unlike her own experience, and she thought the long-term effects might be a problem for the politician. Like Barrett, Kristin had become overwhelmed with the demands of life. In her early 30s, a single mom with two young boys at home, Kristin tried hard to juggle the pressures of child-rearing, homemaking, and holding down her job as a secretary.

At night, she would crawl into bed exhausted, yet she couldn't sleep. When she did doze off, she would suffer night sweats, waking wet and terrified. She worried about her boys, she worried about her job, and she worried about other things that didn't matter in the light of day. Her smoking increased and her appetite was poor. Her health was getting worse and she worried even more. Then she began to shake and cry uncontrollably. Her family doctor prescribed Serzone and it helped a little. Then, one evening, she returned home from work and found the boys had defaced a wall in their bedroom with felt markers. Kristin began to scream uncontrollably. Her boys cowered on their bed until their mom collapsed in a state of exhaustion.

A neighbour phoned 911. When the paramedics arrived, Kristin lay curled in a ball on the kitchen floor. Her boys wept with fear and guilt. Kristin was taken to the emergency department at Calgary's Foothills Hospital. After an examination by the on-duty doctor, she was referred to the Department of Psychiatry. Within a short time, a sensitive young psychiatrist, an increase in medications, group discussions and some stress-management training made a huge difference in the way Kristin felt about herself. A friend was caring for her children, and her boss said he looked forward to her return to work. Kristin Kinnaird was beginning to have some hope for the future.

One out of six people will suffer from some kind of mental disorder.

1980s anti-stigma posters indicate one in six people will suffer a mental disorder. Current projected "lifetime prevelance" is one in five. (Photo courtesy of CMHA)

Five out of six will never let her forget it.

Following discharge from hospital, the young mother returned to her suite, only to find an eviction notice. Her rent was in arrears, the suite had been damaged with crayons, and the neighbours had complained about her frequent yelling. The man across the hall from the Kinnairds privately admitted the neighbours didn't want "crazies" in the building. At work, Kristin was treated differently. People seemed to shy away from her, and her boss gave several of her responsibilities to others in an effort to "reduce the stress." She overheard remarks that she had "gone wacko" and that people felt "fear for her children." Kristin felt unwanted and angry. She began to understand the meaning of the words stigma and discrimination. The single mother knew she would need to remove that stain on her reputation. She would find a new home and a new job where no one knew her background.

The only place Kristin felt accepted was in the support group at the Foothills Hospital. The people there seemed to understand her feelings and rarely criticized her behaviour. Even better, they complimented her on her new-found calm and the changes in the way she responded to her boys. She also found that the stigma around the word "mental" was experienced by almost everyone in the group.

Tracy, a young group member who was still in high school, described sneers, rejection and beatings at the hand of other students. The student described herself as a "leper" and others stayed away from her. The isolation reinforced her own feelings of worthlessness and she needed the regular therapy meetings to muster enough courage to leave her home for the scary world of adolescence. Another group member, Tony, would sneak into the group meetings for fear someone would recognize him. Tony had listened to his friends and workmates talk about the "loonies, nuts, and psychos who were making the streets unsafe"—and he was certainly not about to admit that he might be one of them.

It seemed that many people with mental illnesses and most of their families, dealt with the stigma by hiding the truth. Everyone agreed it wasn't the preferred way, but it was the most practical. Kristin hid her secret except for her time in support group meetings and during volunteer work with the Canadian Mental Health Association. She mustered courage from the understanding of people around her and from attendance at meetings with high-profile people—people like astronaut Buzz Aldrin, who publicly described his fight with mental illness at a community meeting in the Calgary Convention Centre. The event was a bit frustrating for Kristin, as most people seemed to have attended to discuss space travel rather than mental illness. But Aldrin left Kristin with hope. He spoke of sliding into a major depression after achieving his lifelong goal of travelling in space. What would he do now? His solution was to find new goals, one of them being to carry a message that there is indeed life after mental illness.

Kristin admired the astronaut's attitude, drive, and hope. But he had cautioned that it wasn't easy. She also admired Aldrin's willingness to risk discrimination by speaking out about his illness. Aldrin had said that his decision to go public was even tougher than dealing with the depression, at least in the beginning. Kristin wished she had the strength to make that choice.

But for public figures like Aldrin, disclosure was often not a matter of choice. People who "work in public," as Nancy MacBeth had put it, frequently had their illnesses "exposed." One example was Canadian-born actress Margot Kidder, who played Superman's girl-friend, Lois Lane, in four movies. In 1996, Kidder was living on "alcohol, amphetamines, and hot dogs." She was also immersed in a creative, ambitious period of writing when she lost several crucial computer files. It was the last straw. She found herself travelling the streets of Los Angeles and yelling at people. "I was literally all over L.A. for quite a few days," she recalled, screaming at people to "Get off my back! All those CIA agents for one middle-aged woman? How dare you!—blah blah blah."

Margot lived in filthy clothing, slept in a cardboard box, was assault-ed, and lost some of her teeth. Kidder demanded that the police shoot her. "Just get it over with," she pleaded. "Blow me up, but just don't prolong this." Kidder was apprehended and taken to a psychiatric ward at the University of Los Angeles—an event that instantly made headlines around the world. Her private demons made for great pub-lic entertainment. The media hounded her and tabloid photographers snapped pictures in private surroundings. Superman's girlfriend had "lost it" and the world was fascinated.

Canada's skating superstar and gold medal winner, Elizabeth Manley, also "lost it" in 1983 and the country had been interested in that, too. Born in Belleville, Ontario, Manley was an "army brat" who had lived in many parts of the country. The fourth child and only girl, Elizabeth was fiercely competitive. She began figure skating at age five and won her first gold medal five years later. But the pressures of skating—physical, financial and emotional—took their toll.

Following the separation of her parents, a severe case of mononucleosis and several lonely years spent travelling from competition to competition, Elizabeth began to lose her concentration. She sat alone and nibbled on snacks when she wasn't practicing. She began to gain weight. She perceived her coaches as irritable and demanding. Elizabeth responded by avoiding everyone. She was lonely and her loneliness made her feel even more reclusive, which made her even more lonely. "I couldn't break the spiral," she lamented. Nights were hard. She couldn't sleep or alternatively couldn't seem to wake in the morning. She had nightmares, often waking in a cold sweat. She became afraid of everything. Then her hair began to fall out.

By February of 1983, Manley thought she could not go on. She felt weak, her appearance drew stares, and she avoided everyone—both in person and on the phone. The thought of going out drove her into an immobile state of panic. At the urging of her mother, she saw a hair specialist who diagnosed alopecia areata, hair loss caused by "anxiety, stress, loneliness, fear, and depression." It all fit, even the weight gain. The doctor recommended a hair treatment, and he didn't stop there. Elizabeth desperately needed a change in environment, he counseled. She knew her doctor was right, but she didn't want to hear the words.

The young skater and her mother, who also had great plans for Elizabeth, cried uncontrollably. "Mom," she said, "there's something terribly wrong here. Look at me. If this is the price I have to pay for skating, then it's too high. Nothing is worth this kind of pain." Her mother asked her not to make a decision until after she felt better, but Elizabeth was adamant. She put her skates in storage.

The now-former skater hibernated in her mom's apartment hoping "anyone" would call. Most of her friends avoided her. "It's always a painful lesson to learn who your friends are," Elizabeth said. But a few hung in, to cheer her on and give her courage. The media, however, described her as a "has-been" with emotional problems "caused by her parents' divorce." The divorce was only one issue, but the young skater accepted the criticism matter-of-factly. "I guess it's easier to write about stereotypes than about real people with complex problems," she reasoned.

Elizabeth Manley would make a comeback under new coaches who provided extraordinary support, encouragement, and understanding. Friends like Toller Cranston listened and provided advice in her weakest moments. "Skating well is the best revenge," he counselled her. At the 1988 Olympics in Calgary, Elizabeth Manley won a silver medal in the overall competition. But most important to her was the gold she won in the freestyle portion. Manley still needed to be the best.

Elizabeth Manley wins Olympic Gold in Calgary. (Photo courtesy of CMHA)

Can people with mental illnesses be the best? Elizabeth thought so and volunteered to be a spokesperson for the Canadian Mental Health Association. Between skating competitions and Ice Capades, she visited communities and mental hospitals, speaking about her experiences and the need for personal support. Her book, Thumbs Up, described both her pain and passion, along with the necessity of always "remembering your supporters."

Margot Kidder also made a comeback. In a television interview with Barbara Walters, she explained that stigma associated with mental illness had prevented her from looking for help for most of her life. She spoke with intensity about the poor treatment of people with mental health difficulties and accepted speaking engagements across the United States and Canada. She spoke of the need for personal support, alternative therapies, and proper diet. Kidder had been secretly admitted to a number of mental hospitals and was highly critical of their "insensitive shrinks" and "chemical lobotomies." Stress, she said, "is the catalyst for mental illness—and life in the loony bin is the most stressful experience one can have." Her constant advice was for communities to open their hearts. "There's not one of us who doesn't have some dark shadow parts in our psyche," she told her audiences.

Pam Barrett also made a comeback, although short-lived, returning to the Alberta Legislature with renewed enthusiasm and resolve. In a personal letter to a supporter, she wrote: "It is people like you that helped me in my determination to get well again and to be back in the legislature fighting the good fight." When she returned, Barrett received an enthusiastic all-party welcome. Perhaps attitudes were changing, although when she resigned her position early in year 2000 after a "near death experience" in a dentist's chair, some of the media were not as gracious or understanding as they had been.

For politicians like Pam Barrett, such admissions had, in the past, frequently proven to be the end of a career. One of the most notable examples came during United States Senator Thomas Eagleton's bid for the vice-presidency. The revelation of his treatment for depression stopped his nomination in its tracks.

For Margot Kidder, who, as a teen, wrote journal entries wondering if she was crazy, the fear was worse than the illness itself. "You don't want people to know," she said. "It is the only thing that will make people shy away from you and completely invalidate you."

Much of Elizabeth Manley's pain stemmed from suffering in silence. She too was terrified to discuss her feelings for fear of losing her coach and her dream of stardom. She was hypersensitive to the arena crowds and had no confidence in her ability to carry on without the public's adulation.

Perhaps attitudes had become more enlightened, but admitting to a mental health problem was still not easy for anyone. While politician Pam Barrett, actress Margot Kidder and skater Elizabeth Manley received the support of friends and relatives, along with letters from well-wishers and others who had similar experiences with being stigmatized, secretary Kristin Kinnaird did not. With the exception of therapists and fellow patients, her experience with stigma and prejudice was immediate—and persistent. Kristin wondered why some members of the public seemed understanding while others did not. Was it the nature of the mental health problem? Is anxiety better than depression? Was it the intensity of the illness? Is depression better than schizophrenia? Was it the issue of people needing to be able to predict the behaviour of others?

Kristin went to the public library in Calgary to research the topic. While few studies were available, she located an Ontario study that concluded the public was only tolerant toward the mentally ill "in the abstract." Most of the survey respondents said the mentally ill "should be accepted," but later confirmed they would not want the afflicted in their community. The researchers concluded that the "acceptance of a humanitarian notion of the mentally ill" was largely driven by a need to be perceived by others as tolerant and enlightened. The reality of how the public behaved was much different.

Despite the vast numbers of people who have struggled with mental illnesses—and the prominence of many of those people—the public's attitude toward the issue had softened little over time. Everyday descriptions of the mentally ill were still replete with terms like "wacko," "cuckoo," "loony," "nut," and "psycho." Kristin had heard most of them. These words, used in everyday language, were as repulsive to Kristin as taboo epithets like "nigger," "fag," "retard," or "broad." But the "crazy" terms remained in fashion. "They are fuelling the myths that all people with mental illness are dangerous or violent," Kristin complained. "These myths perpetuate the belief that the mentally ill lack intelligence and willpower, that they are weak and unpredictable and not to be trusted." Unfortunately, these myths often become reality for the afflicted.

The evidence of stigma and prejudice existed throughout Kristin's community. Advertisers frequently used words like crazy, insane, and mad to imply that the merchant's mental instability had resulted in such poor judgment that he had priced things too low—and that the public should therefore rush to take advantage of them. Movies and television constantly presented the mentally ill as dangerous—or laughable. Newspapers frequently emphasized a history of illness in high-profile crimes. The public was fed a diet of stereotypes on a daily basis.

These attitudes seemed so firmly entrenched and the conditioning of children started alarmingly early. A 1992 Batman adventure from DC Comics entitled "Shadow of the Bat" depicted life in an insane asylum. The first page showed a procession of devilish-looking men in chains and straitjackets leaving a barred asylum. They were described as "a sad procession of lunatics and freaks, bleak testimony to the fragility of the human mind." The comic book then detailed the asylum director's first experience with a deranged man who committed suicide in front of him, spreading "hot blood and mad man's brains." The death was "destined," the director explained, because insanity is inherited. The doctor then dealt with a "violent schizophrenic" who was beaten with batons until he "accepted his medication." And it was all good for them. The asylum was a "womb." The outside world was the "wilderness." The messages were clear: Insanity is inherited, the insane are evil and violent, treatment must be forced, and violence against the insane is justified. Children were learning early.

Sadly, professionals in the mental health system were also sometimes part of the problem. "Psychiatrists are as guilty as anyone," said Margot Kidder. "Once you're in the bin, or there's something really off-kilter, everything about you that's good becomes invalidated. You are that label. You're crazy."

"Professionals working in the field are often hardest on their own," said Joan Swan, a friend of Kristin's from Edmonton. A registered nurse who suffered bipolar depression, Joan described how she felt "inadequate and rejected" when she could no longer achieve the "health standard" set by her colleagues at the University Hospital. She overheard comments suggesting that she should not be trusted with confidential information and that she should be placed on disability. "Where was the compassion, encouragement and support we were told the patients needed?" she asked.

Even the psychiatrists seem to go to extremes to hide personal problems like depression. A year 2001 presentation to the American Psychiatric Association by researchers from Detroit's Wayne State University revealed that four out of every 10 psychiatrists in their study said they would consider self-prescribing in order to minimize records of their condition. They would also advise travelling out of state in order to ensure confidentiality. Many of the doctors feared prejudice and discrimination—by patients and colleagues.

Members of the Psychiatric Association lamented that few people would discriminate against cardiologists who suffered heart disease—perhaps even thinking it would enhance their practice. But patients would likely be fearful that a potentially depressed doctor might not be able to provide adequate care, even when the doctor was well. The Wayne State study called for more "professional training" on the issue.

Writing in *the Edmonton Journal* in response to news of the Detroit study, respected University of Alberta Professor Larry Pratt described his own fight with depression and how his psychiatrist had recommended treatment in Toronto because of Pratt's stature in the community. "I understood he was trying to protect me," wrote Pratt, "but he was also telling me to run from the stigma. I stayed here." People who suffer from mental illness need to remember they have an "illness of the brain and not a hopeless flaw in their character," said the professor. As a "veteran" let me explain, he wrote. "Don't feel shame, don't apologize for something you can't control." Self-loathing, he predicted "can lead to suicide."

Pratt strongly urged people to take their medication and counselled that "if people lecture about the evils of psychiatric drugs, avoid them like the plague." In the long run the opinions of other persons aren't so important, he professed. "What is important is that you begin to like yourself and accept your illness. When you get well, then you can wonder about this superstitious shaming society of ours." And Pratt's views were shared by many brilliant minds before him.

In 1939, Sir Frederic Banting, the Canadian surgeon who discovered insulin, was interested in the use of insulin shock therapy. He had conducted some of his own studies on brain metabolism and insulin and while he was skeptical about the therapy, he was intrigued by the "mysteries of mental illness." With Dr. Clare Hincks, Banting travelled to mental asylums and hospitals across the nation. "They are going about the job of treatment in the wrong way," confided Banting to Hincks. "I have come to this conclusion after talking to hundreds of patients and observing the activities and attitudes of doctors and nurses. ... I entered these hospitals assuming the attitude I was a patient. I kept asking myself if this or that hospital procedure or this or that attitude on the part of the doctors or nurses would elevate my morale and self-confidence and self-respect." Otherwise, he concluded, he might not get better.

Banting continued. "I chatted over these matters with patients them-selves who all agreed with the soundness of my point of view. Viewing the hospitals from this angle, I found that the attitude of doctors and nurses was all wrong." Banting had still received no vis-ible response from Hincks and so he went on. "They treated the patients as inferiors and not as equals—telling them what to do rather than leading them to self-help, self-respect, and independ-ence. On the other hand, when the patients were by themselves with a minimum of doctor or nurse supervision, they spoke to each other as equals and were really doing a magnificent job therapeutically. The patients, if given a chance, are the real therapists—not the doc-tors and nurses." He then concluded with a sense of despondency: "You'll have to change the attitudes, policies, and procedures in all these hospitals."

Treating the mentally ill as "inferior" was much more pervasive than Banting realized from his visits to the institutions. It happened on the outside, too. In 1994, in the Edmonton community of Mill Woods, hundreds of people turned out for a rally to protest a proposed men-tal hospital on the grounds of the Grey Nuns General Hospital. Community leaders warned that "dangerous nuts would now be found in malls rather than down country roads." The protesters out-side of the hospitals carried placards reading, "No Mad House in Mill Woods." The patients in the hospital's psychiatric unit watched in fear.

But support sometimes appears in unexpected ways. Kristin Kinnaird remembered her own experience with "nuts" in the com-munity. She had attended a community meeting to discuss the pro-posed location of a new housing innovation. It would provide former psychiatric patients with semi-independent living arrangements in northwest Calgary. The young secretary had hoped to live in a pro-posed 14-storey high-rise that would combine rooms for the mental-ly and physically disabled along with the general public. The Canadian Mental Health Association sponsored the meeting in a somewhat naïve hope that the community would accept the project if residents understood what was planned.

Person after person rose to predict violence, theft and a drop in their property values. The organizers, who used statistics and logic to counter emotions, were clearly losing the debate. Kristin sat quietly, her worst fears confirmed. Then a robust woman in her 50s stood, walked to the front of the hall, clutched a microphone and stared at the hundreds in attendance. "I know most of you," said the neighbourhood pharmacist bravely. "You come to my drug store. You come and fill your prescriptions for antidepressants and anti-anxieties. You make it through life the best way you can. Without our jobs, our families, and our homes, all of us would perish." A hush fell over the room. "Give these people the same chance," she pleaded. She then walked slowly back to her chair as the room sat in dead silence.

At the back of the hall, a young woman stood hesitantly and thanked the pharmacist for giving her the courage to speak. She described a horrendous life of poverty, abuse, depression, and homelessness. She explained how a home much like the one being proposed had given her a refuge and a new start in life. The tone in the room seemed to change from anger to compassion, at least for most. Others, sensing the tide had turned, left the hall in disappointment and disgust. When the meeting had ended, Kristin left feeling as she had after the Buzz Aldrin speech—wishing she could have mustered the courage to speak up. Maybe next time.

For some there is no next time. Cameron Wilson, the son of former federal Finance Minister Michael Wilson, killed himself in 1995 during a severe depression. Michael Wilson says his son's fear of disclosing his illness robbed him of the support of others. Cameron appeared to have all the right treatment supports. He was on medication and had a "good physician and a good psychologist." But he was fearful of everyone's reactions, wanting no one to know of his problems. "Dad, promise me you won't tell anyone what's wrong with me—people will think I'm a schiz," he pleaded. "The issue was very troublesome for him," said the senior Wilson. "In the end, he failed to confide in people who might have helped." And then Cameron killed himself.

225

Michael Wilson is now a special member of the Canadian Business and Economic Roundtable on Mental Health, a group of prominent business and health care professionals hoping to educate the business community on the economic cost of mental illness. The information, Wilson hoped, would encourage employers to develop programs to keep employees healthy and to ensure early treatment. But some health care professionals, like Dr. Roger Bland of the University of Alberta, believe the issue is a double-edged sword.

"Industry is well aware of the costs of mental illness," he said "and that is, in itself, a problem." The perception is that mental illness causes absentee rates to be higher, benefit plans to be more costly, and employee reliability to be a factor. With this knowledge, businesspeople avoid employing individuals with any history of illness. The discrimination is "justified in their own minds," said Bland.

However, Michael Wilson thinks that attitudes need to be re-appraised in order to avoid "dismissing the potential of people with mental health problems." The jobs could be made to better fit the employees' capabilities and limitations. One of the things Wilson has in mind is for companies to make workplace "accommodations" as they have for the physically ill. Part-time work, job sharing, mentoring, coaching, and other accommodations would take into account the "cyclical nature" of mental illness and allow people to work when they were well.

Colleges and universities could do the same with their study requirements. As well, employers need to assess their own misunderstandings. A Time magazine report on a study of workplace violence concluded what managers might have known intuitively if they had thought about it: "The factor most predictive of violence is not a history of violence or mental illness; it's being laid off from a job."

Kristin Kinnaird loved Michael Wilson's attitude but wondered how such an attitude shift might ever happen with the general public. She had seen ads on television for "a caring community" and she saw posters in hospitals pleading for tolerance and understanding. But they just seemed to be words. Kristin had even participated in the 1992 "Cutting Words" campaign sponsored by the Canadian Mental Health Association's Alberta division.

226

The project hypothesized that if even a small portion of the 20 per cent of Albertans who suffered from a mental illness—or perhaps their families—were to participate, change could occur. The campaign included pamphlets, posters, a media guideline, and a response form that could be sent to offending parties. Dozens of volunteers like Kristin mailed forms to advertisers, toy manufacturers, publishers, and media outlets that had "reinforced stigma through insensitivity and ignorance." Companies such as The Brick, a chain of furniture stores, were targeted for advertising "Midnight Madness" sales. The CMHA volunteers hoped that these terms and inferences would become just as unacceptable socially as have the offensive words once commonly used to describe race and gender.

They had few successes. A representative of the San Francisco Gifts chain apologized for carrying a Halloween costume of a mental patient and promised it would never be ordered again; he did not, however agree to scrap that year's shipment. A manager at The Brick said he had never before received complaints, but that the company "would certainly react" if there were a public outcry. The Brick received few complaints other than those from the project volunteers, and the ad campaign continued.

A similar American program, promoted by the National Stigma Clearinghouse in New York, involved high-profile participants and received a somewhat better response. Former First Lady Rosalyn Carter persuaded a candy company to pull a "Certifiably Nuts" ad campaign featuring cans of peanuts in straitjackets. John Deere pulled catalogue ads for a "schizophrenic power mower," putting in its place a public service ad that read "the most shocking thing about mental illness is how little people understand about it." A CNN news anchor who had said that people with schizophrenia were prone to violence wrote, "I am sorry to have caused any distress by my ill-informed and off-hand remark; you are right to have objected." Computer software manufacturer WordStar took "loony bin" and "funny farm" out of its thesaurus. But even the American victories were sporadic—and the Alberta program had no high-profile citizens leading the way.

"Changes will only occur," the CMHA's Cutting Words media kit predicted, "when people learn that these stereotypes of illness are grossly inaccurate and when it is unrewarding for individuals and organizations to perpetuate the myths." Those conditions were tough to achieve and little change seemed to occur as a direct result of the campaign. While a few individuals and organizations had responded, others thought the program was petty and that it infringed upon freedom of speech. The Alberta Report complained there were "politically correct people out there who will complain about anything."

Even many former patients and their families were reluctant to participate in the program. "The stigma is so pervasive that people are afraid to identify with an anti-stigma campaign," explained program consultant Dr. Paul Sussman. The real tragedy, he said, is that three out of four people who suffer an illness will avoid treatment because of the stigma. Many of them deny their illness to keep a job, an insurance policy, a friend, or even a family. Indeed, a 1992 survey by the Canadian Psychiatric Association reported that stigma and shame were considered by half of the survey respondents to be the primary barrier to seeking help.

Similarly, a 1997 University of Alberta study concluded that only 28 per cent of mentally ill Edmontonians look for help. According to the authors of the study, a "social stigma" about mental illness was the major factor. And many people who did receive help tried to explain it away by using terms that they thought would be more acceptable to the public. In July of 2001, according to television reports, singer Mariah Carey "checked herself out of a clinic where she has been recovering from a nervous breakdown." Apparently the term "nervous breakdown" was a more palatable term to her publicist.

More than 60 years earlier, Alberta's Mental Health Commissioner, Dr. C.A. Baragar, proposed community education because "the greatest obstacle to early and effective treatment is an unkindly general attitude towards those who are unfortunate enough to be sick or crippled in mind." He predicted the attitude would be entirely changed by dissemination of "correct information." It was obviously difficult, then as now, to get that "correct information" to the public. It was also tiring.

In 1994, after only two years of existence, the Cutting Words program was abandoned; the task was simply too great. Volunteers and staff felt the job was overwhelming—and futile. They were bailing a river. There seemed hardly a moment when the radio, television, magazines, and papers didn't depict damaging stereotypes at the expense of people with mental illness. One American study said that, on average, television viewers see the depiction of three mentally ill or formerly ill people per week—73 per cent of whom are violent.

But Kristin felt the campaign had made a difference—at least for her. She had learned the truth about how many others shared her experience. Misery sometimes did love company—the company of other people whose fear of being stigmatized had affected their relationships, their jobs, their housing, their acceptance in the community, and, of course, their self-esteem. These were people who nonetheless had the strength to look for help, whether they suffered from a serious illness or had simply succumbed to the pressures of living. These were people who truly understood the reality of myth.

There were, of course, people like Cameron Wilson, who gave up and died. The numbers of stigmatized also included people like the Seattle women who leaped from a fifty-metre-high bridge after state authorities closed a busy interstate, "because passing motorists were telling her to jump."

But increasingly, those who lived with stigma were reflective of people like Kristin Kinnaird, who found the strength to fight back against negative perceptions of people with mental health problems. That strength frequently flowed, she said, from high-profile fighters like Elizabeth Manley, Margot Kidder, Buzz Aldrin, and Pam Barrett.

Strength came from people who understood and cared.

References

Aldrin, Buzz. Laguna Beach, CA.—Interview with author, 1974.

Anonymous. Consumer of mental health services—Interview with author, 1998.

Anonymous. Registered nurse—Interview with author, 1998.

Abt, Mary Frances McHugh. *Adaptive Change and Leadership in a Psychiatric Hospital*. Edmonton, Alberta: Ph.D. Thesis, University of Alberta, 1992.

Abt, Mary Frances McHugh. Ponoka, AB. Interview with author, 1998

Associated Press. "Woman rescued after 50-m leap." August 29, 2001.

Balon, Richalor. Presentation to American Psychiatric Association, Wayne State University, 2001

Barrett, Pam. Vancouver, BC. Conversation with author. 2001.

Bland, Roger. Edmonton, AB. Interview with author, 1998.

Canadian Mental Health Association. "Cutting Words, If You Think Your Words aren't Cutting Think Again: People with a History of Mental Illness Deserve your Support—Not Verbal Abuse." Canadian Mental Health Association. Undated.

Consumer/Family Perspectives. *Consumer Support Network News*. Boston, MA: Consumer Support Network News, Center for Psychiatric Rehabilitation, May 1990.

Farrell, Jim. "'Near-Death' Experience More Like a Panic Attack," *The Edmonton Journal*, February 5, 2000.

Goyette, Linda. "A Search for the Holy Grail: The Experience in the Dentist's Chair was Pam Barrett's Third

Brush with Death. She Took This One as a Spiritual Wake-Up Call," *Elm Street*, May 2000.

Griffin, John Douglas. Toronto, ON. Interview with author, 1998.

Jeffs, Allyson. "Barrett Steps Aside as ND Leader ...," *The Edmonton Journal*, January 13, 1999.

Jeffs, Allyson. "Barrett to get $29,000 MLA Severance," *The Edmonton Journal*, February 5, 2000.

Johnsrude, Larry. "Barrett Says 'Sense of Purpose' Brought her Back—She's Out of Politics, But the Warrior for Public Health Care will be Watching," *The Edmonton Journal*, February 4, 2000.

Kidder, Margot. Los Angeles, CA. Interview with author, 1999.

LaJeunesse, Ron. "Mill Woods 'Mad House' Sign is Typical—Mental Illness the Modern Leprosy," *The Edmonton Journal*, April 14, 1994.

Leighton, Alexander H. Caring for Mentally Ill People: Psychological and Social Barriers in Historical Context. London: Cambridge University Press, 1982.

Manley, Elizabeth C. and Oglanby, Elva Clairmont. *Thumbs Up! The Elizabeth Manley Story.* Toronto, Ontario: Macmillan of Canada, 1990.

Manley, Elizabeth C. Belleville, ON. Interview with author, 1990.

Martindale, Carolyn. "Man's Food Stuck in Mouth, Throat; Death Inquiry Told," *The Edmonton Journal*, July 22, 1982.

National Stigma Clearinghouse. *Consensus Statement—Violence and Mental Disorder: Public Perceptions vs. Research Findings.* New York: National Stigma Clearinghouse, September 27, 1994.

Roland, Charles G. *Clarence Meredith Hincks: Mental Health Crusader.* Toronto and Oxford: Hannah Institute & Dundurn Press, 1990.

Simmons, Harvey G. *Unbalanced: Mental Health Policy in Ontario*, 1930-1989. Toronto: Wall & Thompson, 1990.

Wen, Patricia. "For These MDs, 'Heal Thyself' Means Drugs—One-in-Six U.S. Psychiatrists are Self-prescribing to Treat their Own Problems, and Avoid a Record," *The Edmonton Journal*, July 11, 2001.

"Widow of Ponoka Suicide Victim Attacks Hospital Conditions," *The Advocate*, June 19, 1982.

Willwerth, James. "It Hurts Like Crazy: In Movies, in Advertising, Even in Political Rhetoric, the Offhanded Portrayals of the Mentally Ill Add to the Pain," *Time— The Weekly Newsmagazine* (141:7), February 15, 1993.

Chapter 14
Three Ministers
and a Realtor

Chapter 14
Three Ministers
and a Realtor

Three Ministers and a Realtor

1986

It was the beginning of the end. Halvar C. Jonson, member of the Alberta Legislature for Ponoka/Rimbey was appointed Health Minister on May 31, 1996. Born in Athabasca, Jonson attended university and then taught school in rural communities until 1969, when he moved to Ponoka to take a position as a school vice–principal, later becoming principal. As he came to know his students, he also became increasingly aware of how many people lived and worked at the mental hospital and that most of the people in the area had some relationship to the region's largest industry—the Alberta Hospital.

Following a term as president of the Alberta Teachers' Association, Jonson tried his hand at provincial politics, and, in 1982, he was elected to the Alberta Legislature by a huge margin. He maintained a strong constituency association and never forgot the importance of building and maintaining good relations with hospital staff—and, of course, the local businesses dependent on hospital paycheques. Civil servants responsible for Ponoka were quite aware of the MLA's interest in and loyalty to the hospital and decisions were made with great sensitivity to his influence.

The government had, for many years, been sensitive to its rural voters and Ponoka/Rimbey was staunchly conservative. Any Member of the Legislature's view about his or her constituency was critically important and even in the early days of Premier Lougheed's term, and in spite of the Premier's commitment to mental health reform, the local MLA's views were usually paramount in any discussion. It was a lesson learned early by Dennis Anderson, a young MLA from Calgary who chaired the government's Health Care Facilities

233

Review Committee, a body charged with undertaking periodic tours of government institutions and reporting back on conditions. Following a tour of the Ponoka Hospital, Anderson reported to Health Minister David Russell that he considered conditions "deplorable." He recommended that the institution be slowly wound down. Russell replied that the proposal was no doubt proper, but quite unrealistic given the economic benefits to Ponoka and to the strong support for the Tories in the riding.

In the mid-1980s, the government approved the construction of a 64-bed brain injury unit at Ponoka, despite the opposition and concerns of many health care professionals and advocates. Originally proposed for the Ponoka site in 1979 by Minister Bob Bogle, the service was desperately needed but the location was considered wrong on several counts. The opponents argued that most brain injuries occurred in the metropolitan areas of Edmonton and Calgary, that families needed to maintain contact with loved ones, that professional staff were difficult to recruit to rural areas, and that coordination with existing services and a university affiliation for research were vital. Ponoka just didn't make sense to them. Proponents argued that Ponoka had a good pool of nursing staff, specialists could be recruited to a pleasant country environment, a little more than an hour from the city, and program coordination and university affiliation could be arranged. Family travel was admittedly an inconvenience, but it was considered feasible for most people if they really cared. Politically, the government had been searching for some new use for the Ponoka facility since Lougheed's election in 1971, and Jonson strongly supported the plan following his election in 1982. The unit opened in Ponoka in January, 1991.

234

In the southern part of the province, Craig H. Simmons, a realtor, had no knowledge of the politics surrounding the Ponoka hospital nor did he have any personal political aspirations. However, his interest in politics would cause a dramatic intersect with three Health Ministers: Nancy Betkowski, Shirley McClellan, and Halvar Jonson. Simmons could have never foreseen it.

As a young man, Simmons excelled in both academics and sports and after five years of junior hockey and attending university, he returned to his home in Lethbridge, selling real estate and, with partners, building the city's largest realty company within three years. Craig Simmons was conservative, capable, and well-liked—

qualities that made him an attractive political commodity. He was recruited to the Progressive Conservative Party and his abilities moved him quickly up the ranks. In a short time, he was elected constituency president and then served as campaign manager for MLA Dick Johnson, who would later become provincial treasurer.

In spite of denying any interest in being elected himself, many people thought Simmons had a brilliant political career ahead of him. But in 1984, he sold his business and moved to the rural solitude of the mountains near the picturesque community of Pincher Creek. He again caught the eye of local politicians and was recruited to manage a successful election campaign for MLA Fred Bradley. In 1991, Simmons was asked to sit on an Alberta Hospital board of management. Although he knew nothing of the issues and lived some 300 kilometers away from Ponoka, the idea was intriguing and he agreed to serve.

The appointment of a Board of Governors for each of the Alberta Hospitals had been proposed many times in reports dating back to 1966. But the recommendation gained a sense of urgency in 1982 following the release of two highly critical reports. The Minister of Social Services, Bob Bogle, was under heavy media pressure and even his hometown newspaper was referring to him as "Bungling Bob." The first report, by the Canadian Mental Health Association, followed complaints by families, patients, and staff, and the suicide death of young Grant Lee Phillips at the Alberta Hospital Ponoka. The second report was instigated by the Social Services Minister himself and resulted in a Special Report by Provincial Ombudsman Dr. Randall Ivany.

An Anglican priest, Ivany had just completed a review of conditions at the Alberta Hospital Edmonton where he uncovered evidence of "regular abuse" of patients and the intimidation of innocent staff. The Ombudsman found evidence of staff kicking patients in the groin, slapping their faces, and pulling out beard hairs with tweezers. Coincidently, Ivany's report on the Edmonton hospital, like that of the CMHA report at Ponoka, made a total of 25 recommendations designed to improve conditions. Unlike the CMHA report on the Ponoka hospital, Ivany did not see the Edmonton problems as generalized to the whole institution. He cautioned that he would not want the readers of his report to be left with the impression that his findings "applied to the hospital as a whole." He acknowledged that he found staff that could not "cope well," but the performance of the few, he wrote "was not indicative of the staff generally," commending both staff and administration.

The CMHA report was less supportive of administrative staff. It acknowledged that many fine individuals were working under extreme conditions, but then laid the responsibility for conditions directly on the administration, both at the hospital and within the Department of Social Services and Community Health.

The government would act and appointed boards both at the Ponoka and Edmonton hospitals. When the new Ponoka board saw that six executive directors had served over an eight-year period, they searched carefully for the right person. He came in the name of Ken Sheehan from Ontario. Appointed in 1984, he was able and ambitious. The hospital had lost its Canadian hospital accreditation only a month after Sheehan arrived, but the board was hopeful that his experience would help reverse their fortunes.

Sheehan was an authoritarian administrator demanding loyalty in his subordinates, a style which was largely characteristic of the institution's leaders since its opening in 1911. While some of the hospital's organizational difficulties were quickly improved, conditions for many of the patients remained poor. They languished in obsolete buildings, living in dormitories with little or no privacy, extreme temperatures, and bathrooms located "down the hall." When patients were discharged, some left in abject poverty, catching a bus "back home," when in reality many of them didn't have a home.

The new executive director developed a strong relationship with local politicians, including Halvar Jonson, who owned a neighbouring ranch. They shared a similar philosophy regarding the need for "asylum." Community care was fine, they both professed, but large separate psychiatric hospitals needed to be an important and integral part of the mental health system well into the future. The new executive director appeared to work well with his board of directors who believed Sheehan was making good progress. In 1986, the CMHA and the hospital board jointly issued a report entitled simply AHP— Three years later. The report described hospital conditions as "a new beginning."

Sheehan enjoyed the two-year partnership with CMHA, but he had little patience for outside criticism. When the CMHA in 1990 issued a report expressing criticism of the government's plan to rebuild the hospital, Sheehan issued a sharply worded four-page news release attacking the Association's views as "inaccurate and false." The news release detailed the many advantages of institutional care. CMHA President Bill Gaudette acknowledged that progress was being made to improve conditions at the hospital; however his organization's vision was for improved home based care, psychiatric beds in general hospitals, and provincial institutions to serve as a last resort. The relationship between Sheehan and the CMHA would never be the same.

The government's Mental Health Division, which had an over-riding responsibility for the Alberta Hospitals, were also viewed by Sheehan to be obstructionist and a threat to his authority. In a private meeting with CMHA's Executive Director Ron LaJeunesse, Sheehan confided that he would live to see the end of the Mental Health Division, a prediction that would prove to be correct. The relationship between Sheehan and the Division's senior civil servants was constantly strained.

Craig Simmons, the businessman from Pincher Creek, joined the Ponoka Board of Governors in 1991, still unaware of the hospital's history. He regarded Sheehan as a strong manager with an honest regard for the patients and staff in his charge and a laudable vision for improved services in a bigger, better hospital. Improvements in the hospital, such as the new activity centre and the modern brain injury unit, were considered concrete evidence of Sheehan's success.

One of Sheehan's major achievements was regaining the hospital's accreditation. He had consulted as a hospital accreditor and included a continuing role for himself with the Hospital Accreditation Council in his employment contract at Ponoka. He knew the process well, and his knowledge and experience had helped the hospital staff address the right issues. From Sheehan's perspective, one of the "right issues" was rebuilding the aging Ponoka, and he needed the support of the health minister and Cabinet to do so.

The health minister appeared to agree with Sheehan. Nancy Betkowski was an intelligent and ambitious woman with a degree in Romance Languages from Laval University. Elected in 1986 and appointed Minister of Health in 1988, Betkowski was a protégé of Peter Lougheed. Her manner and style had many similarities to that of the former premier, but she had inherited a health system widely considered to be financially out of control and unsustainable. She now faced the formidable task of restructuring and reforming the government's largest department, which included mental health services.

Shortly into her new responsibilities, Betkowski was faced with a proposal to rebuild the Alberta hospitals. In spite of budget constraints, the minister was convinced that poor facilities at both the Edmonton and Ponoka locations required a significant capital expenditure. In 1990, she announced a proposal to spend more than $150 million on rebuilding the hospitals.

The Canadian Mental Health Association had been proposing alternatives to mental hospitals for decades, and its president, Bill Gaudette, was quick to respond describing the proposal as "70 years out of date" and "a blatant waste of taxpayer dollars." Betkowski's deputy minister, Rheal LeBlanc, was not unfamiliar with mental health service delivery, having worked as the director of social services at the Weyburn mental hospital during Saskatchewan's rapid de-institutionalization in the 1960s, and he had his own private concerns about the value of the building proposal. But Gordon McLeod, LeBlanc's assistant deputy minister for mental health, who was a highly respected and capable former executive director at the Alberta Hospital Edmonton, like Sheehan, strongly favoured the reconstruction plan.

Then, in a matter that McLeod said was unrelated to the CMHA's opposition to the re-building, he announced that a portion of CMHA's government grant would not be continued in the next fiscal year. President Bill Gaudette appealed the decision to Betkowski and at a Valentine's Day meeting, Gaudette, along with a full contingent of his executive members, delivered a dozen yellow roses. He also delivered a request to halt the reconstruction plans and to reinstate the government grant to CMHA. "I can't be bought," responded the minister with a broad smile. "But you have come close." The grant was reinstated, and a commitment made to review the re-building plans.

Consistent with CMHA's appeal to stop rebuilding of the mental hospitals were a series of government reports on health reform, all of which proposed a system of community-based care. The Rainbow Report of the Premiers' Commission on the Future of Health Care, the Action Plan of the Premiers' Council on the Status of Persons with Disabilities, the Roy Brassard report Claiming My Future, and the health minister's own "discussion paper" entitled *Mental Health Services in Alberta*, 1988, all proposed a system of community care.

The reports collectively appeared to set the stage for Betkowski to discuss a reformed mental health system with Cabinet. In 1992, she released a government policy paper entitled *Future Directions* which strongly emphasized community- or home-based programming.

By 1993, a strategic planning group was organized to build on the theoretical work. After a year of intense planning, Acting Assistant Deputy Minister Dennis Ostercamp and his planner, Betty Jeffers, were ready to unveil their report, entitled Working in Partnership. It set out an action plan to both regionalize and balance mental health services. Ostercamp, too, had spent much of his career working in a mental hospital but his work in the community created a strongly held commitment to provide services nearer to people's homes. The mental hospitals had an interim role to be sure, but research on other jurisdictions done by Dr. Haroon Nasir, a government mental health consultant, concluded that the need for them would diminish with modern treatments and proper community supports. The 1990 plans to rebuild the mental hospitals seemed all but dead.

Many of the people directly involved in promoting mental health reform were optimistic. Some of the more senior civil servants had changed, but many of the necessary ingredients for reform still appeared to be in place. There was a community consensus on a new direction, a new Deputy Minister, Dr. Don Phillipon, who was focused on improving effectiveness and reducing cost, and a politically skilled new director of the Mental Health Division, Bernie Doyle. Doyle shared the vision of the long-range plan developed by Ostercamp, Jeffers, and the 28 members of the strategic-planning groups. He also possessed an extraordinary ability to move a lumbering bureaucracy to action.

Most importantly, there was a minister who appeared committed to real change. Nancy Betkowski's influence would be essential in convincing a government caucus that remained fearful, as one MLA put it, "of moving more crazies to the streets."

Then Premier Getty resigned, resulting in a leadership race that saw Ralph Klein defeat Betkowski, who then left the government. A virtually unknown junior cabinet minister, Shirley McClellan, took over the health portfolio. McClellan presented herself as a sincere woman with good intentions and impressive volunteer credentials, but there was no indication that she had the political strength to deliver on the controversial mental health reform plan. She would require the backing of the new premier, and advocates feared that a populist premier might not show much interest in an issue that did not hold strong appeal for the public. Many of the people who had been working so hard toward a better system seemed demoralized. One exception was Doyle, who continued to campaign for the reforms with passion and commitment. His efforts appeared to pay off when McClellan expressed a special interest in the mental health reform agenda.

In July, 1994, McClellan announced the appointment of a Mental Health Board of 15 people to oversee the restructuring of services in line with the 1993 report Working in Partnership. The Minister sold Cabinet and the Treasury Board on two controversial issues. She proposed to do the mental health restructuring separate from broader plans to regionalize health services, at least until the programs were developed. After that, they would be transferred to the regional health authorities for management. She also recognized the historic underfunding in the mental health system and protected existing dollars from the dramatic budget cuts proposed for the health system generally.

The minister's action was viewed by many to be an amazing accomplishment. McClellan's support in Cabinet had presumably included Education Minister Jonson. The plan would make sense for Jonson if he wished to influence the public funds in the mental hospital system and ensure against the possible downsizing of the Ponoka hospital by a regional health authority. More importantly, a confidential briefing paper prepared for McClellan to take to Cabinet detailed a plan that included a proposal for a single mental hospital to serve the entire province. The location was not stipulated, but health department officials privately admitted it would be in Ponoka.

McClellan then appointed a 15-member Mental Health Board comprised of at least four members with personal ties to the Ponoka hospital—and to Jonson. The group would be chaired by Conservative supporter and Ponoka board member, Craig Simmons. Officials of the Department of Health opposed Simmons' appointment as chair, noting he was too closely aligned with the institutional sector and that given Simmons' history with the Tories, the high-profile appointment would be publicly perceived as patronage. McClellan didn't budge. Simmons was competent and with the support of Jonson's friends on the board, Simmons could deliver results.

Results, Simmons was told, included a single mental hospital in Ponoka. The Alberta Hospital Edmonton was to be downsized. Ponoka Hospital Director Ken Sheehan would now apply for the position of the board's new executive director. Following an open competition, Sheehan emerged on a short list of three. The board appeared split along community/institutional lines, and some members openly expressed concerns about appointing Sheehan. In the end, the job went to Ontarian Stephen Newroth.

By the time the Mental Health Board released its strategic plan, *Building a Better Future*, in March of 1995, Simmons and his board members had listened to hundreds of "consumers" of mental health services and their families. Simmons had heard a very different version of mental health care than the one he heard while sitting on the Alberta Hospital Ponoka board. Members like vice-chair Bill Gaudette and strategic planning chair Mary Oordt described a metamorphosis in Simmons.

The chairman was no longer trying to direct the board. He listened, supported, and worked towards consensus. "More importantly," they said, he became increasingly committed to a mental health care plan similar to one proposed by Dr. W.R.N. Blair more than 25 years earlier, one which Health Minister Nancy Betkowski had also supported almost a decade earlier. The plan was really quite simple—on paper: determine a role for the mental hospitals, expand the number of beds in general and extended care hospitals, build community supports, and then integrate the programs with the local health authorities. Reducing the number of mental-hospital beds would occur only when it was proven they were no longer needed. Retraining staff, improving standards through outcome measures, improving information systems, and supporting expanded research rounded out the plan.

The board had a difficult beginning and then their ambitions were further delayed by the exit of Executive Director Newroth and the time needed to select his replacement, Ron LaJeunesse. But the board was dedicated and persistent and, in the first year following the release of the board's strategic plan, dozens of important programs were initiated. Mental hospital bed closures that had taken place for years, were stopped until new community-based supports could be put in place. Using a business analogy, Simmons had stated that closing hospital beds before providing alternatives would be a bit like reducing bank tellers before the automated tellers had proven themselves.

Without downsizing, but through efficiencies, millions of dollars were transferred from mental hospital budgets to community programs providing crisis care, follow-up of long-term patients, housing, recreation, and employment. Mental hospitals were required to work toward integrating services with community resources and a tele-psychiatry pilot project provided on-line advice to rural doctors. Consumers themselves received funds for new self-help projects to find housing and employment. A university program to retrain hospital staff for work in community settings began, the psychiatric nursing program was transferred from the Ponoka hospital to Grant MacEwan Community College, and mental health research was expanded by integrating it with the Heritage Foundation for Medical Research. Negotiations were also begun for the transfer of community programs to the government's new regional health authorities. Both the service and the administration would be brought closer to patients' homes and families.

Moreover, plans were in place for a better evaluation of the entire system. The board approved an expenditure of $1 million to design and implement a new computerized information system, and Simmons hoped to use the new technology to look at results. "We spend $140-million," he said, "and it's remarkable how little we know about what we get for that." Bernie Doyle, now the acting deputy minister was pleased with the progress and continued to reassure the minister that Simmons and the board were on the right track.

A board-commissioned independent study of the patient population in the two Alberta Hospitals confirmed that almost half of the patients could live in the community if they had appropriate help. Only dangerous patients who had broken laws and people with the most serious of disabilities would, in the future, need to be held in hospitals. Others could be treated closer to their homes and families. The Provincial Mental Health Board's strategic plan called for the eventual downsizing of the mental hospitals by "up to 50 per cent."

As the board grappled with the controversial issue of when and where to close beds, minister McClellan advised Simmons she was concerned with the delay. Simmons too was concerned with the minister's short time frame for bed reductions, and he proposed a multiyear investment plan which would see a dramatic increase in community funds for five years, followed by repayments to Treasury when institutional costs were reduced. Things came to a head when Simmons advised the minister that he could not and would not deliver on her goal of a single site in Ponoka. Downsizing he said, should occur over time at both facilities. If the government felt strongly that only one hospital should be retained, the Board's research concluded "it should be in Edmonton." The Minister responded by appointing a three-member MLA review committee to review the board's progress.

While cordial, the three MLAs on the minister's review committee appeared disinterested in the Board's plans, according to board vice-chair Bill Gaudette, a former CMHA president. Volumes of written material were requested, but judging from the questions, little of it appeared to have been read. This was evidently a "make-work project in order to justify a conclusion," said Simmons. He was angry at having to travel almost 1,000 kilometres each week to try to influence an outcome that seemed to be predetermined.

Craig Simmons' assumption that a decision on the board's future already had been made, was further reinforced at a public meeting in Ponoka. Mayor Ken Greenwell, several business leaders including Howard Roland, a former member of the Mental Health Board who resigned over potential down-sizing of Ponoka, and five former hospital staff and directors organized a public forum to discuss the future of the hospital. On a cold, blustery night in April, 1996, more than 600 people listened to speech after speech attacking plans to reduce the size of the hospital. They predicted mental health services would receive a "fatal blow" if programs were decentralized and the hospital's expertise dispersed to other parts of the province. The speeches were based on a brief entitled Evolution, Not Revolution that the group had already submitted to the premier.

Representatives of the Mental Health Board, although not invited, sat near the front of the room, available but not asked to participate. MLA Jonson stood quietly at the back of the hall, saying nothing. Calgary MLA Heather Forsyth, stood near Jonson and introduced

243

herself as the "chair of the MLA review team." In a confident voice, she urged the citizens not to worry. "Your government is listening," she assured them.

Board Chairman Craig Simmons requested a meeting with the new Deputy Minister of Health, Jane Fulton. The board's plans needed Shirley McClellan's support, and he wanted advice on how to get it back. Fulton was dismissive of the minister and provided no helpful suggestions. The issue was apparently highly politicized. Confident the end of the board might be at hand, Simmons and other members attempted a massive, last-ditch communication campaign to personally inform every MLA in the province of the board's plans and progress. After all, the board was doing exactly what official government policy had asked it to do.

The first meeting would be with Halvar Jonson. Simmons was directed to a meeting room across the hall from the minister's executive office. Jonson burst into the room and with a stern face, glared at his guests. A hand outstretched in greeting was ignored. And so was Simmons's presentation, which included a booklet entitled The Road to a Better Future. The minister asked very few questions, but he didn't seem to much like the "road," and he made it very clear that Ponoka would be a destination on any future journey.

When Simmons expressed his board's preference for decentralized services, including the eventual downsizing of the two hospitals in Edmonton and Ponoka, while maintaining the remodeled Claresholm Centre, the minister grimaced. "It is only reasonable, Mr. Minister," said Simmons, "to maintain the best buildings in all three locations while decentralizing services as much as possible. It is your government's policy!" When Simmons referred to the excellent buildings in Claresholm, the Minister snapped, "Who rebuilt that place?" Simmons responded, "Your government, sir." The meeting was over.

The minister advised Simmons that he and not McClellan had initiated the MLA study committee and then ended the session with a single statement: "You know what I want." Most of the meetings with the other MLAs went little better. The message was falling on deaf ears. Powerful Cabinet members like Stockwell Day said the public was no longer supportive of closing institutions.

Acting Deputy Minister Bernie Doyle, the Board's strongest advocate within government, had left the province following the appointment of Deputy Minister Jane Fulton. Shirley McClellan was under siege as a result of health cuts and her hope for a "good-news story" in mental health reform was fast fading. McClellan had been under fire for months, and Premier Klein seemed to be increasingly concerned about the public's fear of the broader health-reform agenda.

Physicians across the province, including several psychiatrists at the Alberta Hospital, Edmonton, were mounting an aggressive campaign against the reforms. The Edmonton psychiatrists claimed to support community programs and treatment in general hospitals, but they also wanted to maintain a segregated hospital. They argued that segregation provided special benefits, such as more psychiatric expertise, research, and a quiet rural atmosphere. In other words, the benefits of "asylum."

One of the hospital's most outspoken advocates was Dr. Brian Bishop, a man obviously highly regarded by colleagues and by family members of patients with chronic illnesses such as schizophrenia. His dedication extended from working smoky fundraiser casinos to helping the Schizophrenia Society grow. Dr. Bishop's view of the future of psychiatry seemed more balanced than that of many of his colleagues in the hospital, and he made passionate arguments in favour of improved community services, especially housing. But Bishop had worked at the hospital since 1976 and while he wanted community improvements, he too wanted to protect the mental-hospital system.

Dr. Bishop and many other psychiatrists at the Alberta Hospital Edmonton feared the Mental Health Board would reduce beds prematurely, or worse, close most of the Edmonton hospital. The board's message of downsizing only after the community services had been developed was either poorly delivered by the board or perhaps disbelieved because of the Board's short time frame, or perhaps because of rumours that the board and not the minister, wished to maintain only one hospital at Ponoka. Whatever their reasons, the doctors missed few opportunities to assault the Board's downsizing plans "of up to 50 per cent," and the Schizophrenia Society would provide a great opportunity.

On a Saturday morning in May 1996, Dr. Brian Bishop leveled a major assault on Alberta's treatment of the mentally ill at the society's annual meeting. His speech was well-prepared and emotionally delivered. The families in attendance knew what it was like to have their adult children discharged from the hospital and abandoned to the street. They also knew how difficult getting admitted could be. They loved Bishop for "calling it as it is," and he received a standing ovation.

In his address, Bishop declared "they're going around in circles." He condemned the conditions in mental hospitals, calling them "cuckoo's-nest situations" in "medieval facilities." The solution, according to Bishop, was more acute-care beds and community programs. The implication was that rebuilding the mental hospitals was a big part of the answer to Alberta's problems. From the perspective of hospital staff, Bishop had raised all the right issues, in circumstances where there was no opportunity for clarification or rebuttal. Mental Health Board representatives in attendance could, of course, not have explained their attempts to protect the Edmonton facility and in the process try to maintain the momentum for new community programs. That would have implicated the minister.

The following morning, the front page of *The Edmonton Journal* screamed Bishop's message: "Frustrated Psychiatrist Set to Quit" and "System Abuses Mentally Ill." A shortage of acute-care beds was forcing medical staff to "play chicken with people's lives." Board Chairman Simmons was now totally frustrated. "What about the impact of the $13.5 million the Mental Health Board is putting into new community-based services?" he grumbled. "What about the fact that Edmonton is served by 226 acute care psychiatric beds, while Calgary, with a similar population, has only 170? What about the fact that more than 40 physicians and psychiatrists provided medical services to 400 patients in Edmonton, while at Ponoka only six physicians, most without psychiatric qualifications, served 350 patients?"

Simmons agreed with the need for beds, but beds in the local general hospitals, not in the centralized mental hospitals. And the message of eventual downsizing was again missed. Simmons rued the day the Board agreed to publicize a target of "up to 50 per cent" The business plan target had become the target for opponents.

The Cabinet shuffle of May 31, 1996 and the appointment of Halvar Jonson to the health portfolio, was, for Simmons, a dreaded but anti-climactic end to his hopes. Ministerial control was immediate. The board was ordered to refer all decisions to the minister, and all funding for new community programs was frozen. When he phoned the minister, Simmons was instructed to "arrange a meeting." He called Deputy Minister Jane Fulton and was told that "the new minister is fully supportive of the mental health reform agenda." The next day, Fulton was terminated and replaced by Jack Davis, a long-time civil servant known for his ability to deliver on ministerial wishes. Davis expressed no support for the board's reform agenda. Deputy ministers know what their ministers want.

Simmons booked what he knew would be a final meeting with Halvar Jonson. At the brief encounter, he tabled a list of priorities that he considered essential to the future well-being of Alberta's mentally ill and their families. Simmons had no expectation they would be considered. He also pleaded with the minister to meet with the full board in order to explain how his plans met with the government's published policy. Jonson was unresponsive. The board had been appointed until August, and those appointments would most certainly not be renewed. In Simmons' view, he and his Board had been fired. Jonson would make new appointments to a new "advisory" board reporting directly to the minister. Rebuilding of the Alberta Hospital at Ponoka would once again be high on the government's agenda.

In the end, Nancy (Betkowski) MacBeth left the Tory party, admitting, as had her mentor Peter Lougheed, that "in mental health we have unfortunately left some things undone." Minister McClellan moved to the Community Development portfolio, and Minister Jonson took firm control of the mental health agenda. Simmons went back to real estate and the solitude of Pincher Creek.

Alberta was about to go forward to the past.

References

Aikenhead, Sherri. "Suicides to be Studied by Health Department—Betkowski Criticized for not Meeting Needs," *The Edmonton Journal*, December 5, 1990.

Alberta Government. *The Rainbow Report: Our Vision for Health—Premier's Commission on Future Health Care for Albertans, Final Report.* Alberta: Government of Alberta, December 1989.

Alberta Health. *Mental Health Services in Alberta—Sharing a Vision of Better Health.* Alberta: Government of Alberta, November 1988.

Alberta Health. *Future Directions for Mental Health Services in Alberta.* Alberta: Government of Alberta, February 1992.

Alberta Health. *Working in Partnership: Building A Better Future for Mental Health—Final Report.* Alberta: Mental Health Strategic Planning Advisory Committee, Government of Alberta, August 1993.

Alberta Health. *Action Plan: Services for Mentally Ill Adults with Continuing Care Need.* Alberta: Government of Alberta, March 1994.

Anderson, Dennis. Edmonton, AB. Interview with author, 1998.

Anonymous. Civil servant—Interview with author, 1998.

Anonymous. Former Assistant Deputy Minister—Interview with author, 1998.

Anonymous. Former Alberta Hospital Ponoka Board member—Interview with author, 1998.

Canadian Mental Health Association—Alberta Division. *Mental Health Care: Revisiting the 1920s.* Alberta Division: The Canadian Mental Health Association, 1990.

Clarke Institute of Psychiatry, Health Systems Research

Unit. *Best Practices in Mental Health Reform: Discussion Paper.* Prepared for the Advisory Network on Mental Health 1997. Ottawa, Ontario: Health Canada, 1977.

Doyle, Bernie. Ottawa, ON. Interview with author, 1997.

Holley, H.L. *Inpatient Assessment Project*—Final Report. Alberta: Provincial Mental Health Board, March 1996.

Holley, H.L., Hodges, P. and Jeffers, B. "Moving Psychiatric Patients from Hospital to Community: Views of Patient, Providers, and Families," *Psychiatric Services,* 49(4), 1998.

Hopkins, Stephen. "Medicine for a Sick System— Minister Betkowski Stands Firm as a Money Squeeze Hits Hospitals," *Alberta Report*, October 5, 1990.

Ivany, Randall. Ministerial Order re: Alberta Hospital, Edmonton—Patient Abuse. Alberta: Government of Alberta—Ombudsman for Alberta, 1982.

LaJeunesse, Ron. Edmonton, AB. Personal papers. 1996.

Lisac, Mark. *The Klein Revolution.* Edmonton: NuWest Publishers, 1995.

Mental Health Reform in Alberta. Town of Ponoka. Undated.

"Mental Health Reform in Alberta: Evolution not Revolution"—A submission to the Honorable Ralph Klein, Premier of Alberta and the Honorable Halvar Jonson, Minister of Health. Ponoka: The Town of Ponoka Ad-Hoc Committee for Mental Health. Undated.

Nasir, Haroon. "A Move Towards Community-based Services." Paper prepared for the Alberta Mental Health Strategic Planning Initiative. Alberta: Mental Health Division, Alberta Health, July 1993.

Provincial Mental Health Board. 1995—1996 Annual Report. May, 1996.

Provincial Mental Health Board. Building a Better Future—A Community Approach to Mental Health. Alberta: Provincial Mental Health Board, March 1995.

Provincial Mental Health Board. *The Road to a Better Future.* Alberta: Provincial Mental Health Board, November 1995.

Rockliff Partnership Architects Planners. "Decisions for Mental Health." Consultant's report to the Government of Alberta. Ontario: Rockliff Partnership Architects Planners, September 1976.

Sherlock, Karen. "Treating the Mentally Ill: When Hope Seems to be Out of Reach—Dozens of Mentally Ill Live in the Inner City and They're Just Not Getting the Help They Need," *The Edmonton Journal,* October 14, 1990.

Sherlock, Karen. "Bed Shortage Cost Woman her Life— 29 Beds Cut over 18 Months," *The Edmonton Journal,* December 5, 1990.

Simmons, Craig. Pincher Creek, AB.—Interview with author, 1998

"Special Report of the Ombudsman for Alberta re: Grant Lee Phillips." Alberta: Government of Alberta— Ombudsman for Alberta, February 1983.

Chapter 15
Delusions of Progress

Chapter 15
Delusions of Progress

Delusions of Progress

1998

It was a 75th anniversary celebration. Inside the hospital auditorium, a collection of dignitaries, staff, former staff, and a few patients gathered to celebrate Alberta Hospital Edmonton's anniversary. Edmonton weather had been beautiful for weeks, and the day's activities were scheduled for out-of-doors. But the weather didn't cooperate and many of the events were canceled or were poorly attended.

A small crowd took seats in the Dorran Auditorium; the number of vacant seats left organizers looking uncomfortable. The master of ceremonies introduced the head table, which included a patient, a staff member, some of the government's Mental Health Advisory Board officials, and a collection of politicians from all levels of government. "I bet we have to listen to them all," whispered an elderly patient to the young nurse at his side. He was almost right.

One after another, the dignitaries spoke in glowing terms of the hospital's 75-year history and its contribution to mental health care in Alberta. The final presentation from Health Minister Halvar Jonson was to be the highlight of the event and many in the audience hoped for some announcement reviving the institution's 10-year-old rebuilding plan that had stalled under former Health Minister Betkowski.

They were to be disappointed. The Minister's speech was upstaged by a capable and somewhat emotional speech by a former patient who thanked the hospital staff for her recovery. And Jonson had no specifics to announce anyway. He concluded his comments with a wish that the hospital would provide "another 75 years of dedicated service." While other provincial health ministers across Canada were downsizing or closing mental hospitals in favour of community care and smaller local hospitals, Jonson was rebuilding the Ponoka hospital. He was also wishing the Edmonton hospital staff best wishes for another 75 years—ostensibly in the same buildings.

A senior psychiatrist at the ceremony muttered that the minister's wishes were "hollow." Construction at the Ponoka hospital, although not formally announced, was soon to begin and plans for the Alberta Hospital Edmonton were once again "under review." Staff at the Edmonton hospital had watched the Mental Health Advisory Board under Jonson consolidate its administrative functions in Ponoka, and they feared the Ponoka hospital would soon be the only major psychiatric hospital in Alberta, as it had been prior to 1956. They continued to live with anxiety about their future, but it was nothing new—this uncertainty had been part of the hospital's culture since the early 1960s.

Following the obligatory reception with snacks and drinks, a few people walked to a makeshift museum in the old Number One building, the hospital's very first structure. Built in 1922, it was, quite amazingly, still in regular use. Volunteers and staff had worked hard to collect and display various paraphernalia, writings, and reports from the hospital's early days. It had been a history that swung from commendation to controversy, from caring to callousness. Thirteen years before the Edmonton celebration, the Ponoka hospital had held a similar 75th Anniversary event. The staff produced a commemorative book entitled A History of Dedication and Caring. For some, such as Julius Johnson, the principal author of the book and a former head nurse, that had certainly been the case. But that history of dedication and caring in truth carried some unwritten and disturbing chapters.

The almost 80 - year-old #1 building no longer houses patients but remains in use at Alberta Hospital Edmonton. (Photo courtesy CMHA)

Still, things had improved in both hospitals over the years. Staff were better trained now, more doctors were employed, some buildings had been modernized, and a few relatively new buildings, such as the forensic unit in Edmonton and the brain injury unit in Ponoka, provided patients with a modern standard of accommodation. In addition to the institutions, the psychiatric units in general hospitals provided a range of programs in relatively new facilities. The number of beds in those general hospitals had grown to more than 510 province-wide, with 76 of them serving youth. There were 64 full-time mental health clinics and another 26 "satellite" travelling clinics dotting the province and an array of nonprofit agencies provided programs ranging from housing to crisis intervention.

About 275 psychiatrists served the province, most in private practice. And the majority of the more than 4,800 physicians in Alberta provided mental health treatment. In fact, they billed the government's health plan for more than $80 million every year for mental health-related services. More than 1,200 psychologists and almost 300 social workers were registered with professional associations. They served people who received assistance from the Department of Family Services or who had private health plans or money. Many of these professionals were capable of providing counseling and psychotherapy, and an increasing number was going into private practice. New medications, new treatment techniques and emerging technologies like "brain-mapping" made a huge difference in treatment results. And ongoing research provided even more hope for the future.

Throughout Alberta's history, there have been many heroes who made a contribution to these improvements—people like Clare Hincks, Randall MacLean, Buck Blair, and Peter Lougheed. But the man perhaps more responsible than any other since the mid-seventies could still be found late in the day or, for that matter, early on Christmas morning, in his office at the University Hospital in Edmonton. Dr. Roger Bland, who served as Professor and Chair of the University's Department of Psychiatry in the Faculty of Medicine, and Regional Clinical Director for Mental Health in the Capital Health Authority, first came to Alberta as a student in 1967 from Barnsley, England.

With a medical degree from the University of Liverpool, Roger Bland, with his wife and two daughters in tow, began a search for opportunities in the "frozen north." His first job got them to the frozen north, all right, but he remained unsure about the "opportunity" part, as he worked for several years as a general practitioner in Flin Flon, Manitoba. Neither the climate, the isolation, nor the practice were quite what he had fantasized, and it would not be long before he moved his family slightly south and west to Edmonton. The reputation of the medical school at the University of Alberta made it a very attractive destination for both work and study.

Bland laboured as a resident in psychiatry at the University Hospital, a medical officer at the Alberta Hospital Edmonton, and as staff physician at the Provincial Guidance Clinic in Edmonton. He was immediately popular with professors and staff, who saw him as exceptionally bright and supportive. He was approachable and his patients soon learned that they were his top priority. Splitting his time between three work sites also gave Bland a rounded introduction to psychiatry in traditional institutions, general hospitals, and community clinics.

But skilled therapists rarely remain in front-line jobs for long. Almost immediately after obtaining his Canadian Fellowship in Psychiatry in 1971, Bland was appointed clinical director at the Alberta Hospital in Edmonton. Dr. Charles Hellon, a man for whom Bland had great admiration, had been appointed medical superintendent of the hospital in 1969, and Bland looked forward to working with him. Hellon had been an assistant professor at the University of Alberta and was a team member on Dr. Blair's study of northern Alberta.

Hellon was a strong advocate of community care and had proposed downsizing the mental hospitals by moving geriatric patients to long-term care facilities and alcoholics to the general hospitals. As for the Alberta Hospital Edmonton, Hellon pursued improvements that would lead to its first accreditation with the Canadian Hospital Accreditation Council. His plan of action included the appointment of a professional administrator, restructuring the units into areas of specialty, opening additional outpatient units and "approved homes," and implementing a system of community psychiatric nurses.

Hellon also introduced new psychological treatments like behaviour modification and aversion therapy, and greater use was being made of technology for purposes such as studying brain wave patterns. Occupational therapy was expanded, a sheltered workshop was introduced and a new academic program was begun for the young patients with visiting teachers from the Edmonton Public School system.

Hellon was a good mentor and Bland observed carefully when working with him, first as a resident physician and later as his clinical director. In 1971, following the election of Lougheed's Conservatives, Hellon was promoted to the position of Mental Health Advisor to government; he was promoted again in 1972, this time to the directorship of the Mental Health Division. In that same year, Roger Bland, only 35 years of age, moved to the Ponoka Hospital to become its medical superintendent.

The new superintendent's plan for the future was to have the hospital play a reduced role in the province, serving primarily as an inpatient facility for the central region of Alberta while community-based programs were being developed and expanded. Bland copied most of Hellon's innovations, and the nursing staff responded positively to his presence. "It was like a breath of fresh air hit the place," reported a senior nurse. "He made an impact; he was young."

Some of the medical staff were not so impressed. Their comments about Bland were sometimes nasty, and nurses overheard physicians declaring that they "would never take orders from this young twerp." But Bland was convinced he could win them over. When he started at the Edmonton hospital, the doctors had been described to Bland as "middle-aged, Middle European, refugee physicians whom one could expect to be 'sticks-in-the-mud.'" In the end, he found they had been misjudged. He was to have a similar experience at Ponoka. "They were," he admitted, "a group of people who helped me enormously." The young psychiatrist was admired for his vision and administrative skills, but even more highly respected for his commitment to the patients. He would always make time to see the hospital's sickest patients, adjust medication, try new treatments—and he rarely gave up hope.

The patient count had been dropping for years, but the staff viewed Dr. Bland as a true advocate of the Blair report in that he wanted to ensure that the discharged patients had support services in the community. It was a challenge to find proper community placements throughout the south, but during his three years at the hospital, the patient count dropped from 613 to just over 400. There were bad placements, however and staff brought back "some terrible reports." Bland would have to fix that by working in the community.

In 1976, Bland left the hospital to take on responsibilities as the regional director of Edmonton's community mental health clinics, where he continued to work closely with Hellon. In addition to streamlining clinic services and organizing a more closely integrated program of follow-up with the institutions, he began to learn the complexities of working in large bureaucracies with politicians. Hellon had been fortunate to work for Neil Crawford and Helen Hunley, both ministers who, according to Bland, were "well-intentioned people" who "listened well," wanted to make changes, and wanted to "do it right."

In 1979, Hellon resigned. His move coincided with the appointment of Bob Bogle as Minister of Social Services and Community Health along with the transfer of the mental hospitals to his department from the department of Hospitals and Medical Care. It also coincided with the selection of John Forrester as the first director of the Mental Health Division who was not a psychiatrist. The premier, Peter Lougheed, was also receiving a national award from the Canadian Mental Health Association at about this time—just as Alberta's mental health system was beginning to be swamped by population growth and inadequate resources.

A 1980 report commissioned by a group calling itself the Edmonton Hospitals Psychiatric Studies Committee concluded that throughout northern Alberta the "need for an improved psychiatric service was pressing." Known as the *McKinsey Report* in honour of its authors, Toronto consultants McKinsey and Company, it described an expected Alberta population growth "boom" of up to 40 per cent and warned that programs were already experiencing "lean resourcing" and "fragmented care." The report made 78 recommendations relating to finances, personnel recruitment, and the coordination of services "as near as possible to the population they serve."

Services for children, the report stressed, are "seriously inadequate." It suggested a 10-per-cent incidence of mental illness among children but estimated that "only 2.6 per cent are being served." There were too few hospital beds, too few residential beds, and too few child psychiatrists. Consultations were difficult to get, and only the most severely ill children found help. Early intervention and treatment were rare. What did exist was poorly coordinated and no one had taken a lead role. The recommendations included expanding beds, outpatient clinics, and day hospitals to provide long-term stays for children who needed specialized schooling and therapy. An entire section dealt with the need for "increased coordination and integration." If the government successfully implemented the recommendations, it concluded, the result would simply "provide a service that is at least adequate compared to the standard of care provided elsewhere in Canada."

Two years later, a Calgary group called the Southern Alberta Psychiatric Services Committee contracted with Toronto's Clarke Institute to study "needs and provisions" in the south. Like the *McKinsey Report*, the recommendations, which numbered 58, proposed ways to increase resources, recruit personnel, and coordinate programs regionally. Also, as in the *McKinsey Report*, the population was projected to increase by up to 40 per cent and the need for growth in services was considered to be "urgent." Furthermore, the Ponoka hospital was not to be considered a major resource in southern Alberta. The Clarke Report observed that "for at least three decades, the literature has abounded with incontrovertible evidence pointing to the failures of mental hospitals the world over to achieve the objectives of programming." Instead, it concluded, "they lead to increased chronicity, debasement of human dignity, dependency, separation from families, and even squalor and suffering."

But children were the major priority. There was "no planning or cohesion," child psychiatrists were desperately needed, and there were too few resources. There was, in short, no system. The report made 14 child-related recommendations that paralleled those made by McKinsey for northern Alberta.

Most of the recommendations were aimed at the Department of Social Services and Community Health, but neither Minister Bogle nor his Deputy Minister Catherine Arthur appeared very interested. According to Bland, mental health staff were frustrated by what they saw as "disinterest, micro-management, and political intervention." The minister showed some creativity in his support for new research and for the development of an innovative suicide-prevention program, but overall planning seemed impossible.

Funds were rarely available for new services and when they were, they had to be "doled out in the form of grants" rather than contracts. The minister, according to Bland, wanted to personally deliver the grants to the recipients (with no clear expectations or standards) in order to ensure maximum public exposure. Evaluation and control by government administrators was considered difficult. Although he was well aware of the department's problems, Bland accepted a joint appointment as the Mental Health Division's part-time director, with Mr. Dennis Barr serving as his associate. The co-directors spent their first year "trying to keep the mental health division alive." They were, Bland said, "constantly fighting a rear-guard action."

In 1982, Bland's ability to deliver services "improved substantially" when Dr. Neil Webber was appointed minister. Webber inherited a mess, according to Bland, "but he attacked it with integrity and hard work." He was also cautious. An intellectual man, Webber wanted to weigh and consider all action. And the province was once again in financial difficulty. Rapid population growth and reduced oil and gas royalties, coupled with high inflation and double-digit interest rates, were hammering the economy. Solutions that cost money were hard to sell to the Treasury Board. Webber, Bland, and Barr persevered.

Some controversies continued, particularly around the lack of services for troubled youth, Aboriginal peoples, and the chronically ill, many of who were in jail for lack of alternatives. Nonetheless, the psychiatrist and politician working together made some gains. Institutional beds continued to be reduced as community-service budgets were expanded. Mental health clinics set clear goals and maintained better computerized records, integration with the mental-hospital community services was improved, psychiatric units were expanded in general hospitals, community agencies were funded to take on expanded roles, and more research was initiated and funded.

Overall, the improvement in services was significant. By the time Dr. Bland left the government in 1989, a newcomer to the province would have seen quite an array of programs and services including long-term care hospitals, psychiatric units, clinics, clubs, socialization programs, self-help groups, crisis services, housing programs, and even a few outreach services. Priority was given to providing urgent services to the sickest, but there was still no "system" of integrated care for children or adults.

One of Bland's last initiatives with the Mental Health Division was to begin a strategic planning process that he hoped would create an overall provincial system. The effort would ultimately lead to Health Minister Nancy Betkowski's commitment to mental health reform. The process was one that Bland would watch carefully and attempt to influence subtly from the University of Alberta. He had maintained a position with the University Hospital since graduation and in spite of other responsibilities, worked there full-time after leaving the Ponoka hospital.

Bland's work as physician, educator, researcher, and administrator was supplemented by community service with a range of community organizations. He provided advice to the Schizophrenia Society, the Depressive Disorders Society, and the Canadian Mental Health Association. He was also a favoured speaker at the self-help group, Unsung Heroes, where he made himself available to discuss topics as varied as medication and personal hygiene.

The psychiatrist understood the value of consumer and family initiatives as part of a comprehensive service. He also understood the need for programs in the community, programs managed at the local level. The strategic-planning process he started in hopes of spawning true "systems" reform had been built on the research literature. One of the most influential documents was a report published by the national office of the Canadian Mental Health Association in 1984 entitled A Framework for Support. The report described the "community resource base" necessary to maintain mentally ill people outside of institutions. The model saw families, professionals, government and community agencies, and consumers themselves as having equal roles to play. The base of success in the community, the study professed, was "income, homes, friendship, and recreation." People who had viewed mental health services as meaning only doctors and hospitals were encouraged to begin seeing things differently.

But Bland's hope for a comprehensive "system" of care was now in jeopardy. Health Minister Halvar Jonson would abandon the vision built on the directions recommended in many previous government reports, including Bland's 1988 Cabinet-approved report entitled

Mental Health Services in Alberta, more widely known as the "peach and teal" report for the colour of its pages. A second significant report, a 1997 federal study on "Best Practices," initiated by New Brunswick and Alberta, described the cornerstones of mental health reform. It included "correcting the historic imbalance between institutional and community programs, offering comprehensive services and transferring governance to the local level"— precisely the same recommendations as in "peach and teal."

The federal study described a total of 29 best practices, summarized in a table of core programs and system strategies. The Government of Alberta, through its Mental Health Advisory Board, would respond partially to only nine of the critical strategies. The new board was now planning to rebuild the institutions; virtually ignore the critical determinants of health such as housing, work, and recreation; and continue governing most programs on a provincial basis.

Fearing the Mental Health Board's emphasis on institutions and its potential rejection of best practices, the Canadian Mental Health Association published and widely promoted a report entitled *Mental Health Care at the Crossroads*. The publication provided a history of the government's aborted reform initiative from the early 1990s and made six "common-sense recommendations" to get the plan back on track.

Major stakeholders like the Consumer Network, the Schizophrenia Society, the Alberta Psychiatric Association, the Psychologists' Association of Alberta, and even the Psychiatric Nurses' Association of Alberta, expressed support. It was a gutsy and ethical move for the nurses, most of whom worked in the large mental health hospitals, as the report spoke to eventual "downsizing" of those hospitals and transferring the money to inpatient services in regional hospitals.

Although the report recommended transferring services to the regional health authorities, only the board of the Palliser Health Authority in Medicine Hat provided a formal endorsement. Others conveyed informal support, with some of them expressing fear for retribution from the health minister. The Mental Health Advisory Board's response to the recommendations was a simple brush-off: "There are a number of areas where we agree, on other issues there are some differences." There was no explanation as to what the issues were, nor any apparent consideration of change.

While most advocates and many mental health professionals were becoming increasingly discouraged, the frustration was much more intense for the "consumers" who were living with the deficiencies daily. In frustration, several of them wrote an article entitled the "20 per cent Solution," which was published in the consumer newsletter CCN News.

A hard-hitting satire in the form of a parable, the column began: "Once upon a time there was a land overflowing with natural wealth. . . . The ruler appeared to be, on the surface at least, a jovial and caring character." The story went on to describe the premier's appointment of a "good witch," former Health Minister Shirley McClellan, who had the task of looking after the health of the population. The parable then identified the one in five Albertans who will suffer a mental illness, thereby noting the witch's responsibility for the "20 per cent of the population who had very specific needs," with only a "tiny portion of her resources to meet these needs." Then the premier replaced the "Good Witch" with an "Evil Warlock."

The parable wove a story about Health Minister Jonson's elimination of the original Alberta Mental Health Board ("kill the sages') along with the board's plans to re-build the mental hospitals, which the article derided as "Resource-Eating Monsters." The plan, the parable said, "brought more hardship and pain than had ever been known by the 20 per cent." The 80 per cent would "support and praise" the endeavors, according to the authors, whilst the 20 per cent continued to suffer and die. "The action became known as the 20 per cent Solution."

Few, if any, really seemed to believe there was a conspiracy by government to harm people with a mental illness, but the article was symptomatic of consumer frustration and their felt need to use sensationalism in order to make a point. The authors were also wrong about the 80 per cent of the population who would "support and praise" any plan that would perpetuate hardship and pain for troubled people. In fact, consumer wishes were beginning to be supported by professionals and others as never before in history.

In early 1998, members of the Consumer Network joined with the Alberta Psychiatric Association, the Calgary Health Authority, the Schizophrenia Society, and the Canadian Mental Health Association in order to appear before the government's powerful Standing Policy Committee on Health Planning. The group presented a unified position appealing for a system of services on a regional basis, along with improved funding to compensate for the minister's decision to leave 70 per cent of the currently available funds in mental health hospitals. At the conclusion of their presentation, only one brief question was asked of the group. The health minister said nothing and even the MLAs who had expressed private support of the group's concerns sat in silence.

Then in December of 1998, the government's own "watchdog," the Provincial Health Council, issued a scathing report critical of the fragmentation, the lack of a "whole life focus," the "confusion of roles" and the insufficient money in mental health services. Children were particularly at risk, the council warned. Funding was considered "minimally sufficient to cover treatment of crisis situations only." The Council had found that there were lengthy waiting lists, "transitional issues for children moving from children to adult services," little emphasis on prevention and early intervention, and no clear mandate. "It is not clear," they said, "just who is responsible for the provision of children's mental health services."

The report was a courageous move for a group of political appointees, almost all active Conservatives and supporters of the Klein government. But they were also sufficiently concerned. The chair, Mayor Gail Surkan from Red Deer, had attended the inaugural conference of the Consumer Network and shown great interest in their cause. But the report wasn't released until just before Christmas, a common strategy when governments want to release a document with very little public attention. It was not until mid-January, when CMHA's president and former Conservative Cabinet minister Dennis Anderson prodded the media, that anyone even gave it a second thought.

When approached by reporters, Health Minister Jonson said he had "not yet seen the report," and Premier Klein dismissed it as "flawed" and out of date, though the Premier also admitted he had not read it. The premier said the council couldn't have been aware of his government's new "Alberta Children's Initiative," which would purportedly address the problems. The council, however, was fully aware of those plans and stood by its report anyway. Similar recommendations had been repeated in study after study for more than 30 years. The council indeed noted the announcement of the children's initiative and stated that it would "eagerly await the results." Over at the Provincial Mental Health Advisory Board, Chair Betty

Schoenhofer agreed to review the criticism and provide a response, perhaps "in two months."

The council had made some important observations. It also made a number of very specific recommendations that included the need for a shared vision and the development of a citizen-focused system to support consumers and their families. It recommended no new capital expenditures to rebuild the mental health hospitals until the "role of community versus that of institutional care can be adequately addressed." The council also advised that there should be no infusion of funds for new adult programs until a system could address the "fragmentation and lack of integration" that "probably results in inefficient use of resources." The only exception to the funding recommendation was for children's services, because "lack of investment in this area is a false economy." The problems in the area of children's mental health services were described as "critical."

The report then recommended that the mandate and membership of the Provincial Mental Health Advisory Board be changed to "reestablish its leadership role for mental health services." Services should be transferred to the regional health authorities and ultimately the Mental Health Advisory Board's job should be limited to monitoring standards and performance measures.

The council noted that the original Mental Health Board's plan included transferring the institutions in Edmonton, Ponoka, and Claresholm to the Capital, David Thompson, and Headwaters Health authorities respectively. "This has now been taken off the table," council members observed. "It is not clear why." In conclusion, the self-professed "unbiased external observers of the mental health system" expressed the hope that their comments and recommendations would help to revitalize mental health reform in Alberta.

In stark contrast to these recommendations, the Mental Health Advisory Board restructured and eliminated the regional director's positions in favour of a more permanent corporate model with key individuals responsible for specific functions. The plan was a clear sign that the group was here to stay. Then in November, 1998, the new chief executive officer of the board appointed a new team of managers. CEO Don Schurman, a highly respected former administrator of the University of Alberta Hospital, announced the appointments of chief operating officers Janet Davidson, Sharon Read and

Mary Marshall, each of whom was capable and known to get results. Ken Sheehan would complete the senior team.

President Dennis Anderson of the CMHA expressed concern that the new management team could be "dangerous." Would the results of their efforts reflect what science and the community said was needed, or would it reflect what the minister wanted? Competent people working toward the wrong goals could indeed be dangerous and time would tell.

On March 11, 1999 Health Minister Halvar Jonson announced an infusion of $18.6 million for mental health services. Shortly thereafter, he formally announced that $95 million in capital funds would be spent on rebuilding the mental health hospital in Ponoka. Jonson was proving to be quite adept at getting government money and the problem for the advocates was how he planned to spend it.

Two weeks later, Jonson announced that the Provincial Mental Health Advisory Board would become the "Alberta Mental Health Board," effective April 1, 1999. There would be no new vision, no transfer of provincial programs and resources to the regional health authorities, no re-appraisal of the appropriate roles for institutions, no specific support for families and consumers and no significant change in the board's role, other than a responsibility to serve as "advocates." The only effect of the activism by community advocates was a blast of rhetoric from the health minister assuring

Unlike the Alberta Hospital Edmonton, the Alberta Hospital at Ponoka, experiences a controversial $95 million re-building in 2001. (Photo courtesy CMHA)

Albertans that "with the Alberta Mental Health Board, regional health authorities and community agencies working together as partners, we have the skills, resources and knowledge to improve conditions."

The politicians knew best. Not the recipients of the service and not their families, not the "special-interest groups," not the professionals. Even the mental health advisors in the health department had been decimated. In 1997, after 67 years of service, as Ken Sheehan had predicted 13 years earlier, the department's mental health branch was abolished.

In late 1999, Chief Executive Officer Don Shurman was advised that his contract with the Alberta Mental Health Board would not be renewed. The Board would search for yet another chief executive officer, the fifth in as many years. As Shurman planned his exit, so did Davidson, Read, Marshall and others. After a short search by the board, the new executive director's appointment came as no surprise to stakeholders. Ken Sheehan, a friend, neighbour, and confidante of Health Minister Jonson, assumed his responsibilities in early 2000, bringing with him an entirely new management team—many of them from the Ponoka hospital. Although the Alberta Mental Health Board had just released its Business Plan for 1999–2002 on January 25, 2000, work would begin anew on a plan that reflected the values of the new administration.

As Dr. Roger Bland completed his two terms as chair of the university department in 2001, he could only concede incremental gains during his career. " I have no delusions of progress," he said. In spite of his accomplishments, services were still far from ideal. As to his place in history, he didn't think it important. It's what keeps happening to people with mental illnesses that mattered, and the physician had experienced more than his share of both hope and disappointment. Some of Bland's colleagues called him a cynic because of his persistent negative view of the future. As he looked back on his 32 years in psychiatry, administration, and government service, he concluded that he had "little faith in political promises." Bland, however, saw himself as a realist and not a cynic. While there were politicians who were "exceptions," he explained, "realists don't trust politicians. They have their own agendas."

References

Abercrombie, Sheila. *Alberta Hospital Edmonton 1923 to 1983—An Outline of History to Commemorate the 60th Anniversary.* Edmonton, Alberta: Alberta Hospital Edmonton, 1983.

Abt, Mary Frances McHugh. *Adaptive Change and Leadership in a Psychiatric Hospital.* Edmonton, Alberta: Ph.D. Thesis, University of Alberta, 1992.

Abt, Mary Frances McHugh. Ponoka, AB. Interview with author, 1998.

Alberta Mental Health Board. Business Plan, 1999-2002. January 25, 2000.

Anonymous. Civil servant—Interview with author, 1998.

Bland, Roger. Edmonton, AB. Interview with author, 1998.

Barr, Dennis. Edmonton, AB. Interview with author, 1988.

Canadian Mental Health Association. *Mental Health Care at the Crossroads.* April, 1997.

Carling, Paul J. *Return to Community: Building Support Systems for People with Psychiatric Disabilities.* New York: The Guilford Press, 1995.

Clarke Institute of Psychiatry, Health Systems Research Unit. *Best Practices in Mental Health Reform: Discussion Paper.* Prepared for the Advisory Network on Mental Health 1997. Ottawa, Ontario: Health Canada, 1997.

Clarke Institute of Psychiatry Consulting Group. *Southern Alberta Study of Psychiatric Needs and Provisions.* Commissioned by the Southern Alberta Psychiatric Services Committee. Toronto: Clarke Institute of Psychiatry, January 1983.

Cunningham, Jim. "Provincial Council Report: Province "Urged to Clarify Mental Health Responsibility," *The Calgary Herald*, January 14, 1999.

Fewster, Gerry. *Expanding the Circle: A Community Approach to Children's Mental Health*. Alberta Children's Mental Health Project. Alberta: Department of Social Services and Community Health, Government of Alberta, 1986.

Jenkins, Jonathan. "Klein Rejects Mental Health Care Critique," *The Edmonton Sun*, January 14, 1999.

Johnson, J.O., *et. al. A History of Dedication and Caring 1911-1986*. Ponoka: Alberta Hospital Ponoka, 1986.

Johnson, J.O. Ponoka, AB. Interview with author, 1998.

Johnsrude, Larry. "Improvement Ignored, Klein Says— Recent Children's Initiative Not Given its Due in Report, Premier Says," *The Edmonton Journal*, January 14, 1999.

LaJeunesse, Ron. Edmonton, AB. Personal papers. 2000.

Lisac, Mark. *The Klein Revolution*. Edmonton: NuWest Publishers, 1995.

Lisac, Mark. "Mental Health System Seems Sick Itself— Strange Actions by Government's Own Council Indicative," *The Edmonton Journal*, January 14, 1999.

Leibovici, Karen. *Alberta Hansard*. November, 1999.

Lothian, Jason. " Cash infusion into Alberta Hospital Ponoka wasteful." *Lethbridge Herald*. February 14, 2000.

McKinsey and Company. "The Challenge for Psychiatric Care in Edmonton and Northern Alberta: An Action Program for the 1980s." Edmonton, AB: Edmonton Hospitals Psychiatric Study Committee, Final Report, 1980.

MacBeth, Nancy. Edmonton, AB. Conversation with author. August, 2001.

Ministerial Order. Alberta Health and Wellness. Legal and Legislative Services. MOU # 92/2001. 2001.

National Health and Welfare. *Mental Health for Canadians.* Ottawa: Government of Canada, 1988.

Pedersen, Rick and Struzik, Ed. "Mental Health System Needs More Money, Beds—Report," *The Edmonton Journal*, January 14, 1999.

Provincial Health Council of Alberta. *Mental Health in Alberta—Issues and Recommendations.* Government of Alberta, December 1998.

Ross, Ken. Mental Health in the 21st Century Challenges and Opportunities—Address to the Canadian Psychiatric Association. Chateau Carier Aylmer, Quebec, Friday, August 14, 1998.

Rusnell, Charles. "Mental Health Board Drops Crisis Intervention Team—Service Centralized in Policy Reversal," *The Edmonton Journal*, December 23, 1998.

Struzik, Ed. "A Tireless Advocate for the Mentally Ill— Dr. Roger Bland Speaks Up for Those Who Cannot Speak *for Themselves," The Edmonton Journal*, October 5, 1998.

Struzik, Ed. "Mental Health Care in Disarray: Services Fragmented—Report," *The Edmonton Journal*, January 13, 1999.

Sypher, Lou and A. Farse D.A. "The 20% Solution," *CCN News*. Calgary, Alberta: Calgary Mental Health Consumers' Network Society, 1997.

Trainor, J. and Church, K. *A Framework for Support.* Toronto: Canadian Mental Health Association, 1984.

Trainor, J., Pomeroy, E. and Pape, B. *A New Framework for Support.* Toronto: Canadian Mental Health Association, 1993.

Tyhurst, *et. al. More for the Mind.* Toronto: Canadian Mental Health Association, 1963.

Chapter 16
The Honourables

Chapter 16
The Honourables

The Honourables

2001

"I must find things acceptable to my colleagues." It was a warm July day in the year 2001 and the Honourable Gary Mar, Minister of Health and Wellness, was dressed casually as he sat in his legislative offices. Mar was reflecting on proposals from a new coalition of mental health organizations, the Alberta Alliance on Mental Illness and Mental Health (AAMIMH). The group had recommended expanded community services, decentralized mental health programs through Alberta's regional health authorities, and a new role for the Alberta Mental Health Board (AMHB).

The Minister acknowledged that since his appointment he had heard "from many individuals who are concerned about mental health services in the province." The issues were "consistent," he acknowledged, with most people concerned with the "the lack of coordination and integration of services between the Alberta Mental Health Board, regional health authorities, Alberta Justice, Alberta Children's Services, and other organizations." Gary Mar appeared to be supportive of the AAMIMH recommendations, but he was careful to avoid being explicit about what he might do." I know what needs to be done," he said, "but I must find things acceptable to my colleagues." He didn't seem at all confident he could get it.

Appointed in June of 2000 as Minister of Health and Wellness, Gary Mar inherited a mental health service that was under heavy criticism from stakeholder groups representing professionals, family members, consumers, and advocates alike. Mar's predecessor, the Honourable Halvar Jonson, MLA for Ponoka/Rimbey, had taken a strong and personal interest in the mental health agenda, but from the perspective of the stakeholders, he had done it wrong.

Alberta had a "non-system" of mental health care, they said. In spite of pouring millions of new dollars into the Mental Health Board's operations, the "psycho-social supports" available to the most seriously ill people living in the community remained desperately inadequate. A further problem, which took away from the smooth operation and coordination of services in each community, was the Mental Health Board's central management of a wide range of "provincial programs" administratively separate from the regional health authorities.

The 17 regional authorities ran the general-hospital psychiatric units and some crisis centres and outpatient programs. Although some regions made efforts to make "joint appointments" of senior staff, authority and responsibility for community-based programs and services remained confusing at best. The original scheme, when the first Provincial Mental Health Board was formed, called for the divestment of the Board's services to the local health authorities by 1997. But not one of the health authorities was yet in charge.

In addition, the Alberta Hospital at Ponoka, in Jonson's riding, was being re-built at a cost of $95 million—without "any definition of its role in a contemporary mental health system," said the Alberta Alliance on Mental Illness and Mental Health. The situation seemed to become further aggravated in January, 2000 when Ken Sheehan was appointed CEO of the board. Sheehan was well-known to stakeholder organizations who saw him as "pro-institution," and "non-consultative" in his work. He also seemed to have a strong personal commitment to Health Minister Jonson's agenda.

The new minister, Gary Mar, had been asked to change all that, but former Health Minister Jonson was Mar's senior in Cabinet, and Jonson had a reputation of being favoured by the premier. Mar, however, had great respect for Premier Klein and some MLAs believed Mar's influence was growing. But the AAMIMH members feared that Jonson was still very much in charge of the mental health agenda, although by protocol, when re-appointed, ministers tended to stay well away from any former department. The AAMIMH's concerns were certainly reinforced in September 2000 when the group presented its recommendations to the government's Standing Policy Committee on Health and Safe Communities. The powerful advisory group consisted of 13 government members, including both the Minister and Associate Minister of Health and Wellness. It did not include Halvar Jonson, who was then the Minister of the Environment.

Jonson did, however, attend the meeting and dominated the debate, attacking the views of the AAMIMH Chair, Dennis Anderson, a former Cabinet minister himself. Health Minister Mar rose and left the room, and while committee chair Janis Tarchuk tried to assure members that Mar was "called away," AAMIMH members were skeptical. In the end, the Alliance's request for support of their policy proposals was only "accepted as information." It appeared that Jonson's influence had carried the day. If Mar indeed planned to change directions, he was obviously in a "tough spot," said Anderson, who was now wearing a decidedly "different hat."

As the chair of the newly formed Alberta Alliance on Mental Illness and Mental Health, Anderson felt like he, too, was in a "tough spot." He had held three ministerial portfolios in previous Progressive Conservative governments, and he had worked with the premier, with Jonson and with dozens of other members of the legislature. Anderson's advocacy as a leading member of a mental health coalition was being interpreted by many as "anti-government." "Traitors," as was explained by one of the members of Cabinet, "are not appreciated by caucus." The member was cautioning Anderson as a "colleague and friend," but as a former member of the government, Anderson was particularly hurt by being viewed as a traitor. He did, though, seem to understand. "Defending your colleagues who seem to be under attack is natural," he reasoned, "and politicians have difficulty seeing you as only opposing one of the policy directions. They generalize and interpret your criticism as that of the whole government. They also take it personally."

Personal issues were what motivated Dennis Anderson to challenge the government's mental health policy in spite of the consequences that he described as "covert." "I certainly lost the respect of some people I valued, " he lamented, "and I probably lost opportunities— but I simply had to promote change."

Anderson said he came from a "dysfunctional family" where "the love that was in it wasn't shown." The "interpersonal skills were few," he said, and the family "dwelled on life's negative aspects." Young Dennis became convinced he was loved by no one except perhaps his animal friends. The pain was sometimes so severe he considered ending his life. Only the animals kept him alive.

Anderson left home at a young age and learned to "survive" and see the world "from a different perspective." He was recruited to a church where he was shown compassion and encouragement. Anderson began to develop a little confidence and he could see "some value in what I could give to others." A voracious reader and deep thinker, the young man settled on a "philosophy of life." It was simple enough in concept. "Do all you can do to change families and communities so that people don't experience the pain that I did; never betray anyone and never do work for money alone." At that young age, he convinced himself that the philosophy "fit well with politics." A life of political action was beginning to emerge.

It was now the early 1970s and Anderson began working with government and street agencies to help young people involved in the "drug culture." The work put him in contact with the Canadian Mental Health Association where his volunteer efforts taught him to be "ideal in your goals." The experience also provided him with opportunities to work with people who he described as "fighters." The encouragement he received in the CMHA bolstered his confidence some more and he decided he was ready to challenge a provincial Progressive Conservative nomination.

Anderson would, he thought, make "the world a better place" through politics. And his family would be "proud." He won the nomination and then was elected to the Alberta Legislature in 1979. The young politician was re-elected and then appointed to Cabinet in 1986. He was now the Honourable Dennis Anderson. His mother wondered why all the fuss. Dennis was only a politician and most anyone could do that! And as for "changing the world," that was also difficult in politics. While proud of his many achievements, like many politicians before and after him, Anderson found that "some things were possible, much was not."

Anderson never lost contact with the CMHA and continued to help them "behind the scenes," during his 14 years in the Legislature. When he retired from politics in 1994, he entered yet another contest at the ballot box and was elected to the CMHA's provincial board of directors. In 1998, he was elected president and chairman of the board.

Halvar Jonson had been appointed health minister two years earlier and the Canadian Mental Health Association was locked in an adversarial relationship with the government. The CMHA also seemed to be considered a threat by the government's Alberta Mental Health Board. Partnerships usually worked better than public conflict, but the Association had a long history of disputes with the MLA from Ponoka/Rimbey and efforts to have CMHA's concerns considered by the Board or by the ministry appeared to fall on deaf ears.

The Canadian Mental Health Association's executive director had also served as the chief executive officer of the Mental Health Board, and his return to CMHA following Jonson's appointment seemed to fuel the conflict. Several media reports, quoting the former CEO and other CMHA spokesmen, laid the responsibility for "stopping mental health reform," directly at Jonson's feet. Although the CMHA board of directors had approved of the public criticisms, the strategy seemed to be going nowhere. The board hoped that the election of a former minister in the Conservative government would open the communication lines and eventually improve the CMHA's influence with both the government and the Alberta Mental Health Board. A sort of "good cop, bad cop" approach.

Anderson's experience in government had taught him much. He proposed a "positive, supportive, and encouraging" relationship with Jonson and the Mental Health Board. It didn't work. The agenda had been set, and no one in government appeared to be listening. "We need to generate much broader support for our cause," challenged Anderson. The association had just published a policy paper *Mental Health Care at the Crossroads*, and while it had been endorsed by several community groups, they had "no ownership" of it and there was little follow-up action on their part. There was also no response from the government or its Mental Health Board. "We need to show more political support," said Anderson. Politicians have many demands, he explained, "and they will therefore take the path of least resistance."

273

The need to build this "resistance" and "political support," said the former minister, would require broad agreement on the policies that would be recommended to government. It would also need a groundswell of stakeholders. Their support, Anderson believed, would lead to support from the broader public and then from the politicians. The first step was to develop a consensus on the policies. In August, 1999, Anderson invited the president of almost every provincial consumer, family, professional and advocacy organization to a meeting in which he outlined his proposal to help get mental health reform back on the "political radar screen." The participants were interested.

The senior representatives of the Alberta Association of Registered Occupational Therapists; the Alberta Mental Health Self Help Network; the Alberta College of Social Workers; the Alberta Psychiatric Association; the Depression and Manic Depression Association of Alberta; the Psychologists' Association of Alberta; the Registered Psychiatric Nurses' Association of Alberta; the Schizophrenia Society of Alberta; and the Canadian Mental Health Association spent the next three months debating issues and setting priorities. A nursing association and a children's-services group participated in the initial stages but then pulled out, citing other priorities and fear of government retribution as their reasons.

274   Dozens of the government's own reports back to 1921 recommend no new mental hospitals, but rather emphasize treatment and support in people's home communities.

By late November of 1999, the coalition had approved a vision, mission, and objectives. They also endorsed a name, the "Alberta Alliance on Mental Illness and Mental Health" (AAMIMH). Initially known as the AAMIMH or "AMI," or the "Alliance," the group later expressed concern for the latter name, as the Canadian Alliance political party began to take root. But the Alliance was already developing an identity in the community and there was too much to do to worry about what was in a name. The group elected Anderson of the CMHA as chair and George Lucki of the

Psychologists' Association as vice-chair. They then publicly announced their formation at a news conference where they cautioned that the government was "heading towards a crisis in mental health care."

Minister Jonson agreed to a meeting and when the group attended a session of the Alberta Legislature, they were cordially "introduced to the House" by the minister. The relationship was strained but at least the group's concerns were being acknowledged. As for the Alberta Mental Health Board, chair Shoenhofer was less cordial as she expressed her anger about the "Alliance" criticism. The Board's CEO at that time, Don Shurman, responded quite differently. He tried to work with the Alliance. He was open, communicative and supportive of the coalition's intent, though he couldn't seem to influence his board and little concrete progress was made on the issues.

Then the Alliance completed its draft policy paper entitled *Good People, Good Practices, No System* and developed a "communication plan" in consultation with experts in the communications profession. The Alliance wanted to get a strong message to the public, but they also wanted to remain positive in their report, giving front-line professionals credit where credit was due, and acknowledging that there were many excellent programs. Unfortunately, there were also many deficiencies and the recommended communications plan was a bit less positive than originally planned. The group said it wanted to get the government's attention, and the consultant's advice was to gain media support first. The leaders in the group, many of whose organizations had members working for the government and its Mental Health Board, expressed some concern about a public attack. The issues, however, were critically important and after providing the minister with an advance copy of the Good People report, the coalition held a news conference.

On February 16 of the new millennium, newspapers across the province carried the coalition's message that the government needed to improve the community mental health system, open more acute-care beds in general hospitals, and define the role for mental hospitals in a modern context. In what was probably the first time in history, *The Edmonton Journal* published side-by-side pictures of the head of Alberta's psychiatrists and the head of the consumer/user movement supporting one another and saying precisely the same things. And the other professions, family members and advocates were all agreeing. While the Alliance was highly critical of adult services, they complimented the government on its recent emphasis on children's programs. Premier Klein and his wife Colleen had taken a personal interest in the problem and a wide range of innovations were being planned province-wide.

Health Minister Jonson responded publicly stating that the Alliance criticisms were "unfair." The staff at the Alberta Hospital in Ponoka, he said, do everything possible to provide a home-like setting. As for community programs, he claimed the government had been putting more money into them and the trend would continue. In the Legislature, Opposition health critic Karen Leibovici, a staunch supporter of mental health reform, asked why the Minister of Health was "spending the equivalent of 37 per cent of the mental health budget on the Ponoka hospital, which, coincidentally, is located in the Minister's riding." Jonson responded by saying that spending on community mental health services had increased by 100 per cent since 1993-94. He then extolled the virtues of the Ponoka hospital describing it as "one of the leading health authorities."

Two weeks later, the national board of the Canadian Mental Health Association issued a news release from Toronto. Headed "Alberta returns to dark ages of mental health care," the national association said the Klein government was "out of step with the rest of Canada." The attack on a provincial government by the national level of the CMHA had been unprecedented in more than 50 years. The reason for the decision, according to the national president, was that while other provinces were working at mental health reform by building "community capacity," Alberta was "reconstructing psychiatric hospitals." The CMHA said that the government's 1995 mental health business plan, developed under Minister Shirley McClellan, was "a cutting-edge model for the rest of Canada (but) the plan has collapsed under the weight of politics."

The public debate continued and the Alliance sent copies of their report to every Member of the Legislature in the province. The written material was then supplemented by phone calls and requests for meetings between politicians and Alliance member representatives at the local level. Many government MLAs responded positively, supporting the call for community services. They also defended the "balanced" plan of rebuilding the institutions. The premier described the Alliance proposals as "thoughtful" and comprehensive" but referred chair Dennis Anderson back to the Minister and to the Mental Health Board.

Media coverage was sporadic, but it continued. All of it was supportive of the Alliance position, except for *The Calgary Herald,* where an editorial writer took a supportive view of Jonson's plans. "Some people need to be in an institution because they don't do well outside one," the editorial opined. Since de-institutionalization, "we have become accustomed to encountering people in the community who are clearly 'different.'" Rebuilding Ponoka, said the editorial, seemed a "suitable solution to a sad problem." One Calgarian wrote an angry response, noting Ponoka was close to Edmonton, not Calgary. The editorial, he concluded, "completely breaks with any position the Herald has taken in the past." "How a Calgary newspaper could advocate aggravating a situation already patently unfair to Calgarians is beyond me."

A few weeks later, on April 1, an *Edmonton Journal* editorial asked, "Why no mental health plan?" The problem, the editorial said "was a philosophical one—a government that seems focused on institutional care rather than developing a comprehensive system of support to help the mentally ill to live in the community."

Only four days later, the Alberta Mental Health Board released its draft business plan for fiscal years 2000 to 2003. The plan had been developed with virtually no consultation with stakeholders. It committed $150 million to "replace existing inpatient facilities" and stipulated four goals and 17 vague strategies like, "continuing to support and encourage a collaborative relationship with regional, provincial and government stakeholders"; to "reduce risk variables for clients, families and service providers"; and to establish "strategic plans."

The Alliance members were highly critical of the "non-plan," noting concern with its contents and with what was not in the plan. The commitment to consumer and family involvement, along with new community services detailed in earlier plans, appeared to have been abandoned. At least the words were gone. The business plan also declared that "Changing the mental health system is an evolutionary process and, as such, an end model cannot nor should not be determined. The end model will continuously evolve," it went on to say, "based on the changing needs of consumers and social, economic and political trends." While hardly a business-planning model, the statement that programs would be based on "social, economic and political trends," was clearly a reflection of history and was, perhaps, "an objectionable but honest statement," said Alliance Vice-Chair George Lucki.

The business plan also seemed to move away from divesting services to the regional health authorities. The previous business plan to "complete service divestment by March of 1997" became, three years later—in the year 2000—a commitment to "determine the feasibility of transferring administration of community mental health services programs."

The Alliance members had met with representatives of the Mental Health Board before the public release of the business plan, and they had been given 48 hours to develop a response with recommendations for any changes. Although the coalition met the challenge, none of its proposals were evident when the final printed report was released two weeks later.

The coalition members then took their message to the regional health authorities, hoping they would support the Alliance recommendations. The presentations were well-received across the province, but no health authority seemed to want to go on record disagreeing with Minister Jonson.

Meeting with the deputy minister also appeared to go well, but there was no commitment to any attempt to influence the Minister. Meetings with Jonson himself went nowhere and an attempt to influence him through a meeting with the politicians on the Standing Policy Committee responsible for health appeared to have been blocked.

The members of the fledgling Alliance on Mental Illness and Mental Health were getting frustrated and tired, although some new organizations had joined their ranks and that seemed to bolster the mood. The new members included the Alberta Association for Community Living, the Alberta Committee of Citizens with Disabilities, Edmonton's Boyle Street Co-op and Edmonton City Centre Church Corporation, and even the government's own Premier's Council on the Status of Persons with Disabilities. All of the representatives carried full-time responsibilities outside of the coalition, and they needed more time and energy. In addition to the advocacy with government, the group had other ambitious plans. A public-information web site, research in order to develop an annual "report card" on reform progress and a vision for a major conference involving, for the first time in Alberta's history, all of the groupings of stakeholders interested in mental health care. The group was also trying to develop a policy position on how best to transfer services from the Mental Health Board.

In a bid for help, Alliance representatives approached the Edmonton-based Muttart Foundation. They found the foundation's Executive Director, Bob Wyatt, to have an extraordinary grasp of the issues, probably in part due to his former work with Ombudsman Randall Ivany. The foundation also had established, as a priority, the funding of community efforts designed to combine and coordinate the resources of the voluntary sector. The board of the foundation approved a grant of $105,000 over three years. Combined with contributions from the member organizations, the Alliance could now open an office and employ a professional secretariat, Dr. Haroon Nasir.

Then in June of 2000, the premier announced a Cabinet shuffle, appointing Gary Mar to Health and Wellness. In an unprecedented move, the Premier also replaced almost every senior manager in the Department of Health and Wellness. One of the officials transferred said the premier's office had taken direct control of the department in the wake of the "mishandling of *Bill 11*," the legislation dealing with government contracts with private health facilities.

Whatever the premier's motivation for moving Jonson, the relationship between the Alliance and the minister's office began to change almost immediately. The new minister appeared interested in the issues, his staff were cordial and responsive, and meetings were relatively easy to obtain. Even the Standing Policy Committee on Health now agreed to hear an Alliance presentation.

First elected in 1993 as MLA for Calgary Nose Creek, Gary G. Mar, an articulate young lawyer, rose through the political ranks quickly, serving, in turn, as Minister of Community Development, Minister of Education, and then Minister of the Environment. Mar was friendly and accommodating. He also seemed popular with his constituents, including the Calgary Chinese community where he served as a Director of the Sein Lok Society. The minister's assistants said he was focused on accomplishments and took pride in specific initiatives in each portfolio. A concern to the Alliance however, was the

Minister's alleged ambition. He was often mentioned as a possible successor to the premier. A few former colleagues in government advised chair Dennis Anderson that Mar was particularly adept at smoothing "troubled waters," but he was not inclined to advance unpopular issues. Mar also had many conservative values, such as accepting personal responsibility for one's lot in life. Coalition members had heard for years how people with mental illness needed only to "pull themselves up by their own bootstraps." The new minister had mused about charging for health care when problems were a consequence of lifestyle issues like smoking, excessive drinking and obesity. People did need to assume responsibility for their behaviours, and there were many things that individuals could do in order to protect their mental health, but the notion of personal responsibility for illness seemed to be a simple answer to complex problems caused by biological, psychological, and environmental factors.

None of the concerns about Mar materialized in either his words or actions. If he was ambitious, he also seemed willing to consider action on some of the tough issues. In his view, there were "three basic requirements" for mental health services. "First there must be local access to timely assessment, treatment, and follow-up," he said. Second, there must be community supports "including housing" to enable people to "live independently," and third there must be support for individuals, "their families, parents, and friends." The minister's views were entirely consistent with the "best practice" advice he had received from the Alberta Alliance.

Gary Mar certainly believed in personal responsibility, but he also seemed to recognize that many disabilities were beyond people's complete control. "Mental illness and diabetes," he predicted, "will be the two greatest health challenges in the future." As for mental illness, the minister admitted he was hearing a great deal from Albertans now. Many people had contacted him, he said, expressing concerns about "what they see as the limited availability of community services and supports, especially in remote rural areas of the province." The calls and letters included concerns regarding "the absence of safe affordable housing; the long waiting lists for initial assessment; admission to inpatient psychiatric beds; and access to community services on discharge." Mar was also concerned about "injuries and suicide in Alberta—especially among our young people." They were all problems the minister wanted to address.

As the relationship with the minister grew, Alliance chairman Anderson expected the Alberta Mental Health Board might also present a new position of partnership, but it didn't happen. Instead, the board appeared to be "digging in for combat," said the Alliance chairman. By July, 2000, the coalition members were so angry with the board, they sent chair Betty Schoenhofer a strongly worded letter expressing their "frustration at the apparent lack of co-operation and partnership." The letter detailed six months of communication that appeared entirely one-sided. Anderson sent a copy of his letter to the Minister.

The individual members of the board seemed to be concerned and responsive people, but collectively, they seemed to see the Alliance as the enemy. CEO Ken Sheehan advised one member of the Alliance, that there was too much negative history between the coalition and the board and that a working relationship would "never be possible." "They may as well fold," he said. One of the Alberta Mental Health Board members also confided to an Alliance member that the board members had "too little information to make reasoned decisions," most of which occurred at the "executive level anyway."

By November, 2000, the Alliance was becoming "cautiously optimistic" that they were making inroads with the new minister. On December 4, Mar joined chair Dennis Anderson of the coalition and Bob Wyatt of The Muttart Foundation to officially announce the Muttart grant and to describe for the media "a new era of partnership." Then, the February 12 Throne Speech seemed to provide some evidence of Mar's commitment, announcing the government would "meet the unique needs of persons with mental health issues" by establishing "effective community-based services." The budget also provided the Mental Health Board with an additional $16 million. In addition, more than $106 million over three years would go to special initiatives for children at risk.

In early February of 2001, Alliance representatives presented their concerns and recommendations to the Premier's Council on the Future of Health Care. The Council, a group of 12 "health policy experts," chaired by former Deputy Prime Minister, the Right Honourable Don Mazankowski, had been appointed in August and charged by Premier Ralph Klein with developing recommendations on the "preservation and future enhancement of quality health services." The Alliance presentation was very well-received and the 20 minutes scheduled for questions neared an hour.

That same month, Premier Klein announced a provincial election. With new resources in the form of a secretariat and with a new relationship and confidence in the minister, the Alliance mounted a "positive" election campaign where they provided every candidate with an information package designed to answer potential election questions from the public. The packages appeared to be well-received by government and opposition members alike, and they phoned, wrote and e-mailed, thanking the coalition for the help and "constructive" approach. Mar's re-appointment to the Health and Wellness Ministry in March caused a sigh of relief with stakeholders. There was, however, disappointment that supporters like Nancy MacBeth and Karen Leibovici would not be returning to the Legislature.

The Alberta Progressive Conservatives were re-elected in a landslide. Although history had shown that almost absolute power generally made leaders less responsive to criticism and advice, the coalition members took some comfort that Mar seemed sufficiently concerned with the problems that he would take action anyway. There were issues around the performance of the Alberta Mental Health Board, the reconstruction plans at Ponoka, the need to determine a modern role for both the Edmonton and Ponoka hospitals, the need to emphasize community programs with the money announced in February and, of course, the hope that work with the stakeholders on a new mental health plan would reflect a consensus of opinion.

By this time, the Alliance had finalized its policy on transferring programs to the regions. It supported full divestment of all of the Alberta Mental Health Board's programs to regional health authorities. The board should be reconstituted, it recommended, with responsibilities to determine "mental health policy based upon an explicit vision", to preserve the "integrity of mental health funding," to monitor and evaluate "system performance," and to promote "accountability and standards." Regional health authorities, the Alliance advised, should "provide and integrate" the full range of services. The idea was communicated separately to the departed former management team of Don Shurman, Janet Davidson, Mary Marshall, and Sharon Read. Their opinions were unanimous—"the current board should go."

The recommendations were detailed to Mar, to his executive staff, and to health department officials. They were also relayed to the

Premier's Council on the Future of Health Care in the hope the Council would, at some later date, exert some influence on the premier and his Cabinet if other shorter-term strategies failed.

The Alliance members waited for signs of action. New meetings were held with the minister's staff and senior department officials. The meetings with regional health authorities continued. The Alliance secretariat monitored government activity but little seemed to be happening. The April 9 Throne Speech committed to the pre-election goals announced in February, but no specific mention was made of mental health.

The Alberta Mental Health Board was also fighting back. It sent public relations "fact sheets," detailing their services and accomplishments, to every MLA in the province. Chair Betty Schoenhofer met with the newly elected presidents of both the Schizophrenia Society and the Mental Health Association, asking for co-operation. Some of the pressure on the Alliance members was not so subtle. An employee of the Alberta Mental Health Board, sitting as an Alliance member, was reminded of who paid salaries and the executive director of the Premier's Council on the Status of Persons with Disabilities had to justify his action to his MLA Chair. The executive director was then instructed to clarify that the Council would not be a "member" of the Alliance, but would be "an ongoing participant recognizing the Council's mandate as an objective liaison."

In June of 2001, Mar approved a Ministerial Order extending the appointments of the Alberta Mental Health Board's chair and two other members until September 30. A three-month extension for what was normally a two-year appointment seemed unusual, and Alliance chairman Anderson wondered if this might be the date by which new announcements might occur. The minister's executive assistant cautioned that nothing should be inferred by the decision, but the minister himself had admitted that public complaints to his office included "concern about the Mental Health Board."

The complaints, Anderson knew, were not only from the Alliance. Regional health authorities had openly complained about the board during the Alliance presentations, and frustrated psychiatrists from Edmonton and Calgary demanded a meeting with the minister to ask for "one administrative structure in each region." Edmonton child psychiatrists publicly complained about arbitrary decisions by the board, and community volunteer agencies publicly fought decisions to remove funding. Program transfers and money from the charities had gone back to the Alberta Mental Health Board, causing program disruptions and client upset. The action also eliminated volunteer involvement and increased operating costs as higher government salaries were instituted. The decisions generated controversy and publicity in Grande Prairie, Edmonton, Calgary, and Medicine Hat. In Red Deer, newspaper coverage on front pages went for weeks.

In other cases, community groups expressed frustration that the board was denying funding for needed services. In a June letter to *the Edmonton Journal*, the executive director of Edmonton's ComSup Services and Resources complained the board had "spent over $15 million to build up its administration rather than help the mentally ill in the community." In fact, the Board spent $12.6 million on administration in 2000-01, up 20 per cent or $2.1 million from the previous year.

Anderson began to wonder if the Alliance optimism in the minister was unfounded, and he arranged a "private and confidential" meeting with Mar. Anderson later reported to the coalition members that the meeting was "very positive" and that he was once again "guardedly optimistic." He could say no more at that time.

While Anderson's experience in the provincial Cabinet taught him that members "have to judge whether the cause is worth the conflict," and that members had to "weigh the importance of their cause against their ambitions," there were, of course, other possibilities. Mar might well know what should be done, but he couldn't or hadn't yet been able to generate support in Cabinet. Anderson expressed some hope in Premier Klein's support, citing his wife Colleen's leadership on children's mental health issues. Alberta's premiers, explained Anderson, "have generally been more enlightened than the Cabinet or caucus."

There was another, almost unspeakable, possibility. Perhaps the Alliance had been "duped." It had been kept publicly quiet except for statements supporting Mar for more than 15 months—right through a provincial election and beyond. Mar had a reputation for being "strategic" with every action. Was this all just strategic?

Then in July, 2001, the minister began to share some of his views on a few of the "tough questions." On others, he would remain vague. As to the role of the mental health hospitals, "there is a continuing

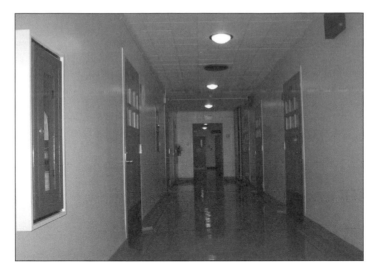

The 40-year-old #9 Building at Alberta Hospital Edmonton remains in use in 2002. (Photo courtesy of CMHA)

need," he said. They provide "specialized services designed to complement and support the inpatient psychiatric units in acute and long-term care settings." The Ponoka hospital redevelopment would clearly continue, but as for renovations at Alberta Hospital, Edmonton, "the Alberta Mental Health Board has yet to submit a capital plan to Alberta Infrastructure."

Would AMHB programs be divested to the regional health authorities? "Seven regional health authorities have expressed interest," the Minister said, and the AMHB was "working with them." The board's work with health authorities, Anderson believed, was around the possible transfer of a few community-based programs. In the plan, provincial programs and therefore most of the money would remain with the AMHB and that was not consistent with the Alliance's recommendations.

It was also not consistent with a resolution of the Alberta Psychiatric Association (APA). In September of 2001, the province's psychiatrists asked the Alberta Medical Association (AMA) to "register support of the Minister of Health and Wellness for the divestment of mental health services from the Alberta Mental Health Board (AMHB) to the regional health authorities while preserving the

AMHB's ability to ensure that mental health funding is protected and to ensure that standards of mental health care are met across the province." The psychiatrists, led by Dr. Richard Hibbard of Edmonton, said mental health care was in "crisis." When they ask for more resources, they complained, the "AMHB states that it is an RHA responsibility." Then, " when the regions are asked, their response is that it is an AMHB responsibility." In the end, "patients and their families will suffer most."

The resolution to support divestment was endorsed by the AMA membership following a passionate presentation by Dr. Brian Bishop, and Dr. Haroon Nasir of the Alliance and by several other physicians.

As to whether or not the minister was listening to the stakeholders, Mar seemed coy. He clearly intended to make changes to the membership of the board and chair Schoenhofer would go. Any substantive change in the board's responsibilities would have to wait. "At present, the Mental Health Board is appointed," he said vaguely. "Its role and function is well-defined."

And what of the minister's commitment to community-based services? He detailed his desire for local access to timely assessment, treatment, and follow up, and community supports including housing and help for individuals and their families, but there was no plan. There were no specifics.

In Mar's defence of the existing mental health services, he identified some improvements in "community treatment teams, outreach services, forensic diversion, telemental health for rural communities, and

six clubhouses." But the minister acknowledged there were many gaps and many of Alberta's psychiatrists certainly agreed with him. The chronically mentally ill, they said in an internal APA briefing paper, were "occupying acute care beds because of shortages of adequate housing and community services." Meanwhile, "acutely ill patients are being held for several days in emergency departments." The patients, they said "were not getting adequate treatment and (are) posing a risk to themselves and staff." Neither the psychiatrists nor the Alliance would be satisfied with a piecemeal approach and they jointly urged the minister to plan for a comprehensive system based on international "best practices."

Money was another issue. The Alliance had never been able to find an answer to Halvar Jonson's February, 2000 claim in the Alberta

Legislature that funding for community services had been increased 100 per cent since 1993—in spite of requests to executive staff, department officials, and the Official Opposition. In the fall of the year, Mar, while presenting to the Legislature's Committee of Supply, said he was pleased to add $10 million "to enhance community programs so people suffering a mental illness can get the help they need to stay in their homes, neighbourhoods, and workplaces." He added that he was pleased to note the "government has almost doubled the funding in the last five years." By early 2001, Ken Sheehan, the Mental Health Board's CEO, was saying community funding had increased by 142 per cent since 1994. Figures could, of course, be adjusted by picking the years that represented the most favourable picture, but the huge dollar increases and the apparent lack of improvement in the community services somehow didn't fit with people's experience.

For many consumers, family members, and professionals, there was very little or no change in the resources they had to work with. And the most tightly resourced group was the voluntary sector. While the board's administration grew, executive staff received large salary increases and labour settlements set new records, the charitable organizations that sponsored many of the community support services would receive no grant increases for inflation or salary adjustments. The "funded agencies" were advised to submit budget requests at last year's level "or don't submit at all." "So much for the International Year of the Volunteer," grumbled a housing-agency manager. Perhaps the answer to the apparent inconsistency in the availability of more money and the lack of new initiatives was within Mar's assertion that the doubling of the dollars "would keep pace with the doubling of Albertans receiving service over the same period." Alberta was indeed growing.

An Alliance request of the AMHB for background detail regarding the various reported dollar increases took months to respond to. Then the table of figures still provided no detail as to what specific new services, if any, had been developed in support of people with severe and persistent illnesses. Certainly children's services had been improved and some innovations like an eating-disorders program were evident, but the coalition's recommendations for a comprehensive system of care based on the world's best practices seemed elusive.

And finding yet more money seemed unlikely. The province did not have infinite resources in spite of the once-high price of oil and gas, which, by mid-2001 was beginning to drop. Premier Klein himself was setting the tone with public statements like "We've got to control our spending" and "Our free-wheeling days are over."

Mar apparently agreed, admitting that his "greatest concern" was the "sustainability" of health care. Mar seemed to be able to get more money from the Treasury Board than other Cabinet ministers and some of them privately expressed envy. "My department's budget of $6.4 billion this year is the largest of any government department," Mar said. We cannot afford to keep putting more money toward health services, he said "without a fundamental adjustment to the way services are delivered."

Had the latter statement been made directly to the Alberta Alliance on Mental Illness and Mental Health, it would have received sustained and resounding applause. But what "fundamental adjustment" Mar would or could make was apparently known only by the Honourable Gary Mar.

In early September, there were some hopeful signs. Community agencies that had been previously denied any grant increases, were provided a 5-percent increase in their payroll costs. The Alberta Mental Health Board was instructed by the minister to begin working with the Alliance and rumours of an imminent review of the Board's activity were widespread.

The Alliance had also maintained ongoing contact with representatives of the Premier's Council on the Future of Health Care and began stepping up efforts in order to influence its recommendations. Discussions were initiated with any Council member who would listen and Council staff and consultants were provided with statistics, research and reports including the *World Health Report Mental Health: New Understanding, New Hope*, all of which supported the Alliance philosophy of care.

Members of the Alliance also increased their communication and contacts with cabinet ministers and with members of the influential Standing Policy Committee on Health and Community Living. The committee's Chair, MLA Mary O'Neill, appeared knowledgeable and sympathetic to Alliance concerns, and media comments to that effect gave Alliance members additional hope.

Then the September 11 terrorist attack on the United States, killing thousands, appeared to shock and change the world. Mar's proposals for a review of the board were apparently bogged down in more urgent Cabinet discussions and budget debates. The world's economy took a nose-dive and with it, Alberta's oil and gas revenues plummeted. When September 30 arrived, AMHB chair Schoenhofer and her colleagues were simply reappointed for another six months. By mid-October, the premier was announcing $1.3 billion in budget cuts with the "possibility of more to come."

By late fall of 2001, most of the members of the Alberta Alliance on Mental Illness and Mental Health believed they had made some gains, but as for the future, they had nothing but "hope." Hope in a Health and Wellness Minister who continued to say most of the "right things," but who had yet to really deliver. There was also hope, and indeed an expectation that the Premier's Council on the Future of Health Care would recommend integrated services and a greater emphasis on community-based programs "We are waiting for the proof of the benefits which come from that level of consultation," said Anderson.

As founding chairman of the Alberta Alliance on Mental Illness and Mental Health, Anderson had been pleased with the group's unity and commitment. He was also pleased that mental health issues were back on the "political radar screen," and that new funds had been allocated in government budgets. Anderson was not, however, at all satisfied with the overall results. He was sensitive to the fact that his work in developing the coalition, the first and only of its kind in Canada, had earned him the national Canadian Mental Health Association's foremost recognition, the C. M. Hincks award for advocacy. He felt he needed to earn the recognition with better and greater "results." But turning a ship can't be done easily or quickly and, as Anderson well knew, in politics "some things were possible, others were not."

Then the art of the possible became evident. The report of the Premier's Council, described as the "Maz" report after Chairman Don Mazankowski, was released on January 8. While filled with controversial proposals for the overall health system, on mental health, the report was everything the Alliance had hoped for. Entitled A Framework For Reform, the report recommended that the government "integrate mental health services with the work of regional health authorities," that they set "clear guidelines to ensure that mental health services receive a high priority in the regions," and that these guidelines include "province-wide standards, performance measures and targets." Of equal importance, the Council recommended that spending on mental health services should be "maintained and enhanced." In a surprise recommendation, the Council proposed an "innovative blend" of services, including "not-for-profit organizations." The Alberta Mental Health Board, with its emphasis on centralized programs, along with its tendency to discontinue funding of community volunteer groups, appeared to be in jeopardy.

The AMHB however was not about to accept the report passively. A news release asked for the recommendations to be studied further, and members of the board and administration contacted reporters and columnists in order to generate public support. The Board demanded letters of support from their consumer advisory council and from the chairs of their regional advisory councils. They got them, in spite of the objections of some of the members.

The Alliance membership saw the Mazankowski report as a watershed, but the battle had not been won. A new round of contacts with MLAs, news releases, and letters to the editors was initiated in order to ask for government support of the "Maz" recommendations. Psychiatrists from the Alberta Hospital Edmonton conveyed verbal support of the Alliance objectives but avoided public comment. Each physician had received a letter from the AMHB's lawyers threatening legal action after a highly critical letter from staff association president Dr. Brian Bishop was published in *the Edmonton Journal*.

290

Health Minister Gary Mar agreed to attend a meeting of the full Alliance membership and, on January 16 told them he was fully supportive of the report recommendations, but that he still needed, as he had said six months earlier, "the support of my colleagues." The following Monday, Standing Policy Committee Chair Mary O'Neill held a private day-long meeting of her health committee. The 14-member group expanded to more than 40 MLAs. The following day, the provincial cabinet considered the committee's recommendations and on Wednesday, the full caucus met to confirm the government's response to the report of the Premier's Council. That afternoon, Gary Mar, the Minister of Health and Wellness, finally delivered on Alliance Chair Dennis Anderson's request on behalf of the Alliance. Mental health services would be "fully integrated into regional health authorities by March 2003," he said. "A transition plan that ensures continuous patient care," he added, "will be developed in the spring of 2002."

On January 23, 2002, as the Honourable Gary Mar left the Alberta legislature for health discussions with the "First Ministers" in Vancouver, the former "Honourable" Dennis Anderson volunteered to attend yet another community meeting to talk about the Alberta Alliance and mental health reform. But his time it would be different. Anderson spoke with hope, confidence and champagne for everyone in attendance. Complete reform of the mental health system "may not happen during my time," admitted the Alliance leader the following day, "but it will happen," he predicted. Anderson's confidence flowed from his personal view that there was "a growing realization of how mental health issues affect all of us—mental illness is not something others have." His confidence also stemmed from his observation that more and more citizens were beginning to speak up about their experiences or those of their family members. "Those who suffer personal pain are more likely to be more compassionate," Anderson theorized, "and from true compassion comes action...The time is right," he added, "for mental health issues to reach an awareness that meets the real significance of their importance in the community."

Could Anderson really predict the future? "Predictions are dangerous," he said, "hopes are easier." As for now, his hope was in the recommendations of the Premier's Council on the Future of Health Care and in the promises of the Honourable Gary Mar. Anderson understood history and the reality of people, politics and power, so nothing was assured. But Anderson now had hope. Hope for a modern mental health "system," one with fewer gaps and earlier access—delivered in the community. A system that would respond "first" to people "who suffer the most," he said. A system that would rely on "political asylums" as a very last resort.

References

Alberta Health Care Insurance Plan. *Statistical Supplement*. Service Years March 31, 1996 to 2000. 2001.

Alberta Mental Health Board. *Fact Sheet—The Alberta Mental Health System*. May, 2001.

Alberta Mental Health Board. *Business Plan, 1999-2002*. January 25, 2000.

Alberta Mental Health Board. *Business Plan, 2000-2003*. April, 2000.

Anonymous. Cabinet Minister—Interview with author, 2000.

Anonymous. Former civil servant—Interview with author, July, 2000.

Anonymous. Former Alberta Mental Health Board employee—Interview with author, March, 2000.

Alberta Hansard, Committee of Supply, November, 2000.

Anderson, Dennis. Edmonton, AB. Interview with author, August, 2001.

Canadian Mental Health Association, *Mental Health Care at the Crossroads*. April, 1997.

Clarke Institute of Psychiatry, Health Systems Research Unit. *Best Practices in Mental Health Reform: Discussion Paper*. Prepared for the Advisory Network on Mental Health 1997. Ottawa, Ontario: Health Canada, 1977.

Davidson, Janet. Toronto, ON. Conversation with author, January 11, 2000.

Faulder, Liane. "Mentally Ill need that $150 million for more community programs, not rebuilt hospitals," *The Edmonton Journal*. February 17, 2000.

Hibbard, Richard. Briefing notes for a meeting of the Alberta Psychiatric Association. Undated.

Johnsrude, Larry. "Latest Tory makeover: back to austerity, *The Edmonton Journal.* August 26, 2001.

Klein, Ralph. Correspondence with AAMIMH. March 2000.

Lucki, George. Edmonton, AB. Interview with author, July, 2001.

Mar, Gary. Edmonton, AB. Interview with author, July, 2001.

Mar, Gary. Written response to selected questions. August, 2001.

Michelin, Lana. "CMHA lays off staff." Red Deer *Advocate.* April 4, 2000.

Read, Sharon. Edmonton, AB. Conversation with author. December 12, 2000.

Sheehan, Ken. Edmonton, AB. Conversation with author. February 29, 2000.

Shurman, Donald. Edmonton, AB. Conversation with author. March 9, 2001.

The Alberta Alliance on Mental Illness and Mental Health. *Good People . . . Good Practices . . . No System—A Discussion Paper.* AAMIMH: Alberta Alliance on Mental Illness and Mental Health, February 2000.

Working Together. Brochure of the Alberta Alliance on Mental Illness and Mental Health. Undated.

Wowk, Roger J. "Mentally Ill Poorly Served by Board— Little Funding Flows to Local Services." *Edmonton Journal.* June , 2001.

Epilogue

Epilogue

Epilogue

The lessons of history should be self-evident. They weren't to me. The research necessary to write this book was an adventure. I had previously heard or read about most of the parts, but somehow I had missed the "whole." I certainly didn't see the repetitive nature of our history. One would think that after working more than 30 years in this field, I would understand people, power, and the influence of politics.

In my work, I have traveled to many parts of the world. In fact, the Muttart Fellowship let me see, firsthand, the "best practices" and most highly rated programs in North America. But it was an earlier trip that was most notable. I was in central Africa where I marveled at the innovations, all of them aimed at the "determinants of health," things like homes, work, recreation, education and training, all completed with virtually no money. I thought the Africans did so much with so little. I could not escape the conclusion that we had a responsibility to do so much more with our resources.

In Alberta, the government's Alberta Mental Health Board spent $220 million in 2000-2001. The 17 regional health authorities spent an additional $197 million (estimated) on mental health programs, and physicians received more than $88 million for counselling and psychotherapy. In summary, Alberta taxpayers now spend $505 million a year on mental health services. That doesn't include the cost of capital construction, drugs or private services. Yet Alberta has many gaps in service, consumers/users have difficulty accessing programs, many sick people live in squalor, and far too many patients experience the "revolving door" of hospital re-admission, treatment, and abandonment to the streets. Is it what we spend or how we spend it that really makes a difference? This is only but one of the many questions I have pondered while researching this book.

Beyond the questions, what have I learned and what do I think we can we do about the problems? As obvious as they may be, I feel compelled to state those lessons of history in explicit terms. The recurring themes struck me like a punch to the stomach—and they shouldn't have. It is amazing what you miss when you are "in the trenches." The "trenches" for me have been varied, and I have had the rather unique opportunity to work at the "front line" in both hospital and community programs and at the most senior level within government, with the Provincial Mental Health Board, in the non-profit sector and as the owner of a franchised restaurant that employed mentally ill people. Members of my family have also suffered with mental illness, and I know firsthand the problems of getting help. In other words I have seen the "system" from almost every angle. My perspectives, one hopes, are not the conclusions of a cynic, but rather, as Dr. Roger Bland put it, the "inescapable conclusions of a realist."

Reform of the mental health system has been an elusive goal for thousands of Albertans for almost a century. Why is that? Perhaps because:

Government decisions are driven first and foremost by the need to be elected—and then by economics.

Political considerations all too often supersede humanitarian concerns.

Mentally ill people are feared and shunned. Only rarely are they considered a public-policy priority.

As a result of stigma and public apathy, mentally ill people have few advocates in the political ranks.

Socially conservative politicians often claim there is no clear consensus on what needs to be done and that the demands for human services are insatiable, no matter what the effort. "Social services" are dirty words.

Stigma results in few consumers or their families who are willing to "stand and be counted," despite the staggering statistic showing that one in five are affected by mental illness. This reluctance to admit illness is, however, changing.

Media interest and government embarrassment has driven reform in almost every situation. As specific services improved, institutional, cruelty, and physical abuse have been largely eliminated. The problems are now more insidious and complex and are therefore lacking in drama. Today's media is less interested because there is rarely an opportunity for good, splashy copy or catchy sound bites—unless, of course, violence is perpetrated by a mentally ill person.

And what do we do about it? At the risk of trying to pass myself off as yet another "expert" in a field already crowded with theories about how to fix things, I will take the plunge because none of the following ideas originated with me. They flow from what I have heard, read, seen and experienced for the past 30 years. Consumers/users, patients/clients, family members, professionals, and volunteer advocates have, for most of the past century, said pretty much the same things, over and over and over again. Designing a mental health system that will help people with the most severe and persistent illnesses is not rocket science. If we listen, we will hear what people want and need.

Income. Like all of us, the first thing the mentally ill person needs is a source of money—preferably money earned from work. Jobs can provide more than money; they can give people an opportunity for social contact, a daily activity to complete. Work can provide a feeling of accomplishment. Even the sick can work if accommodations are made. Job-sharing, flexible hours, personal support, altering time requirements, paying attention to work references, and teaching skills on the job have all been shown to work. Incentives and help to start "alternative businesses" have also had some success. Educational accommodations and support in post-secondary institutions might also improve work opportunities. When work is not possible, a reasonable disability benefit must be available, one which is flexible enough to allow—and indeed encourage—paid work when the illness allows it.

Homes. The second priority is a place to live—somewhere safe, warm, and clean, a place that encourages maximum independence and allows for maximum privacy. Independent living apartments are the most ideal arrangement for most, but shared apartments, group homes, and foster or "approved home" living can work. "Placements" in other people's homes, though, tend to be paternalistic and/or create dependency. They are more appropriate for children than adults. Ultimately, we need to have good options and enough of them to meet the needs.

Drugs. There is an entire "new generation" of psychoactive drugs that are having amazing results by any historic standards. They present great hope and many more pharmaceuticals are in the development and trial stages. The best drugs must be made available, and a prescription insurance plan must help cover the costs when necessary. People receiving disability benefits need to have portable prescription coverage that allows them to maintain coverage if they find paid work.

Outreach. Clinics and office visits don't work for many people with chronic illnesses; there are years of missed and late appointments to prove it. What we need is assertive community outreach in order to meet with people in the places where they live, work and play. Outreach programs should monitor treatment effectiveness, deal with personal crisis and provide training in the many skills of interpersonal life. They can include education on such topics as grooming, budgeting, shopping, polite discourse and safety—in other words, the art of "being normal."

Crisis Response. A non-medical "help centre" to call or visit in times of crisis can prevent serious consequences and avoid costly hospital admissions. Although medical services may be available in such a program, it should not become another hospital emergency department. It is a place to deal with any personal crisis from loneliness to a bare cupboard. Many good program examples exist and they often include a mobile outreach. They are sometimes managed by consumers/users themselves—and they work.

Hospitals. Mentally ill people must have the ability to be hospitalized quickly, whenever they need it. Many mental illnesses require brief, intermittent hospitalizations, and active treatment should occur in general hospital psychiatric units close to people's homes and support systems. Senior citizens suffering dementia should live in extended-care facilities close to their homes and not in psychiatric hospitals. There may be some people with severe and persistent illnesses who want, or even need, a more extended stay in mental hospitals, but their numbers are small and will continue to decrease as other options become available.

Networks. One of the most valuable resources in any mental health system are the people who use it—the consumers/users and their families when appropriate. They need to be involved in every decision. They need to be supported and encouraged to design and run innovative services. They also need "self-help" opportunities, time to be with their peers in order to share common problems, understanding and solutions. And they need an opportunity to advocate.

Medical Care. Family physicians are the primary contact for citizens who suffer a range of mental and emotional illnesses and disabilities. In the year 2000, there were 2,545 family physicians and 277 psychiatrists—an increase of eight per cent over the previous year—(plus 22 physicians with a mental health specialty), all of whom do some form of psychotherapy. (The median payment to family physicians in 1999-2000 was $155,358 and to psychiatrists $148,493.) These physicians need to be made a formal part of the mental health system with ready psychiatric consultation and the support of teams of professionals who can address related needs.

These are the priorities. Of course, much more could be done. Court diversion could redirect ill people in the jails away from incarceration to more appropriate treatment. Clubhouses can provide people with an opportunity to socialize and work in an environment that accepts them, one that they have some control over. Central phone lines could help people to better access and navigate the sometimes bewildering array of services available from government and private agencies by providing a single point of contact in each health authority. The United Way's proposed new universal 211 toll free information and referral number might serve that function. Safe houses could be established to provide people with temporary accommodation, safety, and respite. Alternative therapies could be made accessible to more people. The Alberta government, in the year 1999-2000, spent $87.9 million on psychiatrists and physicians who do mental health work. Could some of the money be used more efficiently—with psychologists, for example? Why are traditional-healing strategies more effective with First Nations people? Are our services culturally sensitive? These are questions that need to be addressed. Public education, starting with our youngest citizens, could help change prejudicial attitudes. Some of the teaching should be done by people who have lived the experience. Anti-stigma campaigns should continue to educate the public about their own negative attitudes and generate greater understanding of mental illness. Research resources need to be improved. We still know so little about the human condition and even less about what really works to improve it. Information systems need to be useful along with stringent laws and policies to protect the privacy of personal records.

Professional education opportunities need to be made readily available to institutional staff in order to ease the transition to community care.

Some of these resources now exist in some communities. They are however, patchy, uncoordinated, under-resourced, and often difficult to access. There is no Alberta system.

So how do we make progress on mental health reform in this century? If we agree that the failures of the past are largely economic, attitudinal, and political, we will need to address the issues on those fronts. People will go to the polls to obtain jobs, ensure their safety, educate their children, protect themselves from higher taxes, or simply because a politician has charisma—but they rarely go the polls to ensure a good mental health policy. That has to change. In the short term, Albertans need to organize in order to generate political will. A strong advocate in government could do it, but intense controversy and massive public outrage may be the only way. Professionals, family members, consumers and advocates will have to work together as never before to urge a minimum of six urgent and immediate actions:

Review the plans to rebuild Alberta's mental hospitals. The cost of rebuilding institutions is repeated every two years in operating costs. At the very least, the millions needed to rebuild hospitals in Edmonton and Ponoka will siphon off scarce resources for another three decades—and the rebuilt institutions will likely become white elephants, with the government once again searching for ways to use the buildings. There are some reasonably good buildings at both institutions and, with minor renovations, they could continue to be used for appropriate services like forensics and perhaps for a small number of very chronic patients who require long-term institutionalization. But acutely ill people and seniors with family contacts should be moved out of mental hospitals and back to programs in their home communities. If we need to build, let's build there. This is not an issue of community versus institution. We need it all. It is an issue of ensuring community supports and then "beds" when they are needed.

Set appropriate priorities on the use of existing dollars or increase the money available for the home and community-based programs that have been described earlier. Mental health services have a history of being underfunded and of making poor use of available funds. Canadian and American jurisdictions that have reputed "best practices" have invested additional dollars in community programs in order to eventually decrease the demands on institutions. In other words, keeping people well in their communities will help break the current cycle of costly readmissions.

Transfer all mental health service delivery to the regional health authorities so that programs can be developed, integrated and coordinated at the local level. Provide the authorities with a "funding envelope" that allows for flexibility when transferring dollars between hospitals and other community programs, including those managed by voluntary organizations, which are often better able to provide creative, flexible, affordable and effective service.

Change the role of the government's Alberta Mental Health Board from providing services to overseeing mental health reform. Functions could include identifying best practices, setting standards and performance measures, funding, monitoring results and evaluating progress. The board might also recommend changes in law and oversee the investigations of the Mental Health Patient Advocate and the admission and treatment appeals done by the Hospital Review Boards.

Continue efforts to improve the Alberta Income for the Severely Handicapped (AISH) program to encourage work and maintain flexible benefits, including portable prescription coverage and rapid reinstatement when an illness recurs.

Continue the Alberta Children's Initiative, coordinated at the health authority level and fast-tracked in order to ensure early programming for emotionally disturbed children on a priority basis.

It is said that a society is judged by its treatment of its most vulnerable citizens. Albertans have made many attempts to care for people with mental illness, but the efforts have fallen short. After almost a full century, we still have political asylums. Consumers/users and their families really don't care about politics, economics, system complexities, or philosophical differences. They care only about getting better.

Their problem is that they suffer with a mental illness, Alberta's modern-day leprosy. That should surely be enough of a burden for anyone.

302

APPENDICES

APPENDICES

Appendix I

Milestones

World

1547	Henry VIII opens Bedlam, first English Asylum.
1751	First North American asylum opens in Philadelphia.
1792	French reformer Philippe Pinel unchains insane in Paris asylum.
1796	English reformer William Tuke introduces "moral treatment."
1834	First Canadian asylum opened in New Brunswick.
1841	American reformer Dorothea Dix pushes moral treatment.
1891	Asylum opens in Brandon to serve Manitoba and Northwest Territories.
1893	Northwest Territories sends insane to Brandon from the territory which will be called Alberta.

Alberta/Canada/US

1905 Alberta becomes a province.

1907 Passage of *The Insanity Act.*

1908 American reformer Clifford Beers advocates humane treatment and forms the first mental hygiene society in the world.

1909 Canada's first mental health "outdoor clinic" opens in Toronto.

1911 Hospital for the Insane opens at Ponoka to treat men and women.

1918 Reformer Clare Hincks forms the Canadian National Committee for Mental Hygiene.

1919 *Department of Public Health Act* passed.

    Mental Diseases Act amended.

1921 Clare Hincks surveys Alberta's services.

1922 First official appointment of a psychiatric social worker at the Ponoka hospital.

    Introduction of Occupational Therapy.

1923 Provincial Mental Institute opens near Edmonton.

304 Inmates from Red Deer hospital are sent to Ponoka.

    Edmonton Education Home inmates are sent to the Red Deer Hospital for Returned Soldiers.

    All active treatment is to be done at Ponoka with refractory patients sent to Edmonton.

    Hospital for the Insane at Ponoka changes name to Provincial Mental Hospital.

1924 Passage of The *Mental Diseases Act.*

1925 First Board of Visitors tours mental institutions.

1927   Official report on staff working conditions in mental institutions.

1928   Survey by Clare Hincks and C.B. Farrar following a patient death in Ponoka.

        Canadian Criminal Code has provision for insanity plea.

1929   *Sexual Sterilization Act* passed.

        Mental Hygiene Clinics opened in Edmonton and Calgary.

        First staff trained in occupational therapy at Edmonton Institute.

1930   Guidance clinic opened in Lethbridge (Medicine Hat and Drumheller will follow in 1933; Ponoka, High River, and Coleman clinics open in 1937)

        Edmonton Institute expanded.

        First formal training in nursing for mental hospital attendants at Ponoka (later becomes RPN program).

        Beginning of three-year psychiatric nursing training in general hospitals.

1931   Psychopathic ward opens at University of Alberta.

1933   Provincial Auxiliary Mental Hospital opens in Claresholm.

1934   First travelling Guidance Clinics.

1935   Building additions to Edmonton Institute to compensate for overcrowding at Ponoka.

        Health Minister W.W. Cross vows to close mental institutes.

1937   Introduction of insulin shock therapy.

        Ponoka hospital population peaks at 1,707.

1939   Exodus of staff to join armed services; by 1944 staff were at 50 per cent of requirements.

Provincial Auxiliary Mental Hospital opens in Raymond.

1941   Volunteer visitations begin at Edmonton's Oliver institute.

1942   Edmonton Institute opens first women's unit.

1943   Unions negotiate return of eight-hour day lost during the Depression.

1945   Introduction of electro-shock therapy (ECT).

        Beginning of three-year nursing program at Oliver.

1947   Discovery of Leduc oil field and the beginning of prosperity.

        Another survey by Clare Hincks is published by government.

        Rosehaven Care Centre opens in Camrose for elderly mentally ill.

1949   General nurses train in psychiatry at Ponoka.

1950   All Oliver attendants require to take three-year program including culture and literacy.

        Introduction of psycho-surgery at Ponoka.

1952   Tuberculosis unit opened at Edmonton Institute.

        First full-time social worker and pastor at Institute.

        An "after-care" team begins operation at Foothills Hospital, using Ponoka staff.

        Plans for new mental hospital in Calgary.

1953   Introduction of group psychotherapy at Oliver and Ponoka Hospitals.

        Alberta Hospital Ponoka (AHP)

1954	Introduction of tranquillizers. No controlled trials until 1962.
	Calgary General opens the city's first psychiatric unit.
1955	The *Mental Diseases Act* revised.
	The Canadian Mental Health Association is founded in Alberta.
1956	Opening of admissions building at Oliver to serve northern Alberta—now considered an active treatment hospital.
	The first "open wards" and an increase in treatment of alcoholics at Oliver and Ponoka.
1957	National Hospital Insurance Plan excludes funding for mental hospitals.
1958	Occupational therapy expands dramatically and art therapy begins.
	Deerhome opens in Red Deer with transfer in of the "retarded" from hospitals.
1960	Beginning of deinstitutionalization.
	Linden House in Red Deer opens to serve emotionally disturbed adolescents.
1961	Books by Goffman, Szasz, and Laing influence psychiatry and treatment.
1962	Insulin shock discontinued and ECT curtailed.
1963	CMHA publishes report *More For The Mind*.
	Farm at the Edmonton Hospital discontinued.
1964	Passage of *Mental Health Act*.
	Hospitals renamed Alberta Hospitals Edmonton (AHE) and Ponoka (AHP) and clinics are renamed "Alberta Guidance Clinics."
	Clinics in Grande Prairie and Red Deer opened.

First foster homes opened in Calgary.

1966   First group homes opened by CMHA in Calgary.

Lethbridge hospital opens first psychiatric unit in a smaller centre.

1967   National Health Plan includes funding for psychiatry.

Reporter Karen Harding's influential reports appear in *The Edmonton Journal.*

Premier Manning and Minister J. Donovan Ross announce Blair study.

1968   Writer G. Tori Salter's controversial article in *Canadian Living Magazine.*

Opening of first sheltered workshop for the mentally ill (28 already existed with the Association for the Mentally Retarded).

Integration of male and female patients on wards at AHE.

1969   Blair report on mental health services published.

ECT refined, including the increased use of anesthetics.

Calgary opens first "Day Clinic."

308   Alberta Alcoholism and Drug Abuse Commission established.

1970   First lay administrator in a mental hospital at AHE.

First school program in a mental hospital.

1971   Conservatives are elected with mental health a platform priority.

Sterilization Act repealed.

Human Rights Legislation passed.

Merger of Health and Social Development consolidated into one department.

Foothills Hospital takes over Ponoka follow-up clinic.

1972   Passage of new *Mental Health Act.*

Research begins at AHE.

Alberta Psychiatric Association begins travelling consultations.

1973   Blair Report II published to evaluate reform progress.

1974   AHE forms a department of neuropsychology and research.

1976   Child Guidance Clinics and mentally ill clinics sponsored by AHE combined.

First mental hospital accreditation by the Canadian Council.

Calgary General Hospital opens forensic beds and expands psychiatric beds.

1978   First accreditation of clinics.

1980   Passage of revised *Mental Health Act.*

Lougheed awarded by CMHA National.

Mental hospitals transferred to Department of Community Health.

Schizophrenia society formed.

McKinsey report published.

1981   Alberta Children's Hospital in Calgary opens psychiatric beds.

Psychiatric Nursing training discontinued at AHE.

1982   CMHA prepares critical report on AHP and Ombudsman reports on AHE.

Boards appointed at AHE and AHP.

Influential reports by *Edmonton Journal* reporter Wendy Koenig published.

Special section in Hospitals and Medical Care opened to support boards and mental hospitals are transferred to Community and Occupational Health.

1983	Report of the Drewry Task Force to review the *Mental Health Act* released.

Clarke report published.

1984	Psychiatric Services Planning Committees appointed.

Publication of CMHA *Framework For Support*.

1987	Calgary general hospitals able to admit under the *Mental Health Act* (Edmonton will follow suit in 1988).

1988	Departments of Hospitals and Community Health amalgamate.

Policy paper Mental Health Services in Alberta released.

Revised *Mental Health Act* passed.

1989	Consumer Network formed.

1991	500 psychiatric beds are now available in 15 general hospitals.

Brain injury unit beds opens at Ponoka.

Mental Patient Advocate appointed.

1992	Government discussion paper *Future Directions* released.

1993	Mental health policy paper *Working in Partnerships* released.

Government appoints 17 Regional Health Authorities to localize service.

1994	Provincial Mental Health Board (PMHB) appointed to restructure, develop, and then transfer services to Regional Health Authorities.
1995	Strategic Plan *Building a Better Future* released by PMHB.
	Psychiatric Nursing program at Ponoka transferred to Grant MacEwan Community College.
1996	Provincial Mental Health Advisory Board (PMHAB) appointed with power limited to ministerial "advice."
1997	Mental Health Branch of government dissolved.
	National *Best Practices* report published.
1998	PMHAB recommends new capital for construction at AHP. AHE to be reviewed.
1999	PMHAB changed to Alberta Mental Health Board, with new mandate to govern provincial programs in perpetuity and to advocate.
	Alberta Alliance for Mental Illness and Mental Health formed.
2000	Health Minister Gary Mar contemplates a reformed mental health system.
2002	Government endorses report of Premiers Council of the Future of health care regarding reform of the mental health system.

311

Appendix II

Legal Table—Mental Health Law

1907   The *Insanity Act* provided for committal by a Justice of the Peace if a person was insane and dangerous. An appeal could be made by a relative.

1919   The *Mental Defectives Act* provided for placement of a "mental defective" in institution upon application to the Minister. The person could not be insane or dangerous.

1922   The *Insanity Act* added a discharge process to the 1907 Act.

1924   The *Mental Diseases Act* expanded admission authorities to include the Minister if "voluntary" or with medical advice. Expanded the powers of physicians and allowed for psychopathic wards in general hospitals.

1927   *Canadian Criminal Code** provided for an opportunity to assess whether the insane were fit to stand trial or not guilty by reason of insanity.

1928   The *Sexual Sterilization Act* provided for sterilization of persons "in danger of transmitting mental disease or deficiency."

1938   The *Mental Defectives Act* redefined the defective person and provided for parole. Expanded discharge criteria to require a capability of legitimate livelihood, the ability to conform to the law and sterilization.

1955   The *Mental Diseases Act* changed the term "psychopathic ward" to psychiatric ward and limited stay in hospital to three months in every 12.

1964   The *Mental Health Act* replaced *Mental Diseases* and *Mental Defectives Acts*. Mental disorder is defined as "suffering from mental illness or retardation," and admission procedures are refined. Apprehension is based on the person's welfare or on the protection of others. Complaints could be taken to a review panel.

1970   The *Mental Health Act* essentially the same Act as in 1964, although it excluded from its provisions people who were "promiscuous or immoral."

1972   The *Mental Health Act* changed the definition of mental disorder to "lacking reason or control." A citizens' Advisory Council was established and a provision made to register therapists. Apprehension was based on a mental disorder and dangerousness. It also legislated certain rights for patients.

1980   The *Mental Health Act* changed the responsibility for mental hospitals from the Department of Hospitals to Social Services, eliminated the provision for therapist registration, and allowed certificates of incapacity to be dealt with through the new Dependent Adults Act. Added a section dealing with confidentiality of records.

1988   The *Mental Health Act* expanded the definition of mental disorder was expanded to include judgment, behaviour, recognition of reality, and meeting the ordinary demands of life. Conditions were placed on treatments and substitute decision-making was introduced. A Mental Health Advocate to investigate complaints replaced the Ombudsman's authority.

314

1991   *Canadian Criminal Code** replaced insanity with the concept of "not criminally responsible on account of mental disorder," refined procedures, and introduced rights of review and appeal.

NOTE: Changes were sometimes passed in advance of the date of the legislation and then written into the Revised Statutes.

* Denotes a federal law. The remainder are provincial statutes.

Appendix III

Health and Social Services Evolution

*Denotes Mental Health Services Responsibility

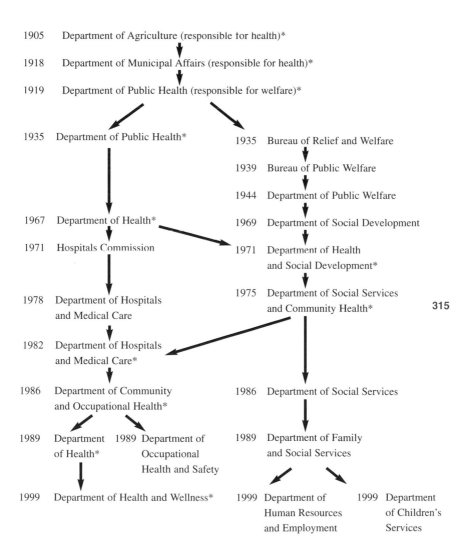

1905   Department of Agriculture (responsible for health)*

1918   Department of Municipal Affairs (responsible for health)*

1919   Department of Public Health (responsible for welfare)*

1935   Department of Public Health*

1935   Bureau of Relief and Welfare

1939   Bureau of Public Welfare

1944   Department of Public Welfare

1967   Department of Health*

1969   Department of Social Development

1971   Hospitals Commission

1971   Department of Health
and Social Development*

1978   Department of Hospitals
and Medical Care

1975   Department of Social Services
and Community Health*

1982   Department of Hospitals
and Medical Care*

1986   Department of Community
and Occupational Health*

1986   Department of Social Services

1989   Department
of Health*

1989   Department of
Occupational
Health and Safety

1989   Department of Family
and Social Services

1999   Department of Health and Wellness*

1999   Department of
Human Resources
and Employment

1999   Department
of Children's
Services

315

Appendix IV

Premiers

1905-1910	Alexander Rutherford Liberal
1910-1917	Arthur Sifton Liberal
1917-1921	Charles Stewart Liberal
1921-1925	Herbert Greenfield United Farmers
1925-1934	John Brownlee United Farmers
1934-1935	Richard Reid United Farmers
1935-1943	William Aberhart Social Credit
1943-1968	Ernest Manning Social Credit
1968 1971	Harry Strom Social Credit
1971-1986	Peter Lougheed Conservative
1986-1993	Don Getty Conservative
1993-	Ralph Klein Conservative

318

Appendix V

Ministers Responsible for Mental Health

1905-1909	W.T. Finlay—Agriculture (responsible for health)
1909-1921	Duncan Marshall—Agriculture
1919-1921	Alexander MacKay—Public Health
1920-1921	Charles Mitchell—Public Health
1921-1923	Richard Reid—Public Health
1923-1935	George Hoadley—Public Health
1935-1957	Dr. Warren Wallace Cross—Public Health
1957-1969	Dr. Joseph D. Ross—Public Health and Health
1969-1971	James D. Henderson—Hospitals
1971-1971	Ray Speaker—Health and Social Development
1971- 1975	Neil Crawford—Health and Social Development
1975-1979	Helen Hunley—Social Services and Community Health
	Gordon Miniely—Hospitals and Medical Care
1979-1986	David Russell—Hospitals and Medical Care
1979-1982	Bob Bogle—Social Services and Community Health
1982-1986	Dr. Neil Webber—Social Services and Community Health

1986-1988	Marvin Moore—Hospitals and Medical Care
1986-1988	Jim Dinning—Social Services and Community Health
1988-1992	Nancy Betkowski—Health
1992-1996	Shirley McClellan—Health
1996-2000	Halvar Jonson—Health
2000-	Gary Mar—Health and Wellness

Appendix VI

Mental Health Division/Branch:

Commissioners/Deputy Ministers/Executive Directors

1930-1936	Dr. C.A. Baragar
1936-1965	Dr. R.R. MacLean
1965-1966	Dr. T.C. Michie
1966-1972	Dr. A.R. Schrag
1972-1979	Dr. C.P. Hellon
1979-1981	John Forrester
1981-1989	Dr. Roger Bland
1989-1991	Gordon McLeod
1991-1992	Dennis Ostercamp
1992-1994	Bernie Doyle
1994-1995	Dennis Ostercamp
1995-1996	Ron LaJeunesse
1996-1997	Frank Langer
1997-1997	Mike Weaver

Provincial/Alberta Mental Health/Advisory Board Executive Directors

1995-1996	Stephen Newroth
1996-1997	Ron LaJeunesse
1997-1998	Nancy Reynolds
1998-1999	Don Schurman
2000-	Ken Sheehan

Appendix VII

CMHA Presidents

1955-1956	Dorothy Cameron and Dr. S.C.T. Clarke (Chair)
1957-1958	Dr. H.E. Smith
1959-1960	Monsignor J.E. LeFort
1961-1964	B.L. Robinson
1965-1966	Eric Morris
1966-1967	G.S. Brant
1968-1969	G.E. McLellan
1970-1971	Vera Ross
1972-1973	Howard Clifford
1973-1974	Vera Ross
1974-1975	Monsignor J.E. LeFort
1975-1976	Bettie Hewes
1976-1979	Dr. Paul Adams
1979-1982	Jean Lowe
1982-1985	Aleck Trawick
1985-1987	Mary Oordt

1987-1988	Dixie Watson
1988-1989	Norman Thackeray
1989-1990	Dr. James Browne
1990-1994	Bill Gaudette
1994-1998	Richard Drewry
1998-2001	Dennis Anderson
2001-	Bob Campbell

Schizophrenia Society Presidents

1980-1980	John Lunn
1980-1985	Mary Fitzgerald
1985-1987	Margaret Shone
1987-1989	Al Rupprecht
1989-1990	Jake Vanderleek
1990-1992	Leona King
1992-1992	Faye Herrick
1992-1993	Faye Herrick and Jim Hunter
1993-1994	Jim Hunter
1994-1996	Doug Nelson
1996-1998	Margaret Hussey
1998-2000	Sharon Sutherland
2000-	Neil Congo

Alberta Consumer Network Leaders

1989-1991	Nadine Stirling
1992-1993	Vince Van de Pol
1993-1996	Karin Kossman
1996-1998	Fran Lawson
1998-1999	Nigel Gates
1999-	Richard Scott

326

Appendix VIII

Nominal Record

*denotes pseudonym

Aldrin, Buzz
Anderson, Dennis
Angus, R.B.
Baker, Perren
Baragar, C. A.
Barrett, Pam
Barton,
Bauld, Edna
Beach, Timmy*
Beatty, Edward
Beers, Clifford
Birks, William
Bishop, Brian
Blair, W.R.N.
Bland, Roger
Bogle, Bob
Bond, Thomas
Boyko, Terry
Braddock, Ian*
Brant, Glen
Brill, Henry
Brown, Edward
Browne, James
Brownlee, John
Byron, Lord
Cameron, Dorothy
Cameron, Ewan
Capp, Shirley
Carey, Mariah

Carnat, Morris
Carter, Rosalyn
Channing, Walter
Churchill, Winston
Clarke, C.K.
Cleghorn, Beardsley*
Clifford, Howard
Conolly, John
Cook, Francis
Cooke, E.H.
Coombs, Walter
Cornish, David
Coster, Frederick
Cranston, Toller
Crawford, Neil
Crawford, Neil
Cross, W.W.
Czukar, Gail
Dangerfield, Rodney
Darwin, Leonard
Dau, Jim
Davidson, George
Davidson, Janet
Dawson, Thomas
Day, Stockwell
Dewhurst, William
Dingman, C.
Dobranski, Karen
Donald, Steve*

McClellan, George
McClellan, Shirley
McGhie, B.T.
McGrath, Judith
McKague, Carla
McKenzie, Charles*
McLean, A.J.
McLean, Duncan
McLean, Randall
McLeod, Gordon
McMurchy, Helen
Michie, Thomas
Molson, Fred
Mulligan, Billy
Murphy, Emily
Murphy, Jon
Nagel, Walter
Nasir, Haroon
Newroth, Stephen
Norris, T.C.
Notley, Grant
Oberg, Lyle
Oliver, Frank
O'neil, Mary
Oordt, Mary
Ostercamp, Denis
Parent, Leo*
Park, Nancy*
Patterson, James
Patterson, John
Pearce, Keith
Perusini, Toni
Peters, George
Peterson, William
Phillipon, Don
Phillips, David
Pinel, Phillip
Plath, Sylvia
Pratt, Larry
Reid, R.G.
Revell, D.G.
Roland, Howard

Rose, Patrick
Ross, J. Donovan
Roxburgh, Peter
Russel, Colin
Russel, David
Russell, Ann
Rutherford, A.C.
Rykee, Gary
Salter, Tori
Saunders, Hank*
Savage, Harvey
Sawyer, Jane
Schacter, Marion
Schrag, A.R.
Sheehan, Ken
Schoenhofer, Betty
Shone, Margaret
Shurman, Don
Sifton, Arthur
Simmons, Craig
Slater, Harvey*
Small, Jennifer*
Smith, Annie*
Smith, Ellen
Smith, Keith
Snipps, Eldon*
Stewart, Charles
Stirling, Nadine
Strom, Harry
Surkan, Gail
Sussman, Paul
Swadron, Barry
Swan, Joan*
Szasz, Thomas
Tarchuk, Janis
Thornton, R.S.
Trawick, Aleck
Tuke, William
Tyhurst, J.S.
Urich, J.M.
Van de Pol, Vince
Walker, Emil

Walker, Robert
Wani, Jagan
Webber, Neil
Weitz, Don
Werry, Len
Wilson, Michael
Winkley, Randy*
Whitton, Charlotte
Wrigby, Frank
Wyatt, Bob
Yu, Tim*
Yurko, Allan
Yurko, Chad

The Muttart Fellowships

Ron LaJeunesse
1998 Muttart Fellow

Ron LaJeunesse has more than 30 years experience as a counsellor, educator, advocate, and administrator within mental health systems in Alberta and Saskatchewan. He has held leadership positions as executive director of the government's Provincial Mental Health Board, executive director of the Mental Health Branch of the Department of Health, and executive director of the Alberta Division of the Canadian Mental Health Association.

LaJeunesse has visited and reviewed mental health systems in every Canadian province, numerous American states, the United Kingdom, and Africa. He was educated in psychiatric nursing, education, and business administration at the Universities of Saskatchewan, Alberta, and Calgary. He has worked in mental hospitals, community clinics, and volunteer community organizations.

The author has also served in an advisory capacity to the RCMP, Corrections Canada, and the Canadian International Development Agency. In addition, he has served six years as an elected school trustee, currently serves on the Edmonton Police Commission, and owned and operated a franchised business.

331

The parents of five children, Ron and his wife, Wendy, live in Edmonton.

LaJeunesse is a 1998 recipient of a Muttart Foundation Fellowship.